# LOST BANFF
## AND BUCHAN

✳

# LOST BANFF AND BUCHAN

*Daniel MacCannell*

BIRLINN

First published in 2012 by
Birlinn Limited
West Newington House
10 Newington Road
Edinburgh
EH9 1QS

*www.birlinn.co.uk*

ISBN: 978 1 78027 054 8

British Library Cataloguing-in-Publication Data
A catalogue record for this book is available
from the British Library.

Design: Mark Blackadder

Printed and bound by Gutenberg Press, Malta

This book is dedicated to
Professor Teshome Gabriel (1939–2010),
who taught me never to ignore
'the weather as a character'

# CONTENTS

# CHAPTER 1

# INTRODUCTION

The region north of Aberdeen and east of Moray, guarded on its southern flank by the ancient earldom of Mar, cannot readily be pigeonholed as highland or lowland, depopulated or populous, sleepy or chaotic. Superficially it is unchanging, almost 'backward' or inward-looking. The name of its code-like dialect, 'Doric', originated as an insult by persons from Edinburgh – the 'Athens of the North' – who wished to suggest that North-easterners were the modern equivalent of ancient Greek country bumpkins. 'Architecturally,' Charles McKean has written,

> it sometimes feels as though we are studying an independent principality, pursuing its own policies separate from the rest of Scotland: peaceful against turbulence elsewhere, rich whilst the rest of Scotland is beggared by strife, and preserving a homogeneous face against interlopers.[1]

Antique farm equipment and tiny seventeenth-century harbours are still in daily use, and people of all classes seem to share a pre-modern love of horses, as well as a terribly un-British love of military-grade firearms. The area feels lightly policed. With depressing regularity, boy racers kill themselves and others on the roads, noses are broken at a Turriff drinking establishment known jocularly as 'Fight Club', and shipments of heroin pass through Fraserburgh on their way to customers in the cities of the south. Yet, the stranger feels perfectly safe – at least in regard to *people*, who are reliably civil, even welcoming. It is *things* that are disturbing: the schist at Rhynie, containing the oldest fossil organisms known to man; huge caches of illicit whisky, hidden so cleverly from the Excisemen that even their owners never found them again; ruined fortresses perching impossibly on sea cliffs; megaliths, erected for human sacrifice, completely

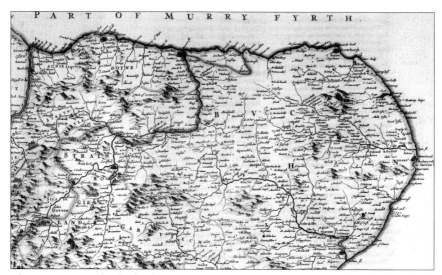

*The region covered by this book, as mapped by Joan Blaeu in 1654. It is much larger than the old Banff and Buchan district council area.*

hidden by dark and tangled woods; the woods themselves.

In some senses, the entire region is 'lost'. Clay pipes of seventeenth-century type were smoked within living memory in Methlick, but tangible oddities of this kind sit oddly against the loss of so much of the region's documentary history. The parish registers of Aberdour were 'the oldest in the Church of Scotland' – at least until 1815, when their entire pre-1698 portions were lost 'by some unaccountable accident'.[2] Many others no doubt suffered the same fate as the registers of Alvah, which in 1718 were either burned or carried off by the last Episcopalian minister, George Campbell, who was ejected in that year. A rent roll of the lost parish of Forvie disappeared from the library at Slains Castle some time between 1830 and 1858.[3] After George Skene, historian and laird of Rubislaw, died unexpectedly at the age of forty in 1776, the iron chest containing his papers

> was left in a low damp apartment, or rather cellar, with an earthen floor, which, in the period of one-and-twenty years that it was suffered to be exposed to damp, so completely rotted the bottom of the chest, that upon its removal, the bottom remained on the ground, reduced to an ochry clay, and with it a layer of about three inches thick of the old family parchments and papers, in a state of destruction utterly irredeemable, in fact resembling a mass of rotten tobacco, which fell to pieces on being touched.[4]

Other, equally priceless collections of papers were destroyed intentionally during civil strife or inter-familial feuds. Yet oddly enough, the process of destruction was not continuous, and the brave new world of the nineteenth century is still a living presence, thanks largely to the absence of postwar prosperity. 'If you wish to discover what Lowland Scotland was like back in the 1950s, before so much became overcrowded and plasticised, noisy, tourist-oriented, money-mad and fake, then Banff and Buchan is the place to visit.'[5] Those words are no less true now, almost a quarter century after Charles McKean wrote them. But this is only half the story. Impressions of backward-looking isolation are belied by the long-standing intensity of Buchan and Banffshire's global connectedness: to the Continent, Scandinavia, England, North America, and even Germany, Poland and Russia. Doric is in fact a mixture of Middle Scots, Gaelic, Norse and French. In 1660, at a time when some English historians still maintain that the area had no roads and no wheeled vehicles, Banff was importing wheels from abroad and paying duty on them at a standard rate of fourpence per pair. Duff House is a baroque palace, to be compared favourably with Blenheim, Castle Howard, and the Royal Naval College at Greenwich; yet many well-educated Britons would not recognise a picture of it, or even that it is in the United Kingdom. Never inhabited by the man who commissioned it, – who refused, indeed, even to look at it – it served as a hospital, prisoner-of-war camp and hotel before being finally becoming a museum. Likewise, Fyvie Castle is one of the world's finest small art museums, as good in its own way as Boston's I.S. Gardner, The Hague's Mauritshuis, or the Paris Orangerie. This does not appear to be generally known, either among the local tourists who flock to Fyvie, or non-local tourists, who mostly do not.

Catholic survivals here are as profound as those of Lancashire in England – the lost-and-found mercat cross of Banff (illustrated p. 102) being merely the tip of the papalist iceberg. Yet, the region has been marked equally by a pugnacious anti-establishment Episcopalianism: Protestantism as actual protest. Between 1760 and 1790, when the Scottish Episcopal Church was vigorously suppressed, the number of Episcopalians living in Peterhead grew in both absolute and percentage terms. But many also emigrated to British colonies, which were overwhelmingly either Anglican or non-denominational; or (in a seeming paradox) joined the British armed forces, which had no non-Anglican chaplains before the mid-nineteenth century.[6] The extremely wealthy Forbes family of New England, which includes recent presidential candidate Sen. John Forbes Kerry, originated in Buchan and went to the colonies as part of the mid-eighteenth-century Scottish Anglican diaspora – as did James Ramsay, native of Fraserburgh and an early and passionate advocate of the abolition of slavery.

Alongside Catholicism and Episcopalianism, the region has seen an equally strong survival (or in some places, revival) of what might be called pre-Enlightenment Puritanism, both inside and outside the Church of Scotland. In 1890s Newburgh, the school curriculum still included very exact memorisation of the Church of Scotland Shorter Catechism of 1648. Upholstered furniture was regarded as 'opulence' even in families living on capital gains, and food 'was not to be enjoyed'. One exception was Newfoundland dried cod, in a sauce made by crushing mustard seed in milk using an iron cannonball; the process 'lasted hours'.[7] One minister there, 'at the close of one of his lurid depictions of Hell' said to the congregation,

> and when ye are suffering all this, ye will raise your eyes to the Lord and ye will say unto Him, "Oh, Lord, we did not think it would be as bad as this". And the Lord will look down upon ye and in his infinite compassion and mercy will say unto ye, "Well, ye ken noo".[8]

At least one of his parishioners believed the Tay Bridge disaster of 1879 was God's response to sin – specifically, the sin of travelling on a railway train on the sabbath.

Historical preservation for its own sake has never been the North-east's

*Traditional arrangement of gable ends to the street alongside more modern houses in Low Shore, Banff, 1901.*

strong suit. The town of Banff boasts 'the clearest undisturbed medieval plan, still occupied by substantial numbers of pre-1800 buildings, to be found in Scotland';[9] but even Banff has more than its fair share of haters of the past, and its dedicated Preservation and Heritage Society has faced nearly fifty years of toil. 'Many ancient coins' were ploughed up on the site of the lost burgh of Rattray, but were 'generally gifted away to the curious' and no record of their age or appearance was made.[10] For every settlement such as Rattray or Forvie that was destroyed by accident, several others have been destroyed on purpose. Cullen was razed and rebuilt on a different site in 1822. This was done, not for reasons of public health, say, but to get it out of sight of the house of the earl of Seafield, who felt the town's presence violated his privacy. Old Cullen was also the victim of a prevalent idea – now, fortunately, overthrown – that the traditional Scottish townscape of houses with their gable ends to the street 'offends the eye of the traveller'.[11]

Substantial ruins of the medieval church of Auchindoir were retained after the construction of a new church in 1811, and the Fergusons of Pitfour famously saved the Abbey of Deer by deeming it an orchard and enclosing it with a garden wall; but these are exceptions proving the rule, and even the Fergusons have been criticised for 'heedlessly' using part of the abbey stones to build a mausoleum in 1854.[12] Churches here that were thought too small, too dark, or too draughty – and even some that were not – were generally pulled down the moment funds for a new building became available. In the eighteenth century, Rev. George Gordon wrote that the medieval church of Mortlach was

> venerable . . . only because it is old; having none of that magnificence, nice architecture, or elegant decorations, which we so justly admire in the more modern cathedrals of after times. . . . [I]t will probably be found adviseable to get over the veneration for its antiquity, and new model it into a more convenient form.[13]

Rev. Gordon's attitude was in the mainstream for ministers of his time. Of Belhelvie's four pre-Reformation churches, two were removed without trace by 1840 and a third was gone before 1900; the lost ones were located at Hatton of Millden, Ardo and Muirton. The first Protestant church of Ordiquhill was built over a chapel of St Mary. The medieval church of St Olav on the south bank of the Water of Cruden was wrongly stated to have vanished without trace in the *Statistical Account* of 1793; in fact, it was not 'barbarously demolished' for road-making materials until 1837 – an operation no doubt made easier, morally speaking, by the building's official non-existence.[14]

*Boddam Castle in 1784. Considerably less of it remains today.*

Wind has been almost as great a destroyer of the built environment as man. As far inland as Delgaty I have known fierce, uncanny winds that alter only imperceptibly in speed and direction, sometimes for twenty-four hours or more at a stretch. 'The Easterly winds here bring rains . . . which often come on early in the Evening, continue all night and sometimes for whole days, and are very disagreeable', tourist Richard Pococke wrote to his sister in 1760;[15] substitute 'snows' for 'rains' and it would be an accurate statement outside the tourist season as well. Wind patterns also made the sea here a favourite haunt of enemy privateers during any war in which sailing ships were used – though one fortuitous gale in October 1757 undoubtedly saved Banff from being looted and burned by 800 French marines. There was in the north-west corner of the parish of Aberdour 'a small neat and convenient harbour' in the 1740s, but fifty years later it was 'totally destroyed, not a vestige of the piers remaining, but the stones of which they were built . . . which have so entirely filled up the former bason, that it is with difficulty that the fishing boats, 3 in number . . . can land.'[16]

Storms from the east were not the only villains: hurricane-force winds from the south-west 'unroofed many houses' in January 1773.[17] In all, since 1400, the unfortunate combination of powerful winds and abundant sand have cost us at least three fishing villages, two castles, a medieval burgh, a sea loch, and the entire 1,700-acre parish of Forvie. The fabulous golf hotel in Cruden Bay, with its own private tramway, lasted only forty years. Wind was in large measure to

*King Edward VII arrives in Lumsden. The region is prone to fierce winds, a problem exacerbated by its many new towns' excessively wide streets.*

blame for its underwhelming popularity. Having learned nothing from this episode, or perhaps in ignorance of it, a certain American tycoon is erecting another golf resort on the same coast, at Menie. When the Menie deal was first announced, a young radio reporter was sent there with a portable recorder and microphone to get local beach users' reactions. Having searched for any such persons in vain for half an hour, in bitingly cold gale-force winds and penetrating sand, she at last saw a lone man approaching her.

He was holding a microphone too.

Few regions of Europe can boast of having been burned to the ground by their own king, but the Comyn family's opposition to the rule of Robert the Bruce led to their earldom of Buchan receiving this treatment in 1308. Bruce's famous command, 'bryn all Bowchane/ Fra end till end, and sparyt nane'[18] took in not only castles such as Auchterellon, Dundarg and Rattray, but the houses of the common people, and even – according to legends still widely believed in the eighteenth century – mighty oak forests. The blackened appearance of trees found in the region's many peat bogs was ascribed, not to natural tannins in the water table, but to deliberately set fires. And for every historical observer who blamed Buchan's relative treelessness on the unseasonably strong and cold May winds, you can find another who blamed it on Scotland's fourteenth-century hero-king.

An argument could easily be made that the North-east 'knuckle' never fully

*The lavish, fifty-five-roomed Cruden Bay Hotel was founded in 1899 and demolished in 1952. Its plush private tramway was the northernmost tram system in the United Kingdom.*

recovered from Robert I's mistreatment, and that to a greater or lesser degree, it has been out of step with the rest of Scotland ever since. It formed the core of what Gordon Donaldson famously called 'Scotland's Conservative North', siding with the doomed King James III against his upstart son, the future James IV, in the Sauchieburn campaign of 1488.

> Indeed, the list of James III's principal supporters – Huntly, Errol, Atholl, Crawford, Sutherland, Caithness, Marischal, Forbes, Ogilvy, Grant and Fraser – could almost as well be a list of royalist leaders of the seventeenth century or Jacobite leaders of the eighteenth.[19]

Our Reformation, in contrast even to Angus's and Elgin's, was slow, not especially destructive, broadly Lutheran rather than Calvinist in tone, and at the end of the day, pluralist. Yet when the south of Scotland accepted the rule of the Presbyterian, but foreign, prince of Orange after 1688, Buchaners opposed the change of dynasty violently and for generations. Rightly or wrongly, the new government blamed this new oppositional stance on Buchan's long-standing preference for Episcopalianism. As a result, Episcopal chapels were systematically destroyed, and a 'deeply resented military occupation' resulted in an 'atmosphere of subjugation' as late as the 1770s.[20] Nevertheless, by the 1790s, when religious nonconformity on Deeside (for example) had been all but rooted out, Episcopalians made up a third of the population of Cruden, twenty-seven per cent in Peterhead, twenty-five per cent in Crimond, twenty-two per cent in Old Deer, sixteen per cent in Lonmay and Turriff, thirteen per cent in Rathen, and a remarkable forty-five per cent in Longside. When Britain set forth to found a second empire in the wake of the loss of the Thirteen Colonies, the militarily talented men of Buchan and Banffshire were as likely to be found serving in foreign armies and navies as in those of their own country. On the eve of the First World War and the Russian Revolution, our economy was heavily weighted toward trade with Germany and Russia. The 1920s did not 'roar' here, and the 1950s did not 'boom'.

For now, the tables are turned. Thanks largely to the oil and gas industries, Aberdeenshire has one of the lowest unemployment rates in a recession-weary Britain, and consistently scores well on a range of other recent measures of well-being. Yet even today, to inhabit this lost region is to feel viscerally that you have wandered outside the mainstream of Scottish, British, and European life – with all the good and bad that might imply.

*Like a postcard from an alternative universe, a German-made statue of a notorious Jacobite stands serenely on guard over Broad Street in Peterhead. (Photo by Barry Robertson)*

# CHAPTER 2

# 'FRINGED BY ROCKS AND SAND DUNES AND INHABITED BY SURVIVORS'

## LOST BOUNDARIES: 'PROPER' BUCHAN, FORMARTINE AND BANFFSHIRE

Foreigners and the young can be baffled by the fact that the Isle of Wight is part of England but not part of Great Britain, or that the Isle of Man is part of the British Isles but not part of the EU. Such anomalies were once commonplace. In our own region, the parish and village of St Fergus lie in the heart of Buchan, but were for administrative purposes a detached part of Banffshire until 1891. St Fergus and similar 'exclaves' – the opposite of 'enclaves' – mostly dated back to the late Middle Ages when they were owned by the powerful Cheyne family. Other examples included the part of Newmachar called Strolach (still in Banffshire for tax purposes in the nineteenth century), and the lost parish of Fetterangus, absorbed by Old Deer in 1618.

If the River Ythan formed a firm boundary between the earldom of Buchan to the north and the thanage of Formartine to the south, as most people now suppose, a number of awkward questions are raised. Bethelnie and Kelly – located south of the Ythan, and since renamed Old Meldrum and Haddo, respectively – were part of the earldom of Buchan in the Middle Ages. So was Newburgh.[21] The pretty town of Ellon, located very much on the border of Formartine, has billed itself as the ancient 'capital of Buchan' for decades,[22] despite its once-famous Earl's Hill having been flattened in the Queen Anne period to make way for an inn and stables (and by the 1950s, a 'public convenience and bus shelter'[23]). Before the sixteenth-century construction of Peterhead and Fraserburgh, the only other town with a pretence to being Buchan's 'capital' was Turriff, which is certainly located in Formartine.

The writings of Alexander Simpson, eighteenth-century schoolmaster of King Edward, consistently use 'Buchan' to mean Buchan and Formartine.

George Cruden, in 1842, argued that Buchan had always extended to the Don. The idea that it stopped at the Ythan, he said, was a novelty of the seventeenth century. This is not to say that everyone in the seventeenth century believed this, either. Marischal College, founded in 1593, divided its student body into 'Naciones' based on their place of origin, and anyone hailing from north of the Don and south of the Deveron was part of the 'nation' of the 'Buchanenses'.[24] The pre-Reformation Deanery of Buchan included the Formartine parishes of Slains, Logie-Buchan, Ellon, Foveran, Methlick, Tarves and Belhelvie.[25] John Pratt, writing in the 1850s, stated that four of the above-named Deanery of Buchan parishes, plus Forglen, Auchterless and Fyvie, were only 'partly' in Buchan[26] – a fairly sure indication that the Ythan was not yet an important regional boundary in the high Middle Ages when the parish system was established.

None of this should be any great cause for anxiety, however. Alexander Grant's research on medieval Scottish thanages shows that these were not 'estates' in the usual sense at all, but royal bases for tax collecting, run (not owned) by thanes who were appointed by the king, usually for five- or six-year terms. In some respects the thane was pre-feudal Gaelic society's version of the sheriff. Thanages, moreover, 'penetrated all the earldoms from Fife to Moray', and some thanes were even employed *by earls* rather than by the king.[27] In other words, it is possible simultaneously to accept the real and distinct existence of Formartine, *and* that the earldom of Buchan reached as far south as the River Don – just as the existence of the concept 'the North of England' does not somehow negate either England as a whole, or County Durham in particular.

In terms of traditional clan lands, Auchindoir is the 'hinge' of the region, in that it was traditionally owned by Grants, Gordons and Forbeses, marking it as the border between the predominately Grant/Gordon culture of Highland Banffshire and the Cabrach, on the one hand; and on the other, the Gordon/Forbes culture of Lowland Donside. Likewise, at some point on one's north-eastward journey from Mar into Buchan, one stops counting Forbes houses in a sea of Farquharsons and Gordons, and starts counting Grant houses in a sea of Gordons and Forbeses.

Banffshire, of course, is a whole 'lost county', divided nearly down the middle in 1975 and gobbled up by Aberdeenshire and Moray. But much of what later became Banffshire had also been part of the earldom, or what might be called 'greater Buchan'. As Alistair Mason points out, the county of Banffshire was a novelty of the twelfth century, before which the Celtic province of Buchan butted directly against the province of Moray; 'so in 1975, when the old county was carved up, we were almost going back to what was before'.[28] Yet sadly, the lost world of Banff as a genteel, Jacobite-dominated county town hosting endless balls, classical music concerts and plays can scarcely be imagined, still less recovered.

## THE TOWN-MAKERS

Aberdeenshire's heavy concentration of still-inhabitable renaissance castles, unparalleled elsewhere in the British Isles, can easily blind us to the relative newness of the rest of the built environment. From his schoolhouse windows in the 1890s, the teacher, folklorist and novelist Gavin Greig

> could see little that was not in some sense man-made. The very landscape was raw and new, torn from the naked heath little more than a generation before to create one of the most advanced and efficient farming systems in Europe. The coastal districts were likewise in ferment as the rise of the great herring fishery swept aside the accumulated cultural patterns of centuries.[29]

Castles aside, so new are the houses and villages of northern Aberdeenshire that a visitor from another planet could be forgiven for thinking it was not part of Britain at all, but a British colony founded at the same time as New Brunswick or New South Wales.

In or by the early eighteenth century, a thriving, literally 'cottage' industry in textiles, combined with a mediocre transport network, had created an almost uniquely dispersed and centreless population, in which even the smallest hamlets were nearly self-reliant in most everyday commodities. As recently as the 1790s, it was commonplace for parish ministers throughout the region to remark that their charges were wholly rural, or that 'there are no villages within the parish',[30] or that a lone village 'is erecting'.[31]

An astonishingly high percentage of Scotland's post-1745 planned villages – about one in five – are concentrated in Buchan proper and the lowland part of Banffshire, though the Highland village of Tomintoul was also 'a bleak and barren moor' until 1750, and Lumsden on Donside was founded on a similar site in 1825. Out of just 127 such planned communities nationally,[32] local examples have included Aberchirder, Burnhaven, Charlestown of Aberlour, Collieston, Cuminestown, Crovie, Deskford, Dufftown, Fetterangus, Findochty, Gardenstown, Gordonston, Inverallochy, Longside, Mintlaw, New Aberdour, New Byth, New Deer, New Leeds, New Pitsligo, St Combs, St Fergus, Sandhaven, Stewartfield and Strichen. A prominent sign by Banff Bridge celebrates the bicentenary of the town of Macduff (1783–1983); visitors from, say, Pennsylvania will find this sort of thing immediately familiar in a way that English visitors will not.

The town-making craze also affected ancient centres. In the second half of the eighteenth century, thanks to investment of £1,800 by the earl of Findlater, the medieval royal burgh of Cullen rather suddenly became a linen centre with seventy-two looms; and this occurred several decades *before* the town was knocked down and rebuilt on a new site half a mile away. Huntly was similarly re-conceived as a textile town, in 1770. Buckie, established in the 1640s, remained 'a fishing station only' until its first shop opened in 1750; but before the end of the eighteenth century it had a hemp factory and eight merchants with a turnover of £5,000 sterling a year, 'exclusive of grain'.[33]

In 1801, inland Aberdeenshire north of the Don had only three villages that were more than a century old and had more than 360 inhabitants. These were Huntly, Old Meldrum and Turriff. In Banffshire in 1791, the landlocked parish of Keith was extraordinary in that 54 per cent of its people lived in villages, as opposed to isolated cottages and farmhouses. But its only settlement 'of old standing', Kirktown of Keith, was 'greatly on the decline, and almost a ruin' with a population of just 192; whereas New Keith, founded by Lord Find-later in 1750 on a 'barren muir', was 'tolerably thriving' with a population of 1,075. Fife Keith would not be built until 1817.

Charles McKean's description of the town-building process closely echoes triumphant narratives of colonisation from the British dominions beyond the seas:

> The new settlements are formal, man-made, and exemplify rational Improvement thought. These were not charitable foundations, but commercial enterprises designed to attract to the wastes of Buchan men of skill and enterprise who could generate a local economy. That they succeeded, in large measure, must be attributed to the courage of those who ventured out to an unknown future in remote hinterland.[34]

Not all of them succeeded, of course. Capt. Alexander Fraser of the King's Dragoon Guards, whose father had laid out the successful new town of Mormond (later called Strichen) in 1764, created a new town of his own on the lands of Whig-About in the years around 1800. Called New Leeds because it was intended to rival or surpass Leeds in Yorkshire as a manufacturing centre for wool, it never achieved anything of the kind, and almost immediately became a haunt of outlaws and smugglers. By 1852, Christian Watt found 'some of the first inhabitants . . . living in shacks of divots and tattie boxes.'[35] Then again, not every new village was principally economic in purpose. The Disruption of 1843 was so severe in Cruden that the Free Kirkers withdrew to a newly built separate village, Hatton, originally known as the 'Free Kirkton of Cruden'.[36]

As late as the Napoleonic Wars, more than two-thirds of Aberdeenshire's population still lived in hamlets of a hundred persons or fewer, and typically of around fifty people. Whatever else it achieved, the 'Age of Improvement' here tended to reduce these tiny villages to the status of large individually held farms, and to move their 'excess' population either into the new towns, or abroad. This consolidation took place mostly between 1755 and 1826. In addition to those former villages that collapsed to a single point – such as the farms called Old-Town of Carnousie and Kirktown, both in the parish of Forglen – there were at least seventy hamlets that existed in 1696, but which have since disappeared altogether, even as single dwellings; even, indeed, as names.

This collapsing-down is better remembered, however, than a previous phase of single communities dividing. Between 1590 and 1696, Achmacoy split into four places, named Meikle Achmacoy, Little Achmacoy, Achmacoy and Mains of Achmacoy. Fedderate grew from one place to five over the same period. The record for the highest number of splits – from one name to six – is shared by Birness, Ellon, and Knaven in New Deer. In Cabrach, the same splitting process occurred much later: 'Geochelarg',[37] the Cabrach's *de facto* capital and late seventeenth-century population centre, would divide by the nineteenth century first into two – Gauch and Largue – and then into four, with Letterfury splitting from Largue, and Reekimlane from Gauch, as the population expanded to fill the labour needs of the illicit distillers there.

The place-name Middlethird, found in various places in Buchan, commemorates three-way splits, usually dating from the seventeenth century. Other names, like Oldtown of Newmill (found in both Rathen and Keith), show how complicated the process of splitting and renaming might become. In part, this reflects the region's unsustainable population growth between the mid-sixteenth and mid-seventeenth centuries – a phenomenon that would bear strange fruit in our enormous commercial and military emigrations to northern Europe (see *The lost armies*, p. 161). The creation of the park around Pitfour House necessitated the destruction of Mill of Leggett and Pilmuir, and Rattray House was built over the ferm-toun of Broadland; but '[i]n the main . . . it is not possible to match with any specific cause most of the places which disappear from the record before the modern period'.[38] In modern times, however, and especially

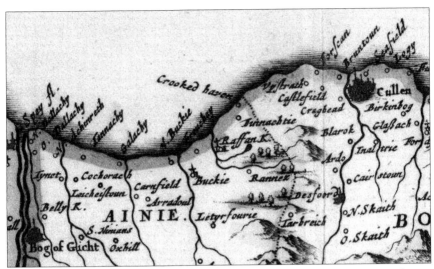

*Drastic change in the positions, names and numbers of coastal villages has occurred since this map was engraved in 1654.*

after 1750, the gentry's widespread desire to erect whole new communities, and then people them with skilled workers, has been one of the most powerful drivers of change in the region's mental and material landscape.

Far from being an exclusively inland phenomenon, the building of new towns actually began on the coast. The region's first and most successful new town, Fraserburgh, was partly built over prior settlements called Broadsea and Faithlie, the former retaining its independent legal identity until 1872. Fraserburgh's early success was deeply resented by Aberdeen, whose burghers from 1573 to 1616 doggedly asserted in the courts that Fraserburgh's trading privileges infringed on their own, or even that the creation of a new burgh on this part of the coast was inherently illegal. Peterhead, another sixteenth-century new town, absorbed the villages of Rehill and Blackhouse and the *c.*1200 Norman manor of Roanheads, while Peterhead prison obliterated one of the most recent new villages in the area: Burnhaven, built in the 1830s by George Mudie of Meethill at a cost of £300. St Combs was laid out in 1771 as a replacement for Corsekelly, which like Rattray, Rattray Castle, Lonmay Castle and the lost parish of Forvie, had become untenable due to shifting sands. Pitscur in Cruden went earlier, some time in the second half of the seventeenth century.

OVERLEAF. *The lost village of Burnhaven, now entombed beneath H.M. Prison Peterhead. Similar sea-towns all along the coast disappeared for a variety of less dramatic, sometimes unrecorded reasons.*

*Pennan, seen here in the nineteenth century, became world famous in 1983 as one of the two major settings of the feature film* Local Hero. *The other was the Arisaig/Mallaig area in Inverness-shire, 150 miles away on the west coast.*

The villages of Collieston and Inverallochy 'were already involved in fishing' by the 1590s, but Cairnbulg may not predate the 1700s.[39] Coastal Banff-shire saw similar developments, with the establishment of Buckie in the 1640s, Portknockie in 1677, Findochty in 1716, and Portessie in 1727. Though a small kirktown may have existed there as early as 1513, Gardenstown was founded as a fishing village by Alexander Garden, laird of Troup, in 1720. A similar initiative in St Fergus began – and ended – in the 1770s. Twenty years later, the only two fishing villages in Lonmay (which did not yet have names) were described as 'lately built' by the Gordons of Buthlaw.[40] Fifty years after that, one of them had become St Combs and the other had disappeared. The people for all of these new settlements needed to know how to fish already, and so had to be brought in from elsewhere, even from a different county: for example, from Cullen (in the case of Portknockie), Fraserburgh (for Findochty) and Findhorn (for Portessie).

Cruden's Oldtown of Ardendraught and Oldtown of Auquharney have 'no corresponding "new" settlements now', suggesting that planned villages of some distant era failed there.[41] Meikletoun of Slains was chartered as a town, but never developed. Likewise, Doun – chartered in 1528 – never developed any urban characteristics until it was re-founded as Macduff two and a half centuries later. Place-names beginning 'Bog' or 'Cott', or which include 'Commonty', refer specifically to colonisation of former waste ground: a phenomenon we will re-visit in *Crofters all*, p. 45. Yet on the whole, the dozens of new villages and towns founded in this region between the 1540s and the 1830s were connected with one or the other of just two activities, fishing and 'the textile industry . . . before it had moved from cottage to factory'.[42]

## SEA-LAIRDS

'The rocks on this coast are generally high, and indented in a strange manner, with immense and terrible chasms', Alexander Farquhar wrote in the eighteenth century.[43] Seven castles, four of them in the immediate vicinity of Fraserburgh, were already in ruins by the mid-1820s, and it is 'perhaps ironic' that these 'most prominent deserted settlements are those of the upper social classes'.[44] One of the most striking features of Buchan past is the building of castles on its 'huge and horrid ridges' overlooking 'deep and ghastly' precipices[45] – a practice which

*New Slains Castle, as rebuilt by 'Tudor Johnny' Smith in the 1830s and left to rot in 1925. 'The outline of the building was clearly silhouetted against the glowing west . . . He had expected something old and baronial. But this was new, raw and new, not twenty years built. Some madness had prompted its creator to set up a replica of a Tudor house in a countryside where the thing was unheard of. All the tricks were there – oriel windows, lozenged panes, high twisted chimney stacks; the very stone was red, as if to imitate the mellow brick of some ancient Kentish manor. It was new, but it was also decaying. The creepers had fallen from the walls, the pilasters on the terrace were tumbling down, lichen and moss were on the doorsteps. Shuttered, silent, abandoned, it stood like a harsh* memento mori *. . . The decadence of the brand-new repels as something against nature, and this new thing was decadent. But there was a mysterious life in it, for though not a chimney smoked, it seemed to enshrine a personality and to wear a sinister aura. He felt a lively distaste, which was almost fear. He wanted to get far away from it as fast as possible.' –John Buchan,* Huntingtower *(New York, 1922), pp. 67–68.*

LEFT. *Tarlair in 1901.*

BELOW. *Gardenstown in the nineteenth century, with fishing lines drying in the left foreground and Gamrie Head in the distance.*

Bram Stoker, Irish author of *Dracula*, found particularly atmospheric and inspiring.[46]

Unlike on the west coast of Scotland, noblemen and lairds here did *not* operate private fleets of galleys or wage private naval warfare against the crown, one another, and various foreign countries. During the Flodden campaign of 1513, Sir James Gordon of Letterfourie in Banffshire commanded 'sixteen ships with tops and ten smaller craft',[47] but this probably represented Scotland's entire navy at the time. And the sixth earl Marischal agreed to provide naval transport for Britain's war with France in 1627 'on condition that he was granted a licence to engage in privateering'.[48] But similar incidents were rare. Thus the positioning of Buchan's sea-cliff castles is sometimes remarked as strange by historians. Even small castles were enormously expensive to build and maintain, and their sites were hardly chosen for the view. It seems more likely that castles such as Old Slains and Boddam were built to defend fishing communities, which were themselves founded to exploit white-fishing and bait-gathering rights which had been granted to nobles and lairds by the crown. (Mussels in general, and Ythan mussels in particular, were considered the best bait found in the area.) In the early days, the landlords took percentages of the fish caught in return for military protection; and in 1744, it was noted that 'Every one knows the Power which Gentlemen have over their Fishermen – who generally hold their Huts, their Acres and their Boats, by no other Tenure than the Master's Good-will and Pleasure'.[49] In 1795, the duke of Gordon himself was described as owning three Buckie fishing boats and a yawl.[50] In Buckie and elsewhere in the parish of Rathven at the same date, the cost of buying a fully equipped fishing boat was

*Boddam Castle was the birth-place of Sir William Keith, fourth baronet of Ludquharn (1669–1749), who became an influential early colonial governor in Pennsylvania despite his family's extreme Jacobitism. Photo by Barry Robertson.*

£24. More than half of this was in sails, rigging, nets and so forth, since replacing the hull (which was done every seven years) cost only £11. In return for the laird's capital, which was used regularly for hull replacement as well as the initial purchase of the whole boat, the mariners would 'bind themselves to serve in it' and to pay an average annual rent to the laird of £5 3s 3d plus '6 dried cod or ling'.[51] Lairds' control of fishing communities was mitigated by acts of Queen Anne and George III which granted fisherfolk free use of the foreshore. The village of Crovie's unexpected (and sometimes dangerous!) proximity to the high-water mark may originate in this legislation.

By the 1840s, in common with many other aspects of feudalism, 'teinds' of fish had been converted into cash fees; for example, £1 per man in Rosehearty and £1 5s per man in Pittullie for the privilege of landing fish and gathering bait. In Slains, the conversion of teinds to cash fees took place around 1780; the fees then quadrupled (from 5s to 20s) by the end of the century. A generation later, the mussel-rental alone had reached £3 per year per man under age 60, and £2 for the over-60s. In some places, the original process reversed itself, with families who had become wealthy from whaling acquiring landed estates, as the Hutchisons did at Cairngall in Longside.

## FISHERFOLK: A 'RACE APART'?

Until quite recently, with few exceptions, fishermen's sons became fishermen and married fishermen's daughters. It was not unusual for whole sea-towns to have only two or three surnames within them. Powerful belief in good and bad luck was nearly universal, and many ordinary words and practices were considered taboo. People living just half a mile inland not only failed to share these beliefs but could be unaware of their existence. Even where out-marriage did take place, women with red hair tended to be avoided as unlucky, and I have seen few photos of nineteenth-century herring-girls who were very fair. Attitudes to modern medicine also differed significantly from those of the landward population, with Banff and Buchan fishing people frequently noted as refusing inoculation. They were also exposed to different medical risks; in the fishing town of Collieston of Slains in 1832, twenty-three people out of a population of three hundred and fifty were killed by cholera, which had come into the town directly from Leith, and did not spread beyond it. Buchan's American-style fundamentalist 'religious revival' of the late 1850s, led by a Peterhead herring-curer named James Turner who personally converted 8,000 people in two years, seems to have affected fishing communities almost exclusively. Writing in 1896, Alex McAldowie – a Deesider with roots in St Fergus – stated that fishing people

> were of a distinct race from the rest of the inhabitants of Aberdeen-shire, towards whom their social relations resembled those of the Jews and the Samaritans. Their customs and superstitions were likewise distinct in most cases. Their most binding oath was, 'May my boat be my bonnet next time I go to sea.' One instance I recollect when, to the horror and dismay of the judge on circuit, this oath proved more potent in extracting the truth from several witnesses than the one administered in due form by the court official.[52]

The idea that they were a 'distinct race' could easily be dismissed as rhetoric in this case, but it was a common theme in writings of Victorian and earlier periods. In eighteenth-century Slains, a confused Alexander Farquhar reported, hollyback were called turbot and turbot were called *rodden-fleuck*. William Donald stated that, while some of the fishermen and pilots in Roanheads could be 'reasonably supposed' to be biologically descended from the original population of Peterhead burgh, in Boddam the people appear 'both from name and remaining habits, to be of Dutch extraction'.[53] Certainly, the Dutch fished very close to the Buchan coast – nearly leading to a fishing war in 1786 – and even used to fish in the Loch of Strathbeg when it still connected to the sea, *c*.1600. But Donald's comments could be as unfounded as those of William Greig, who wrote that the people of Buchan in general lack both the 'liveliness of imagination' and the 'warmth of feeling' found in other parts of the country, and that they were more like Dutchmen than they were like their fellow Scots.[54] The idea that sailors from the Spanish Armada colonised part of Buchan will be discussed in the next chapter. Rosehearty, meanwhile, is still widely believed to have been 'founded by a group of shipwrecked Danes'.[55]

Be that as it may, in this nation of dog lovers, fishermen's attitudes toward dogs were as alien as could be, as recently as a hundred years ago when these lines of verse were written in the vicinity of Portknockie:

> Weel div I min' fin my dog was young
> He barked and growled and seldom held's tongue
> I fed him on porridge until he did grow
> A very good size for a haddock line bow.
> He grew up in sax month as fat as a pig,
> Wi' a nose red's a carrot an' a fine curly wig,

Employed a neibour tae tak's skin o'er his howe,
An' get him made intae an aul' dog bow.
I steeped him nine days in a cog amon' strang,
Then the hair cam' aff wi' the tip o' my han',
I tied his legs in his neck for a tow
An' blew him up tight, my aul' dog bow.
I hung him ootside tae dry on a pole,
The sun made him black, black as a mole. . . .
I took him tae sea tae pit on my line
An' tried him oot ower wi' an unca lang string.
He caved up an' doon like the wings o' a gow –
The pride o' my heart wis my aul' dog bow.

Later in the poem, the fisherman and his family do 'murn' for the dog – but only *after* the fishing-float made from its skin is lost at sea.[56]

The characterisation of most eighteenth-century fishing as 'inshore' does not mean that the fishermen were not intrepid long-distance sailors. The men of Cullen personally took their cured cod, ling, skate and haddocks to Montrose, Forfar, Dundee and Leith, and returned from these voyages with 'hemp, wool, and salt for their own use'.[57] Half of the fish caught off Slains were likewise sent to Dundee, Leith and Perth; the other half were consumed locally, or else taken 'by the women' over land to Aberdeen and Old Meldrum.[58] Pitsligo crews

*A 'race apart' or no, the toughness of our fishermen cannot be gainsayed. Gardenstown-born Joe Watt, skipper of the Gowanlea (FR105), was just twenty-nine when his Admiralty-requisitioned thirty-five ton boat was attacked by three Austrian cruisers. He and his eight-man crew successfully fought them off and escaped, and Joe was awarded the Victoria Cross and the Croix de Guerre.*

*The* Novara, *one of the enemy warships that attacked the* Gowanlea *(and wished they had not) on 15 May 1917. In all, 675 British fishing boats were sunk and 1,127 fishermen killed by the enemy in the First World War alone.*

brought their surplus catch to the Firth of Forth, and as late as the Victorian era, some of the Rosehearty herring boats also caught cod off Tiree in the Western Isles, sold it in Glasgow, and came home laden with coal in time for the start of the herring season. Men from the small Rathven ports typically served six weeks a year (late July to early September) in the Caithness herring fishery, where they were paid in a combination of cash and whisky. The whisky rate was a bottle a day, and the money either a flat fee of £9 2s for the season, or 10s per barrel, at the crewmen's option. The daily exertion required in dragging boats up and down the beach was 'very hurtful to the boats, and sometimes fatal to the men.' Findochty and Buckie alone lost fifty-seven men drowned at sea since between 1755 and the end of the century. All in all, George Donaldson wrote, '[a] more industrious, intrepid, adventurous race of mariners . . . is nowhere to be found in his Majesty's dominions.'[59] Even now, a year hardly passes without a fatal accident.

## THE LOST FLEETS

The unique lighthouse at Kinnaird's Head, Fraserburgh was the first to be built on the Scottish mainland, in 1787. One of the first four lights planned by the Northern Lighthouse Trustees, it is also the only lighthouse set atop a sixteenth-century castle, and was the first to issue warnings to ships via radio, on 20

March 1929. The original light was powered by whale oil, and was so heavy that it caused damage to the castle's structure. This led to it being replaced with the current version in 1824, at which time various castle outbuildings were also removed. The light's purpose, of course, was to prevent shipwrecks, and in this it has been relatively successful. At the time of its construction, not all fishing boats carried compasses, and navigation relied heavily upon visual identification of landmarks such as Binhill in Rathven, Cant's Kirk and Stirlinghill. This was, of course, impossible on moonless nights or in thick haar.

On a coastline which as a whole has been reckoned a 'severe hazard to shipping', the most dangerous sector was from Fraserburgh to Cruden, where about 400 major shipwrecks have been recorded since the mid-sixteenth century.[60] Smugglers alone lost thirteen ships here in the six decades immediately preceding the construction of the light. One of the most spectacular incidents of the pre-lighthouse era was the November 1556 wreck of the *Edward Bonaventure*, in which a Russian ambassador bound for England with a load of exotic presents for Queen Mary Tudor ran aground in Pitsligo Bay. One of a lucky minority, the ambassador survived the wreck only to see his £20,000 cargo picked clean 'by the rude and ravenous people of the Country'.[61] Much the same happened in January 1628 to the *Sanct Marie*, a German ship full of Spanish wine. Driven aground just north of Peterhead, it was being ransacked by the local outlaws when the redoubtable countess Marischal arrived to restore order.

This is not to suggest that Scottish ships were not also plundered. When the *Hope* of Leith was wrecked on the Sands of Cairnbulg in 1672, 'the local inhabitants descended on it like a swarm of locusts and carried off everything they could lay their hands on.'[62] A schoolmaster from the Newburgh area plundered the anchor and mast from a wreck in 1703, from which other upstanding citizens stole 'wool, candles, brandy and hats'.[63] Even the clothing of the drowned was taken, and distress signals fired by ships in the early eighteenth century sometimes served only to alert landlubbers to the rich pickings. Attempts were always made to arrest and prosecute pilferers of wrecks, but the local gentry acting alone against whole guilty populations could do little, and the great majority of such crimes went unpunished or undetected. In fairness, it should be mentioned that unlike in some other parts of Britain, there is no record here of the people using false lights to wreck ships on purpose, or murdering survivors to prevent them giving evidence – though the mob of Cullen 'offered Violence' to a survivor in in 1728. A persistent legend also states that the people of Boddam once executed a monkey so that the ship it came from would have no living survivors, and thus qualify as a wreck under a legal precedent of 1674.

In eighteenth-century Crimond, where there was no suitable landing place even for fishing boats, many ships were lost. The 'lower ranks' of society, William Gall reported, 'pilfer and carry off from the wreck whatever they can lay hold on, sometimes in a very barefaced manner'.[64] By the 1830s this behaviour had ceased 'almost entirely', which is another way of saying that some folk were still doing it.[65] The people of eighteenth-century Foveran, perhaps by way of contrast to their neighbours or their forebears, were described as 'humane and compassionate to the ship-wrecked'.[66]

None of this is to suggest that the majority of cargoes were recovered, even by thieves. At Fraserburgh in 1677, a ship carrying more than a year's worth of the rents-in-kind from the whole of Orkney and Shetland was sunk with the loss of the entire cargo, and all but one crewman. A storm that began on New Year's Eve 1799 and lasted several weeks caused more damage at sea than the much more famous floods of 1829 did on land, with three ships destroyed at Belhelvie on the first day alone, and only one survivor between them. Three more ships were lost at Collieston four days later.

*Buchan fishwife and child.*

Truly, the sea is in the blood here. Perhaps uniquely, George Hamilton-Gordon was simultaneously an earl and a merchant seaman. On a visit to his uncle, the pompous and autocratic lieutenant-governor of New Brunswick, the young man fell in love with the sea and the New World. By the time he became sixth earl of Aberdeen in 1864, Hamilton-Gordon was working as a lumberjack under the name 'George H. Osborne' in New Brunswick, where he did not wash for three weeks. He was swept overboard and drowned off Nova Scotia, aged twenty-eight, while hauling up a sail on the merchant ship *Hera* of Boston, Massachusetts. It was not the sort of life, or death, that anyone would have expected for a man born in Holyrood Palace and raised at Haddo House, grandson of a prime minister.

One of the region's most persistent oral traditions states that certain Buchan families are descended from survivors of the Spanish Armada ship *Santa Caterina* or *Santa Catalina*, wrecked 'under the cliffs between Whinnyford and Collieston'[67] in 1588. The truth of an Armada ship having been wrecked near Slains Manse was corroborated, for John Pratt, by the raising of a four-pounder cannon from the sea there in 1855. It was just under eight feet long, and loaded, with 'ball and wadding . . . in a perfect state of preservation'.[68] Other observers point out that the only two ships from the Great Armada with similar names to *Santa Catalina* both returned safely home; that no Armada ships were reported wrecked anywhere within sight of the Buchan coast at the time; and that any guns recovered could have come from a Danish ship wrecked in 1666. However, David Ferguson speculates that a Spanish galleon could have been wrecked at the same spot in 1594 'while bringing Spanish arms and ammunition to aid the Earl of Erroll's rebellion'.[69]

Pratt was also of the opinion that Peterhead's Meikle Battery – already dismantled by the time his book was written in 1858 – had contained 'seven brass cannon, taken out of the *St Michael*, one of the Spanish Armada, which was wrecked . . . in this vicinity'.[70] Rightly or wrongly, more recent observers have conflated the *St Michael* and the *Santa Caterina*: Ian Whittaker's *Off Scotland* mentioning only the former, and R.N. Baird's *Shipwrecks* only the latter. However, given the furore that attended the wreck of the Armada ship *San Juan de Sicilia* in Tobermory Bay, Isle of Mull for a century and a half and more,[71] the idea that any Armada ship was wrecked here (let alone two) seems questionable at best.

Lighthouses were hardly a cure-all, and many shipwrecks continued to occur. In 'by far the worst shipping disaster' in North-east history, the 1,433-ton warship HMS *York* went down with all 491 hands in a 'hurricane' off Kinnaird's Head on Boxing Day 1803.[72] Part of the 1903 River-class destroyer HMS *Erne*,

*Wooden hulls and dangerous rocks.*

beached without loss of life in 1915, is still visible within a mile of Rattray Head lighthouse today. Rattray Head alone was once responsible for twenty-four sinkings in the space of twelve years. In the hoist-on-own-petard category, a theory exists that the Nazi submarine U-1206 sank eight miles off Slains because it struck the wreck of the *Martaban*, an Aberdeen steam trawler sunk by an Imperial German U-boat in the previous war.

The region's first lifeboat house, known initially as the Shipwreck Institution, was established at Newburgh in 1828, and closed in 1961. The war artist James McBey, born a mile outside Newburgh in 1883, remembered shipwrecks of the late Victorian period vividly:

> If a rocket, fired from the lifeboat-house a mile distant, exploded above the village it was a signal that a ship was in distress and that every able-bodied person had to drop tool or implement and hurry across the Links to man, or help launch, the lifeboat. The postman left the mail where he was delivering at the moment and the school was closed. . . . To launch the lifeboat in the river was, as often as not, impossible, as the bar was a mass of curling breakers and the tide running in. The boat on its broad-wheeled carriage might have to be pulled for miles along the coast in soft sand and blowing spray which bit and stung exposed skin.[73]

The North Sea, with its 'steady muttering drone', was 'the background of sound against the silence in which we all lived.'[74]

*The original Kinnaird's Head lighthouse, painted by William Daniell in 1822. The sixteenth- or seventeenth-century crowstepped doocot at left was later destroyed by the fury of the sea. Scotland's last manned lighthouse was automated in 1998, and Kinnaird's Head now houses a museum. Solar-powered, unmanned lighthouses are in prospect.*

It is well known that Peterhead was at one time the leading whaling port in Great Britain, but I was surprised to learn how late the industry began there. The town's 'fleet', established in 1788, consisted until 1802 of a single two-masted ship, the *Robert*, which caught no whales in its first two years, and never more than eleven in a year. From there, however, growth was steady, to a total of sixteen ships, which killed 268 whales, or 17.9 per ship, in 1823 – also the first year with a yield in excess of 2,000 tons of oil. The all-time record number of whales killed by a single British ship in a season (forty-four) was set by Peterhead's *Resolution* in 1814. She was lost in the Davis Strait along with Peterhead's *Hope* and seventeen other British whalers in 1830.

In the seventeenth century, whales were taken opportunistically in Scottish waters and their meat eaten, sometimes under the name sea-pork. Government subsidies for whale-oil commenced in 1750, and commercial whaling in the Arctic began thereafter out of Aberdeen, Peterhead, Fraserburgh and Banff. The right whale was the main quarry: called 'right', as in 'correct', because it was oil-rich for its size, 'buoyant in death, and ... relatively easy to kill'.[75] In addition to oil, baleen was sold as corset-boning and skirt-hooping material. The hunting method was, initially, in precisely the classic style made famous by *Moby-Dick*. This barely changed over the 105-year history of the industry, as harpoon guns were deployed only after 1864.

> In Peterhead the whalers docked at the Blubber Box Quay in the south harbour and the barrels were carted a short distance to the boilyards on Keith Inch. The blubber was boiled in copper vessels of up to 10 tons or more capacity. These were round in section and raised about 6 feet above a furnace. A pipe, fitted with a stopcock, led from the boiler to wooden coolers lined with lead or cement and each capable of holding 10 tons of oil. Oil was run from the coolers directly into casks. By the time the ships arrived in port, much of the oil had separated from the firm, fatty blubber. The contents of the barrels were simply poured directly into the boilers, filling them almost to the top. The fire was then lit and the oil brought to the boil. Throughout the heating the contents were stirred with a wooden pole to prevent any solids sticking to the sides and burning.[76]

There was also a bone-mill in Longside which ground whale jawbones into fertiliser. This was not, however, considered 'equally efficatious as ... the bones of land animals.'[77]

*A group of men, thought to be Peterhead whalers.*

*Kekerten whaling station, Cumberland Sound, Baffin Island in 1897. Established on a commercial basis by Peterhead explorer and whaling captain William Penny II (1809–92), who also encouraged Moravian Church missionaries in the area, the station is now a whale-watching facility. Penny's patriotic efforts helped ensure that Baffin and other Arctic islands passed from British to Canadian, rather than US, control in 1880. Remarkably, Penny made thirty-three voyages to the Arctic and never lost a ship.*

The whale fishery might well have been stillborn if the *Robert* had not brought home a hundred seal carcasses, with valuable oil as well as pelts, from her whale-less maiden voyage in 1788. 'Sealing' continued to grow alongside whaling and the *Union* of Peterhead, though primarily a whaling ship, brought home 7,500 seals in 1847 alone. In terms of yields, the high point of Peterhead whaling *per se* was actually reached in the two decades before 1827, with 20,000 tons of oil landed. The peak size of the town's fleet, however, coincided with a later period (1848–67) during which the number of whales caught had declined by two-thirds, but the oil yield remained stable due to a 35-fold increase in the slaughter of seals, to more than one million animals. Some ships from Fraserburgh also participated in this later, seal-intensive phase. The 'inexorable decline' of the Peterhead fleet from its peak size of thirty-one ships in 1857 was due to 'the over-exploitation of seals' as much as 'the near extinction of whales'.[78] Having gone, the industry remained gone for good. Our region took no part in Scotland's inshore industrial whaling boom of 1903–29, or in the Scoto-Norwegian Antarctic industry that flourished from 1904–63.

*The* Windward, *Peterhead's last whaling ship, in 1885. After her final voyage eight years later, during which only one whale was caught, the town's whale fishery closed for good. While still a medical student, Arthur Conan Doyle served for seven months as ship's surgeon on a similar Peterhead-based whaling ship, the* Hope. *Ice was a more dangerous foe than the whales, and claimed one-fifth of Britain's whaling fleet in 1830 alone.*

Peterhead is still the leading white-fishing port of Europe, with more than five hundred men employed at sea and at least five fish processing firms. The original sixteenth-century feuars were apparently all fishermen, and the town was actually run by an English fishing company for a decade immediately following the earl Marischal's forfeiture for Jacobitism. Pre-industrial white fishing was very individualistic. Despite boats operating with regular crews, usually of six to eight, each man

> was responsible for his own line. He and his family had to prepare it for the fishing season, maintain it in working order, gather bait for it, process and attach the bait to the hooks, clear the lines after a day's fishing . . . and then repeat the whole operation daily throughout the season.[79]

Mackerel were baited using feathers, but almost all other fish were caught using some other sort of sea creature, chiefly mussels. When mussel populations collapsed locally – as when the valuable Ythan beds were damaged by floods – these shellfish were imported from as far away as Ireland and the Netherlands. In contrast to landward districts, where linen-spinning and stocking-knitting prevailed, bait-gathering and dealing with their menfolk's fishing equipment seem to have been the full-time work of women in eighteenth-century Buchan's coastal villages. Codlings, haddock and plaice were caught relatively close to shore on lines 2,000–3,000 feet long with 600 to 1,000 hooks. Ling, cod, and halibut were caught farther from shore using much longer lines, with larger hooks spaced slightly farther apart. The long-line technique carried over into the era of steam-powered boats, introduced in Aberdeenshire in the the early 1880s.

White fishing had gone on here since at least the fifteenth century, but the herring fishery in Banff and Buchan was mostly a new development of the period 1810–20.[80] In the eighteenth century, the world market in herring was dominated by the Dutch. British government subsidies of 2s per barrel, introduced in 1786, piqued fishermen's interest, but except perhaps in Rosehearty, the herring fishery here did not achieve industrial proportions until the end of the Napoleonic Wars, when the bounty was doubled for a period of fifteen years. While line-fishing was 'almost certain to yield a catch of some kind', herring could only be caught at night – and first had to be found.[81] Various techniques were used, including following porpoises and gannets, listening for the *plowt* of a single herring jumping, and even sniffing the surface of the water. In Cullen it was a feast-or-famine affair, with annual catches yo-yoing wildly from less than a hundred barrels, to more than 5,000, in the 1830s alone. In 1835, Banff's catch having declined by a third compared to the previous year (and by two-thirds compared to 1832), the town laid off 101 of its 162 herring workers and idled 14 of its 22 boats. The cod and haddock fisheries, in which most of the same men and boats initially participated, were more stable, but the haddock population also experienced short-term collapses. Remarkably, the nascent herring industry survived the one-two punch of the withdrawal of government subsidy in 1829, and the abolition of the slave trade in 1833 – herring and other cured fish having been a staple food of slaves in the West Indies. (In spite of, or because of, this connection, many people here were fervent Abolitionists.) Banff's fishing never really recovered, but the number of boats operating out of Fraserburgh more than quintupled, to 626, between 1820 and 1872.

Salmon fishing around Portsoy was profitable enough in 1903 that Adam Gillan could afford a villa 'of impressive size' with a large garden, servants and an upstairs bathroom, despite having only five men working for him.[82] Herring skippers, too, were becoming wealthy enough by the same date to own their houses as well as their boats. There was considerable knock-on employment, and not merely in gutting and packing. Scotland had seven factories producing wooden barrels for herring in 1907, of which five were located in Peterhead or Fraserburgh. By that time, sadly, Scottish fishing (except at Peterhead) was virtually a herring monoculture, and seasonal line-fishing, which had been far less destructive of the marine ecosystem, was mostly a thing of the past.

Overproduction caused a worldwide glut and herring recession for ten years from 1884. Losses were made good due to the opening of new markets in Germany and Russia, until they in turn closed in the 1910s amid war and communist revolution. Over the course of 1919, the price by weight of herrings landed at Fraserburgh declined by ninety-five per cent; and when the Admiralty auctioned off the 324 steam drifters it had requisitioned for war service, not a single soul bid on one. As stability returned to their countries, Germans and Russians established their own fishing industries, and the glory days of Scottish

*Peterhead women gutting herrings, 1890s. For every half-dozen men employed at sea by this date, three women were employed on land – two gutters and a packer. In addition to wielding the knife, it was up to the gutters to place each fish in one of seven categories based on condition and size. Accidental cuts were treated using poultices of bread and sugar. The alarming practice of rearing dogs specifically to be slaughtered and have their skins turned into herring-net floats was known here, at least on the stretch of coast between Buckie and Portknockie.*

herring never returned. Pound for pound, it is now dwarfed by salmon farming nationally, though in Buchan specifically, mackerel and prawns became important from the interwar years onward.

Today, in strong contrast to the Georgian age, there is a strict divide between skippers and crews. Enclosed in their cabins, fishing boat captains communicate mostly by radio, with each other, while their deck hands 'have virtually nothing to do with decision-making'.[83]

Lobstering began in the later eighteenth century in Peterhead, Fraserburgh, Pitsligo and Cullen, with Peterhead reporting catches of 4,000 a year in the 1790s and larger catches in an unspecified earlier period. The main market was London. Pearl fishing was conducted in the Ythan with some success, especially before 1770; in 1762–63, individual specimens were worth from 1s to £3 sterling, with 6s to 10s apparently being the norm. The largest pearl in the crown of Scotland was widely believed to have come from the Ythan – at a particular spot which local people could indicate to visitors as recently as the 1830s. Long ago the subject of a royal patent issued to the prominent Buchan of Auchmacoy family, pearling on the Ythan was already in steep decline by 1800 and 'practi-

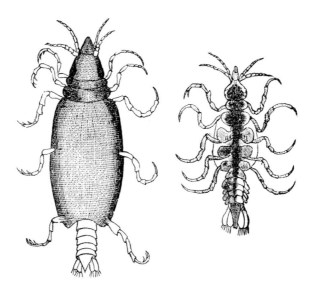

*Despite being a shoemaker by trade with no formal education beyond the age of six, Banff's Thomas Edward learned to read and write as an adult, and 'discovered, by much labour and perseverance, many specimens of Crustacea in the Moray Firth . . . new to science.'[85] When he proposed to quit his scientific endeavours and return full-time to shoemaking due to a lack of funds in 1876, his humble origins and meagre income came as a complete surprise to many who had read his work. Prime minister Disraeli and the queen arranged for him to receive a generous annuity.*

cally in the hands of vagrants' a century later.[84] On the Ugie, at around the same time, it was the preserve of a single family, the Stewarts. Consisting of a father and three sons, one of them a blind veteran of the Boer War, they were all pipers as well as pearlers. If they never found anything of great value, locals remembered, it was certainly not for want of trying. Pearls were also found in the Deveron, but were small and of generally poor quality. Oysters do not seem to have been eaten here, though they may have been used, like mussels, as bait for sea fish. Their status as a gastronomic delicacy came later.

Like our ferm-touns, our ports were economically self-sufficient in certain crucial areas. Banff in 1798 had its own shipyard employing twelve workers, a ropeworks (on and around the site of the present-day Ropeworks Cottage), sail makers, and a fleet of twenty-two ocean-going ships of 60 to 210 tons. Rope making also flourished in nineteenth-century Peterhead, with two firms employing up to three dozen men. In the year ending 5 January 1796, the port of Banff landed 5,258 gallons of foreign spirits, 282 tons of English coal and 3,880 iron bars, and exported a wide range of agricultural products as well as locally-made bricks and tiles. By 1857, Banff's fleet had grown to 142 ships. The craftsmen of early-Victorian Cullen were also capable of producing ocean-going ships of up to 110 tons, as well as more than forty fishing boats per year. However, Banff shipwrights never adapted to the post-sail era, and shipbuilding there was described as a 'lost industry' as early as 1906.[86]

## THE LOST INDUSTRIAL REVOLUTION

Peterhead was a new town founded in 1587 (during a century that saw no new towns founded in England). It quickly became an important centre of trade and fishing, an entrepot for cod and ling caught in the Hebrides and sold at Barcelona, as well as for various goods smuggled from Holland and Sweden. The town's shipping fleet grew from just three ships in 1720, to six in 1727, to twenty-eight by the end of the century: 'more than double the shipping of Banff, a royal burgh, the metropolis of that county, and a town of great opulence'.[87] This comment underestimated the size of Banff's fleet by a third, but the sense that Peterhead was coming up in the world was basically accurate. Its whaling fleet, as we have seen, expanded from a single vessel in 1788 to the largest in Britain by 1857. But this nautical focus is not the whole story, by any means. By the 1790s, Peterhead was also home to an impressive, but now forgotten, industrial base.

According to some sources, the first factory in Peterhead – making white

*The Crosse and Blackwell factory, Peterhead, operated for a century and a half down to 1998.*

thread that was 'as much esteemed as any in the kingdom' – was started by two ladies surnamed Park in 1764.[88] But a visiting Irish bishop noted that a 'small manufacture of linnen yarn, & of thread and woorsted Stockings and Gloves' was already being carried on there by 1760.[89] The Park sisters retired in about 1790, but not before fifty-two similar 'twist-mills' appeared in the town, employing at least 334 people directly and 800 indirectly as spinners: which is to say, thirty-eight per cent of the entire urban population of men, women and children. Not all of these people would have worked for the factories full-time, and some probably lived in the rural part of Peterhead parish, but the sheer numbers are nonetheless astonishing. If cotton mills are not counted, the twist-mills included:

| Firm | Mills | Employees |
| --- | --- | --- |
| J. Arbuthnot, Scott & Co. | 18 | 117 |
| J. Burd & Co. | 15 | 99 |
| C. Cummine & Co. | 8 | 52 |
| J. Robb & Co. | 6 | 39 |
| Alex. Johnston & Son | 4 | 27 |

Much of the raw material for Peterhead's industry came from the inland parishes of Old Deer – where there were three fulling mills, two linen mills, and a set of bleaching machinery, all water-powered – and Longside, where half of the working population were engaged in the cloth trades rather than agriculture. One of the Old Deer linen mills was reckoned among the most successful in the country. But this is not to say that the industrialisation of Peterhead and its hinterland only involved linen and cotton. Nails, tin goods, household furniture 'in the neatest and most substantial manner',[90] and woollen cloth were all also manufactured, and there were five bleachfields, mostly supporting the twist mills. But less than fifty years later, the parish minister remarked that 'manufactures have not hitherto been introduced'![91]

What happened?

Unlike in southern Aberdeenshire, where knitting woollen stockings on a piece-work basis was the main work of women in the eighteenth century, and linen-spinning was virtually unknown, linen was king in the northern part of the county. Stocking-knitting still took place in a small minority of parishes here – notably Rothiemay, King Edward, Turriff, Ellon, Udny and Old Deer – but by the 1790s it was always as an adjunct to linen-spinning, not the main event. The stockings made for sale in Banff and Buchan (in contrast to Deeside and Donside) were called 'market or cargo hose', the latter term presumably because they were exported to Europe and America.[92] The two trades were evenly matched in the north Donside parishes of Auchindoir and Forbes, but in Strathdon, where the women had been primarily employed in stocking-knitting in the 1760s–70s, this had by the 1790s 'given place to spinning coarse lint'.[93]

In comparison to the stocking work, linen-spinning was 'exhausting' due to the 'great quantity of saliva' required.[94] Writing from Foveran in the 1790s, William Duff noted that the proceeds of stocking-knitting have grown 'scanty', and hoped that linen-spinning would soon replace it.[95] In St Fergus in 1840, stocking- and mitten-knitting paid 2½d to 3d 'per cut of worsted' but only 'a few poor women' still did it.[96] In Georgian Methlick, the main source of cash for rents was knitting stockings 'with wires', a task for which most women and 'old and infirm men' received as much as 36d per pair; but by the early 1840s this had fallen to as little as 3½d per pair.[97] In Turriff at the same date, the wages for hand knitting stockings had become so 'miserably low' (around ninepence for a week of six days) that they were accepted only by women too old for other work of any sort.[98] In Ellon, the stocking-knitting was worth more than £5,000 sterling per year in the 1770s, but twenty years later the linen-spinning was 'easily' worth more, and by 1841, stocking-knitting was 'long since . . . discontinued' there.[99] In Old Deer in 1800, 'any woman could have found more work . . . than it was in her power to accomplish',[100] but within a generation, stockings made by machine outwith Aberdeenshire changed the balance of power completely. By the early-Victorian era, one of the region's social ills commented on most frequently by ministers of the Kirk was the new phenomenon of female unemployment.

Linen-spinning, like stocking-knitting, had begun not in mills but as a cottage industry. In eighteenth-century Mortlach, it was the main employment of the women, and money earned from it was instrumental in staving off starvation during the near-famine of 1782. In Botriphnie, people spun yarn from a mixture of flax they grew themselves, and imported Dutch flax. The latter was generally preferred: by manufacturers because of its greater fineness, and by growers because flax was 'thought to exhaust the soil more than any other crop'.[101] In spite of, or because of this, flax was 'a precarious crop upon the east coast of Scotland', and good harvests of it were produced only in exceptionally wet seasons.[102] Fraserburgh's linen yarn was spun from Dutch flax exclusively. The women of Botriphnie, whose activities led three men to become full-time spinning-wheel makers, wholesaled their finished yarn at a local fair held annually in February, to middlemen who sold it on to big manufacturers in Paisley and Glasgow. In Monquhitter, linen yarn was 'spun for the merchant almost in every family', in spite of the linen factory of Cuminestown having been 'dropt'.[103] Likewise, virtually every family there raised flax, which was made ready for use by the local linen mill at a charge of 2s per stone. Individuals' weekly earnings from yarn-spinning in Botriphnie, Rothiemay and St Fergus ranged from 1s 8d to 2s – lower by a third than Deeside and Donside stocking-knitting, but still respectable at a time when crofts (which the vast majority of manual workers had: p. 45) rented for as little as 20s per year.

In 1790s Strichen, there was apparently a seller's market in linen yarn, with 4,000 spindles sold annually, mostly at the yarn fairs held in March and May. Locally-made linen cloth, as opposed to yarn, was sold at fairs in Huntly in July, and Keith in September. Huntly and Banff also had their own linen manufacturers, who particularly favoured yarn spun by the women of Forglen. Huntly's explosion of population – to more than 2,000 in 1800, thirteen per cent of whom were textile workers – was the intended result of the Duke of Gordon's rebuilding the town, specifically as a textile centre, beginning in 1770. Banff linen was sent by sea to Edinburgh once every three weeks, 'and from that place . . . carried on to Nottingham by Land', the bishop of Ossory told his sister in 1760. 'The town subsists by this linnen yarn and Shops.'[104] (The king's officers would have added, 'and smuggling', but that is another story: p. 173.) The linen business had been brought to Banff in 1753 by the English firm of Robinson and Illingworth; one of the Robinson family's townhouses is now the Town and County Club, and their linen works was next door. At one point, Banff alone imported £11,000 worth of Dutch flax, the spinning of which gave employment to 4,300 people and yielded a profit of £19,000.

> At Nethermills of Stryla, a small village in the parish of Grange, the people raised a kind of short flax, which is now entirely banished out of the country, but of which they formerly raised great quantities; the drying, breaking, scutching, beating, heckling, spinning, weaving, and bleaching of which, not only afforded employment to men and women, at certain times of the year, when they could not work at the lime trade; but brought in a great deal of money in those days, and Keith market was formerly resorted to from all parts of Scotland for purchasing linen-cloth.[105]

At one time in Keith, almost every tenant had an acre of flax, and one gentleman had sixteen.

In Old Machar, thread-spinning, weaving and bleaching was carried out at Gordon's Mills and Printfield; cotton-spinning and bleaching at Grandholm Haugh; and flax-spinning, weaving and bleaching at Rubislaw and Broadford, by a total of four different companies. A bleachfield at Tyrie, which cost £1,000 to set up, bleached more than 500 spindles of yarn and 13,900 yards of cloth per year in the 1790s. Deskford, with a population of under 800, had a linen mill, ten acres in flax, a horse-operated bleaching apparatus processing 3,200 items per year, and eighteen weavers. The population of Turriff in 1794 included thirty-four weavers (only one of whom was self-employed), two dyers, three linen-millers, seven flax-dressers and a bleacher, in addition to more than a dozen tailors. A thread factory at Gask was described as new in the same year, and a new linen mill in Logie-Buchan (housing that parish's only alehouse) was reported as operating at less than its full capacity, due to meagre availability of raw flax. The villages of Deer and Stewartfield produced 3,000 yards of finished cloth per year. Even before 1800, the industrial scale of this activity was being noticed as a cause of pollution, Alexander Johnston reporting from Monquhitter that trout were 'daily decreasing in number' due to contaminants, including especially 'essence of steeped flax'.[106]

The end of cottage industry, in which individuals working in their own houses produced a finished article more or less from scratch, was paralleled throughout Europe at around this time. The curious feature of the changeover to a factory system in Buchan and Lowland Banffshire is that the factory system

*Local tailors in Glenbuchat, early twentieth century. A hundred years earlier, nearly every person in upland areas made whatever small items they needed, 'like the famous Crusoe'.*[107]

itself was not sustained, and that the factories and other buildings associated with it, and indeed the existence of the linen industry itself, are now all but forgotten.

A hundred yards from my former home in Burnside of Delgaty, the linen mill and bleachfield operated by Peter Garden Esq. of Delgaty from 1767 to 1777 is now semi-ruinous and in use as a cow barn; potential visitors are strongly advised to avoid it during the black-fly season (and to avoid wearing red. Recent media dismissals of the 'myth' that bullocks will charge at a person wearing red either do not apply to Delgaty bullocks, or themselves constitute a new myth of a rather idiotic kind.). A more enticing example, the pantiled Old Lintmill of Boyne in Boyndie, was described in 1977 as 'remarkably complete' despite also being in use by cows; by 1988 it had been converted into a house.[108] Most of the examples that were not totally demolished probably had similar fates. The afore-mentioned bleachfield of Deskford, founded in 1752, had ceased operating by 1836 and was 'converted into corn-land'.[109] A former linen mill at Byth was converted into a Presbyterian chapel as early as 1793.

The population of the parish of Keith fell by fifteen per cent in the eight years after 1783, likely due to a slump in flax-dressing and spinning, which caused layoffs, the unemployed leaving the area. Causes of the slump included Irish spinners undercutting prices at Glasgow, 'the principal mart for Keith yarn';

ABOVE. *Edwardian grouse-beaters wearing what appears to be a mixture of locally-made and store-bought clothing.*

LEFT. *Former linen works at Burnside of Delgaty. A carpet factory also operated on an unknown site in Turriff from 1760 to 1780.*

increased costs of the raw flax imported from Holland; declining quality of the Keith product; and the decreasing cost of finished cotton products.[110] Weaving and bleaching, the third and fourth branches of the Keith linen trade, were less hard hit than the other two but still suffered. In Monquhitter, it was the Germans and Dutch rather than the Irish who were blamed for undercutting the price of yarn.

By 1798, Banff's linen industry had largely evaporated in the face of mechanisation and war, and by 1803, the Robinsons had gone bankrupt. The overall quantity of linen cloth woven in the parish of Turriff was 28,000 yards per year for many years down to 1840, but output fell to below 16,000 yards in 1841, and further still in 1842. Wages of female linen-spinners working at home there (and in Deskford) had been driven down by seventy-five per cent or more 'for the same quantity and quality of thread', leading them to take outdoor work 'ill suited to their constitution and character'.[111] In Boharm, 'the competition of machinery' rendered the profit from flax-spinning 'insufficient for the barest subsistence'.[112] Between 1834 and 1841, indeed, flax ceased altogether to be given out for hand-spinning in that area.

Given that the Banff and Buchan linen industry seems to have come and gone in the space of less than a hundred years, the obvious question is, why did it start so suddenly and on so massive a scale? The answer, as so often in such cases, was partly political. While some debatable evidence suggests the town of Old Meldrum was a linen-making centre by 1701, no flax was grown in neighbouring Fyvie before 1782. The linen boom came overwhelmingly after, and because of, the 1745 Jacobite Rebellion, and was the brainchild of government. Scottish skippers were leading importers of tobacco, and needed a home-grown product they could sell in North America, instead of sending their ships back across the Atlantic empty. Linen filled the bill. The Commissioners of Forfeited Jacobite Estates – echoing Edmund Spenser's plan for Ireland a century and a half earlier[113] – stated that 'nothing was more likely to civilise the inhabitants of upland Aberdeenshire and Banffshire than the plantation of villages, all with linen works, post-offices, market and prison'.[114] At best it was, as Christopher Harvie puts it, 'a "controlled" process of "proto-industrialisation" in which productivity was increased while traditional relationships [between lairds and tenants] remained'.[115] At worst, it can be seen as part of an attempt to create a repressive internal colony, and proof of recent sociological theories that rigid control of the workforce's day-to-day behaviour is sometimes more important to managers than even profit itself. If the people of Banff and Buchan largely forgot their linen industry, perhaps it was not something they felt was worth remembering.

## CROFTERS ALL

One sense in which the post-1745 society was *not* repressive was in its almost universal provision of agricultural land. This was probably at its most systematic in the parish of Keith. In New Keith and Old Keith, every feu came with two to six acres of attached land, so that every household was self-sufficient in milk, butter and cheese, and sometimes also in oatmeal. In the village of Fife Keith, these town crofts ranged from four to six acres, while in Newmill, the plots were uniformly of five acres.

In Deskford in the early nineteenth century (but not earlier), improvement crofts of eight to twenty acres were let rent-free for the first seven years, and thereafter for nineteen years at a token rent of not above 27s per year. One of Belhelvie's three private schools had an endowment in the form of land, on which the schoolmaster may have been allowed to keep livestock. The minister whose congregation met in the former linen mill of Byth asked for, and received, enough land for a horse and two cows. The parishioners of Strichen gave eight acres to their schoolmaster. The Rathven poorhouse, established in 1226 and still operating in 1795, gave each of its six occupants half-acre plots of land that would have rented for 21s a year each. In eighteenth-century Cullen, burgess James Lawtie gave the poor a house, garden and croft, also worth 21s a year. The Burnett of Dens family gave the lands of Andieswells and Backhill to the poor; if rented, these would have fetched £18. Others imitated their example and by 1840, the quantity of land made over to schools, hospitals, poor relief and other charitable causes had grown to nearly twenty per cent by value of all the land in the parish of Old Deer.

Even where crofts were not provided free of charge, they were quite affordable. In Marnoch, where no true farm was available for less than £8 a year in the 1790s, a croft could be rented for £1. In late-Georgian Rothiemay, tradesmen and 'mechanics' were said to mostly 'cultivate a few acres'.[116] In the whole parish of Aberdour, there were only three tradesmen who did not have a croft; and in Turriff, all the weavers but one had 'small pieces of land', the cultivation of which took up 'the greatest part of their time'.[117] At around the same date at Nether Kinmundy in Longside, successful woollen manufacturers Thomas and Robert Kilgour were said to 'give houses and gardens' to the forty families who worked for them on a full-time basis. When this once 'flourishing' enterprise came to an end in 1828, the Kilgours' workers reverted to a primarily agricultural mode of life – suggesting that their holdings were actually quite a bit larger than the term 'garden' would nowadays suggest.[118] Many of Marnoch's late eighteenth-century crofts were relatively new subdivisions of former 'extensive' farms; the new crofting system was said to have increased the population and brought more rental income to the landlords. 'There are no houses uninhabited, and many more have been lately built than pulled down.'[119]

Opinion was sharply divided over whether subdivision of the land into crofts was a good or a bad idea. From eighteenth-century Alvah, George Sangster wrote that

> One principal cause of depopulation in this parish is, the eagerness of some improvers to take all their land under their own management; by which means mechanics, and even day-labourers are deprived of their crofts; and, as there are no villages within the parish, betake themselves to other places, where they can find accommodation.[120]

But between 1811 and 1841, Alvah's population grew by more than forty per cent. Andrew Todd explained that clearance *per se* had failed in the parish, and that the real work of agricultural improvement was being carried on by crofters:

> Large farms on such a soil are entirely out of the question . . . But the improvement of waste lands by small tenements is of a more permanent and useful nature; and, though at first it may not be done to any great degree of perfection, its progress is gradual and sure. A crofter once set down on the poorest land, or land altogether waste, seldom or never fails to make an independent livelihood, and to bring up his family, and give them such an education as fits them for becoming useful members of society.

It went almost without saying that the system also supplied 'our surplus population with places of abode'. Todd even went so far as to suggest that relocating weavers from large factory towns to crofts in Lowland Banffshire might prove a 'valuable experiment'.[121] A thirty per cent increase in the population of the parish of Ordiquhill from 1805 to 1836 was ascribed solely to 'the improvement of waste lands', also presumably by crofting families;[122] and in 1840, George Garioch wrote that Meldrum's only really significant population increase within living memory was 'in consequence of a number of crofts being set on previously uncultivated land'.[123] A savings bank for crofters was established in St Fergus in 1824.

Sangster's and Todd's views of the positive value of the new crofts were echoed by James Innes in Marnoch, William Gall in Crimond and Alexander Johnston in Monquhitter – the latter writing that most workers of whatever sort have a croft, and 'gradually rise to easy circumstances, as their children become capable of relieving the hand, and assisting the industry of the mother.'[124] But in Fyvie, where crofts outnumbered farms by nearly three to one, William Moir complained that crofters were exploited, paying higher rents per acre than people with larger holdings. Similar price-gouging occurred in Rayne, where farms rented for 20s and crofts for 30s per acre/year. Other complaints could be made: in Methlick by 1842, farmhouse roofs were all slated, but croft houses had only thatched roofs. Rev. William Greig, meanwhile, thought it ridiculous that the average farm size in Longside was just seventy acres, and that up to four tenants would club together to buy one plough. Specifically, Greig recommended that the crofters be 'converted' into day-labourers for new tenants 'of substance and knowledge', to be brought in from the southern counties.[125]

In the end, of course, it was Greig's intolerant and frankly uncivil attitude that won out. Big farmers from other parts of Britain did indeed settle in this region; crofters did largely become wage-labourers or emigrants; and over the course of the 1860s, the population of the parish of Ellon fell by a quarter, a decrease

> mainly caused by the suicidal policy of doing away with so many crofts, which were excellent nurseries for agricultural labourers of the best class. When I was at school I could count more than 40 children, mostly crofters' children, within one mile of Broomfield, and on my return from abroad in 1912, both the crofts and the children were gone.[126]

By November 2008, the average farm size in Aberdeenshire had risen to 440 acres. But people's basic desire to remain connected to the land remains strong, and even as commercial farms get bigger and bigger, there has been an equally rapid growth in the number of 'very small holdings (part-time, equine and hobby farms)'.[127] A croft by any other name. . .?

## KELPERS

Various types of seaweed known collectively as kelp can be burned to produce soda ash, a material so versatile that it is still used today in the manufacture of products ranging from glass and soap to toothpaste and ice cream. Due to the very different experience of other parts of northern Scotland, kelp-gathering and burning are now viewed stereotypically as a particular phase of the Highland Clearances. However, kelp was profitable – albeit briefly – even in

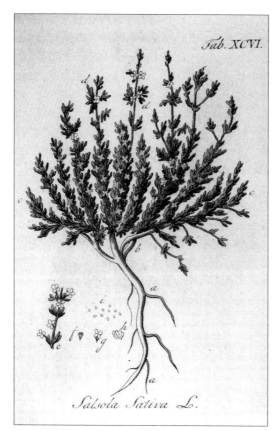

*Jab. XCVI.*

*Salsola Sativa L.*

*The local kelp industry was ruined by the availability of barrilla, a collective name for a group of continental plant species which could achieve the same results at a lower cost. Engraving by Adolphus Ypey, 1813.*

areas such as Banff and Buchan where mass clearance did not occur. At the end of the eighteenth century, Peterhead still exported up to 100,000 pounds of oily blue kelp-ash annually. At £30 sterling per ton, Peterhead's haul alone was worth £1,339. Fraserburgh also counted kelp as a leading local manufacture, and the smoke of kelp kilns was called 'very disagreeable to those who live in places nearer the sea'.[128] In other parts of Scotland the typical kelp kiln was four to five feet in diameter, but no remains of any have been identified in Aberdeenshire or Banffshire.

By 1840, the trade had all but died; profits had been steady 'during the late war' but no longer.[129] The culprit was free trade. The work of seaweed could equally well be done by Spanish *barrilla* – a class of (land-growing) plant also known in English as saltwort. In Lonmay, the lowering of import duty on *barrilla* was blamed for the end of kelping, the parish's only manufacture, which had employed a chiefly female workforce of thirty for two months per year. Twenty former kelp workers were prominent among the unemployed in Aberdour in 1835. By 1840 the business had been abandoned entirely in Rathen, while in Fraserburgh it lingered on, but was so unprofitable that the rent of the kelp beaches had fallen by ninety per cent, to just £15 a year. Kelp was still manufactured in some quantity on the estate of Sir John Forbes in Pitsligo at the same date, but 'more for the purpose of giving people employment than for realizing a profit'.[130] Up until 1820, the same site had been a going concern, employing seventy and producing 140 tons of kelp ash a year.

## TATTIES AND HERRING

Two hundred years ago, meat-eating in this region was largely the preserve of the upper classes. In Forglen, the eating of meat had only recently become commonplace, and its price had increased by a third 'in the space of a few years' in the 1790s.[131] At the same date, people in Highland Banffshire were reluctant to eat sheep's flesh that could be traded elsewhere for money; and in King Edward, meat was still consumed only on holidays. From early-Victorian Alvah, Andrew Todd reported that the working classes seldom ate any meat or even fish, and '[t]he effects of hard labour, and under-feeding, become very perceptible on the approach of age.'[132] Consumption of bird flesh was not generally discussed, presumably because it was normal among all classes; but in 1760, it was noted that the people of the coast around New Slains ate seabird chicks, as well as eggs.

The meat-eaters of Forglen were not alone, however, and mutton and beef were suddenly being consumed even in coastal areas like St Fergus. It seems odd that civilians would have doubled up on meat consumption at precisely the time when army and navy consumption, particularly of beef, was rising sharply and driving up prices across the board, but the evidence for this is strong. Gentlemen like Todd, and Boharm's L.W. Forbes, were quick to condemn the prevailing vegetarianism. Forbes claimed that a mostly vegetable diet led to various complaints ranging from constipation to cancer – a litany curiously similar to the complaints now associated with excessive consumption of meat. On the other hand, when the previously meat-rich ferm-touns of Auchterless faced starvation in 1782, 'three-fourths of the people lived for several months almost wholly on [Royal Navy surplus] pease-meal' – and enjoyed the best health of their lives.[133] Doctors were few, and accurate medical information was correspondingly scarce. In St Fergus, vegetables in the diet were credited with the elimination of scurvy, and in Rayne they were blamed for causing it.

In any case, our recent forebears were not the voracious meat-eaters we are today. As the late-Victorian song would have it:

Oh ye Scots working men, ye've gone crazy, I fear:
Every day ye maun hae yer bit beef and yer beer;
But ye dinna ken noo, and you're maybe no' carin'
That yer natural food is but tatties and herrin'. . .
When the harbour o' refuge was first thought aboot,
Aberdeen and Stanehive, they were fair pitten oot
Fan they heard that the convicts were gettin' best farin'
O' guid Buchan tatties and Peterhead herrin'!
*Tatties and herrin', tatties and herrin',*
*O' guid Buchan tatties and Peterhead herrin'!*
Fan the queen's wantin' men tae gang fecht wi' her foes,
It's nae tae the roast-beef devourers she goes,
But awa' tae the north 'mongst the brave and the darin':
Tae the lads that were brocht up on tatties and herrin'.

## THE MOSS: A LOST WAY OF LIFE

One-fifth of Scotland's surface was once covered by peat bogs. The peat works at Blackhills of St Fergus is now commercialised, and its owners, the Northern Peat & Moss Company, appear to be the only firm of this sort in greater Aberdeenshire. Just two sites in St Fergus, one each in Pitsligo and New Pitsligo, and one in Whitehills had permission for peat extraction as of 2003. As recently as the 1960s, however, farmers cut their own peat for domestic fuel at the Black-hills site, and carted it away themselves. This ancient practice once dominated the lives of whole communities during the summer months, not just in St Fergus but throughout the region.

Buchan's mosses are the remains of ancient forests of oak, alder, birch, hazel and willow trees, preserved in groundwater but still highly flammable if dried – or even during dry weather, as residents of Grange found out the hard way in 1826. Mosses' size, quality, and customary access restrictions varied sharply over relatively short distances, as did attitudes toward peat's value and sustainability as a fuel, and peat-cutting's effects on the local population. In eighteenth-century Kirkmichael in Banffshire, supplies of peat were distant, and in any case already dwindling toward zero. From the neighbouring parish of Inveraven, however, it was reported that good quality peat was plentiful – indeed, 'inexhaustible' on Cairnocay – and peat-fuelled lime kilns were found 'on almost every farm in Glenlivet'.[134] Heather and turf were both used extensively as domestic fuel on upper Donside where peat was scarce; Tullynessle

*Aberdeenshire peat sledge, early twentieth century.*

had exhausted its peat supplies completely before 1800 and was in the process of switching to coal for some purposes. Cullen had exhausted its local supplies by 1842 but was continuing to import peat from round about, as well as coal and wood. In 1790s Mortlach, peat was running out rapidly and people hoped vainly that a local supply of coal would be discovered in time to meet their needs. Where coal was inappropriate, such as in kiln-drying, brewing and baking, peat was usually replaced by heather. Inverkeithny, meanwhile, had no peat at all, and obtained its supplies from Auchintoul in the parish of Marnoch (which was 'fully provided'[135]), and Foudland in Forgue. Itinerant peat merchants were apparently so commonplace as to be beneath suspicion. During the Cromwellian occupation, a royalist assassin disguised as a peat seller killed the Covenanting provost of Banff and escaped 'on the horse that had carried the peats'.[136]

Aberdeenshire's rapidly changing eastern shoreline meant that peat was even found under the sea: as at Belhelvie, where the ferocious storm of December 1799 dislodged huge blocks of it, the largest being 1,700 cubic feet in size, and cast them up on the shore. In Cruden, the peat mosses 'were once thought to be inexhaustible, but are now fast wearing away', Alexander Cock reported in 1840.[137] As a replacement, coal was brought by sea via Ward of Cruden (but only in the summer), Newburgh and Peterhead. Peterhead itself had nearly replaced peat with coal by the same date. The smoking of haddock over peat fires, which allowed them to be exported in edible condition to the primary markets in Portugal and Spain, was invented here and spread to other parts of Scotland later.

In the 1790s, two mosses in Gartly supplied all of that parish's own peat requirements, and those of the town of Huntly as well. But half a century later, the moss of the Braes there was 'almost exhausted'.[138] Huntly residents also obtained peats from Rothiemay, but this was done 'clandestinely, or merely by indulgence . . . not by stipulation and right.'[139] Peat was virtually unavailable within the parish of Turriff before 1800, yet it remained the main fuel source, since 'most of the people have a right to moss in some of the neighbouring parishes'.[140] Perhaps as a result of this, mosses in Old Deer were severely overexploited and 'left an unseemly waste', while grouse and snipe populations declined in locked step with the size of the bogs.[141]

The use of limestone for fertiliser would have accelerated this process, since before being applied to the fields, the stone was burned in peat-fired kilns. In Grange, where 60,000 bolls of limestone were burnt for sale annually in the 1750s, output was intentionally reduced by the 1790s to under 40,000 bolls, so that the moss would not run out so fast. A similar restriction was enacted in Deskford, but such regulation merely postponed the inevitable. Even if a living forest were available (and were allowed to die without its wood being harvested), new peat could not have been generated at a tiny fraction of the rate humans were using up the old. As early as the seventeenth century, a salt-panning operation on the Boddam estate failed because it exhausted the local supply of peat.

James Simmie and Andrew Youngson were among at least half a dozen Georgian writers who condemned our use of peat as wasteful of time and labour.

*Men and women cutting peat, Rora Moss.*

In many places, digging and drying it was reported as taking up 'most of the summer'.[142] The situation in eighteenth-century Aberdour was made somewhat worse by a requirement that the tenant farmers provide 'leet peats (as they are called) for their landlords'.[143] Hauling a certain amount of peat for the laird was a condition of tenancy on some estates. In Fraserburgh and Rosehearty at the same date, peat was sold by the 'leat' or 'leet': a large trapezoidal heap, twenty-four by twelve feet in base and twelve feet high, but narrowing to a yard wide at the top. These cost £5 each, which the minister of Fraserburgh found hard to bear, yet understandable since peat was locally scarce. If bought in Turriff, peat cost 10s 6d per 480 square ells laid out flat – an amount known as a 'spade's casting'. (The ell and other obsolete units of length, weight and volume are explained in *Lost measures*, p. 54.) For most people, paying such sums was simply impossible, and in Tyrie, the elderly frequently moved house in order to remain as close as possible to the 'superabundance of fine fuel' which the mosses provided free of charge to those with the energy to dig.[144] The very poor gravitated to Deskford for similar reasons.

In at least some areas, there was a considerable economic incentive to dig out the mosses as quickly as possible, quite apart from the high value of peat as fuel. This was the belief that the land found at the bottom of fully worked-out bogs was of superior quality for agriculture. Writing in 1842, Harry Leith and William Webster argued that the waste ground in Rothiemay was fit only for planting trees – with the exception of moss bottoms, which should be tilled. At the same date, the 180-acre Moss of Banff was an undivided common – but the ground underneath it belonged to the Forglen estate. It was clearly in the estate's interest for the moss to be exhausted as quickly as possible, so that the 'bottom' or 'under strata' could be brought into cultivation.[145]

Fir trees were not found in Buchan's mosses, but an extinct fir forest provided employment in Banffshire, where people dug up and sold ancient fir roots for interior lighting. In early-Victorian Strathdon, too,

> some of the poorer classes, who cannot afford other light . . . go to the moss, and with a long probe something like a rude auger, search for trunks of trees buried perhaps six or eight feet deep. These, often of a diameter of 12 or 13 inches, are dug up, carried home, and cut into splits. Then being dried on the *kilchan*, or on a kind of round brander with spiral bars, they are made use of in place of candles . . . and when lighted, the rosin boils out at the root of the flame like a torch. In provincial language they are termed candle, or fir-candle, in contradistinction to a tallow-candle, which is denominated 'white candle.'[146]

Fir candles were commonly sold at the St Lawrence Fair in Old Rayne, but were virtually unknown in Buchan's coastal villages, where lamps fired by the liver oil of 'sea dogs' were used universally.[147] This term could refer to seals and walruses, but more likely to the spurdog, a type of small shark. An individual spurdog fisherman could catch three hundred in a day, yielding fifteen Scots pints of oil or about seven and a half imperial gallons.

The Royal Navy's anti-submarine airbase at Lenabo, three miles south of Longside, was built on an enormous peat bog by thousands of workmen in 1915. It was a self-propelling operation, reminiscent of a Terry Gilliam cartoon, in which the steam scoops and bucket cranes used to clear the site were powered by the very peat they were taking away.

Use of peat by the whisky industry has been on a downward trend for some years, and now accounts for only half of one per cent of UK consumption; most of the rest is now being sold as potting soil. Concern about Britain's mosses as habitats is widespread, yet planning permission was granted last year for a wind farm on St Fergus Moss. Ironically perhaps, if they had been left alone, our peat bogs would eventually have turned into coal.

## LOST MEASURES

Supermarkets today sell items using an arbitrary riot of kilograms, ounces, avoir-dupois pounds of 454 grams, the so-called metric pound of 500 grams, and apparently subjective measures like the 'large' egg (which in fact must weigh 63 grams or more). Though the metric system is relatively new, the lack of a single coordinated system is, in fact, traditional. The Cromwellian Excise officer Thomas Tucker wrote in 1656 that one boll of 'Lithquo measure' was found to be 'very neere, or . . . somewhat lesse' than the English barrel of eleven Scots gallons.[148] Similar, horribly confusing attempts to define defunct measurements using *other* defunct measurements were sadly common. Perhaps the unwieldiest such description I have ever seen, from eighteenth-century Forglen, stated that 'The Banffshire firlot is 32 Scotch standard pints, and the medium of a boll of oats of said measure is 14 stone Amsterdam weight'.[149] This 'Amsterdam weight', John Swinton complained in 1789, 'is commonly reckoned the same with Scotch Troye, and is divided in the same manner; but it seems to be a little heavier'.[150] This is by no means to suggest that a Scot would only encounter the Amsterdam pound (of 1.09 pounds avoirdupois) when travelling abroad. In Old Deer in 1793, a stone of hay was stated to weigh twenty pounds Dutch, and a peck of potatoes, two stone Dutch. 'Amsterdam' was in fact the usual measure of weight used before 1824 in Rathen, St Fergus and New Deer, as well as in the city of Aberdeen. Local variations were also popular, however. In Banff, a pound of meat weighed seventeen ounces and a pound of butter, twenty-four ounces. The pound of butter used in Udny was almost double normal weight, at twenty-eight ounces avoirdupois; while the Udny stone was, at twenty-eight pounds, either double or quadruple the size of a modern stone, depending on whether it consisted of avoirdupois or Udny butter pounds.

Fans of drinking lore are probably already aware that the old Scots pint was equal to about three English pints, and that the Scots gallon was larger in proportion. The *anker*, a type of barrel favoured by whisky smugglers, held nine or ten gallons. The dry measure most frequently encountered was the *boll* of six bushels, weighing (in the case of Cabrach barley) about 125 pounds. The Rathven *leet* of peat was only one-third the size of the Fraserburgh and Rosehearty leet previously described. Herring was measured by the *cran*, a barrel of 37.5 (imperial) gallons and generally weighing 3.5 hundredweight – not 350, but 392 pounds avoirdupois.[151] In eighteenth-century Grange, a weight of nine stone was described mysteriously as weighing '157½lb. Avoirdupoise', that is to say, not fourteen but 17.5 pounds per stone. The writer probably had in mind the *Dutch* stone of *sixteen* pounds, each Dutch pound weighing 1.09 pounds, which would indeed make 17.44 pounds avoirdupois.

Knowing that the fishermen of Buckie, Portknockie and Findochty fished up to sixteen leagues from shore in winter and twenty-three leagues from shore in summer is helpful only if one knows that a league was three Admiralty miles, or 2.99989 nautical miles, or 3.45221 modern land miles. A 'sea mile', different again from the nautical and Admiralty mile, was also known; it varied between 6,000 and 6,080 feet depending on latitude. On land, English, Scots and 'computed' miles were all used here. Sadly, writers of early-modern documents frequently failed to specify which mile they were talking about. Scotland's basic unit of length – applied to cloth-making and house-building as well as distance travelled – was the *ell* or long yard of 37.06 modern inches. Six ells made up a *fall*, forty falls equalled a Scots *furlong*, and eight Scots furlongs the Scots mile of – usually – 1.12 English miles. The 'computed' or 'country' mile, theoretically of 1,500 paces, equalled 1.42 English miles, and was used in England as well as in Scotland.

Land area measures were very idiosyncratic and tended to be based not on the standard measures of length/distance, but on how long an area took to plough, or how many fighting men it could feed. Typical of this was the *davoch* or *daach*, still seen occasionally as an element of place-names, which consisted of thirty-two *oxgangs*. Each oxgang was the area which, based on actual local experience, an ox could plough within a certain amount of time. In the event, davoch size generally fell within the range of 400 to 650 acres. All this being said, there was also a measured Scots acre equal to about 1.3 English acres.

Prior to the Jacobean union of the crowns, the value of the English pound fluctuated against the Scots pound like any other foreign currency. In practice, it only tended to fluctuate in an upward direction. Having been worth £3 10s Scots in 1526, sterling rose to £5 Scots in 1560, £8 Scots in 1579, and £10 Scots in 1597, before being fixed permanently at £12 Scots in 1603. Prior to the twentieth century, when coins became in effect paper money that happened to be printed on (cheap) metal, the value of money was dependent on the intrinsic value of its metal content. English coins as small as a penny therefore had to be made of sterling silver in the seventeenth century, but the Scots penny – being worth only one-twelfth as much – could be made of copper. In practice, coins worth less than a bodle (tuppence Scots or two-thirds of an English farthing) were too small to be of practical use, and do not seem to have been made in the Jacobean period or afterwards.

The Kirk, as a weekly collector of money, became expert at detecting and handling a bewildering array of coins that were underweight, clipped, obsolete, base – or even out-and-out fakes like the 'Inverness halfpenny' and the local Aberdeenshire 'maggierobbs'. Many were sold to merchants at steep discounts from their face values, to be melted down or even, perhaps, passed right back into circulation.

*In the century after the 1603 union of the crowns, Scottish coins did not imitate English ones, either in value or in design. Note the patriotic thistle and St Andrew's cross on this 1678 copper sixpence or 'bawbee' (left), and 1681 silver 'sixteenth dollar'. The Scots dollar was traditionally £3 Scots, so one-sixteenth of a dollar was 45d Scots or just under 4d English. Naturally, English silver 4d coins of the same date were about the same size. Author's collection.*

## LOST ONLY LATELY: THE FEUDAL ECONOMY

Scottish feudalism was much in the news in recent years, due to its abolition by Holyrood in November 2004. The essence of feudalism had been landholding as a reward for current and/or future military service, so in a sense it became incompatible with law as soon as private armies were abolished in 1746. The 'fiction of . . . land being held from a superior lord',[152] military in inception, had by the twentieth century 'degenerated from a living system of land tenure with both good and bad features into something which, in the case of many but not all superiors, is little more than an instrument for extracting money.'[153] When the moment came, feudal forms of landholding were easily swept away. The real 'teeth' of the feudal system had lain elsewhere.

I have already mentioned the rents or tithes of fish that fishermen paid to sea-lairds well into the nineteenth century. Tenant farmers throughout the region laboured under arrangements that were similar, but altogether more complicated. Rents in work, called *bondages*, were distinguished from rents in butter, ducks, hens, sheep and a whole smorgasbord of other commodities, called *customs*. The widest variety of customs was seen in Lowland Banffshire. Bondages, payable to the laird, typically included (but were not limited to) haulage of dung, ploughing, reaping and peat-cutting. Walter Chalmers complained from Deskford that they

> often occasion interruptions to urgent domestic concerns, sometimes prevent the seasonable cultivation of the fields, and not unfrequently hazard the safety of their produce. It is astonishing that heritors, in many respects liberal minded and indulgent . . . still continue this pernicious vestige of feudal slavery.[154]

Bondages were further distinguished from labour *taxes* payable to the crown, primarily in the form of road repair. In 1669, imitating English laws introduced in the mid-sixteenth century, the Scots parliament decreed a system of forced labour for highway maintenance, run by the justices of the peace. All tenants and their servants in a given county had to work on the roads for a number of days each year, usually four. Statute labour, as this was called, 'was effective, at least in some rural areas, but was naturally unpopular.'[155] Locally, the results varied considerably, being called excellent (Strichen); 'good' (Fyvie and Botriphnie); tolerable (Foveran, Methlick and Rayne); 'not wholly sufficient' (Slains); superficial (Crimond and King Edward); bad (Peterhead); 'most wretched' (Forbes and Kearn); and 'a mere farce' (Mortlach).[156] The roads of

Keith were likewise 'very bad', but largely because the statute labour was evaded there, not because it was badly performed.[157] Local acts of parliament could commute the statute labour into money taxes, but the use of these was patchy down to 1845. Abolition finally came with the Roads and Bridges (Scotland) Act 1878, which 'abolished the remaining statute labour trusts and assessments and placed all turnpike roads, statute labour roads, highways and bridges under the control of a single road trust for the landward area of each county'.[158] In Aberdeenshire, however, the 1878 Act was only enforced in 1890.

All of these demands for unpaid work must have been irritating enough, but the lairds' monopoly on grinding grain was even more onerous, as well as more complicated. In Turriff there were seven mills to which every person who grew grain was assigned, so that *multures* – tithes of grain, similar in concept to the fish teinds – could be extracted. The head of Scotland's Cromwellian Excise department, Thomas Tucker, baldly stated in 1656 that 'none can grinde any malt privatly', and legally at least he was probably right.[159] There were three kinds of multure: *thirlage*, collected on behalf of the landowner, usually one-thirteenth of the amount milled; *knaveship*, a similar proportion, but collected by the miller himself 'for working and keeping the machinery of the mill in repair'; and *abstracted* or *dry* multure, one-seventeenth of 'grain sold unmanufactured'.[160] (In eighteenth-century Udny, all farms paid mill multures of between one-eleventh and one-twentieth of their grain, 'whether the corns are carried to the mill or not'.[161]) In all, centuries before the invention of a formal income tax, these various charges accounted for a little over twenty-one per cent of the grain grown by tenant farmers; and the system was 'the practice generally through Buchan [including Formartine]' at the end of the eighteenth century,[162] as well as in the neighbourhood of Clatt. A little farther to the south, the exactions came nearer ten than twenty per cent but were still bitterly complained about, sometimes because millers took even more than they were entitled to:

> if all these measures were accurately fixed and proportioned, there would be less injustice; but that is not the case. The multurer is allowed to mend [measuring devices such as the *cog*] or make them anew, or alter them as he pleases.[163]

It was not only the ancient or rural settlements that were affected. Ellon's new town, begun in 1815, required anyone building a house there to grind their grain at Auchterellon Mill.

Low-level resistance to these practices was commonplace. In the baronial

*Mill Croft of Glenbuchat, twenty years before its closure in 1927.*

*Old Glenbuchat Lodge, as it looked from c.1840 to c.1900.*

court of Ardgrain in July 1633, the miller of Cauldwalls sued Alexander Airth, William Smith, Alexander Pattersone and Alexander Lawrensone, 'all in Ardgrain'. Airth paid the claim against him, while the other three defendants failed to appear.[164] The miller received some satisfaction from the same barony court in December, however, when he pursued (for the same cause) 'Wm.

Smyth, Adam Smyth, Wm. Airth, Wm. Sym, James Sangster, James Kelman, Wm. Aiken, Alexr. Lowrenstoun, Alexr. Paterson, James Hutcheon, all in Ardgrain', and three other men on three other farms nearby. Only Airth was let off, on the grounds that he had already paid his fine to the laird of Kermuck, 'his Maister'.[165] A century later, the miller of Glenbuchat complained to the baronial court of Kildrummy that his living had been rendered 'altogether precarious' because 'many if not most of . . . the Tenants of the Lands of Glenbuckett did daily and yearly abstract their grindable corns from the Miln, and . . . kept Quirns & other Machines for grinding their Corns at home'. A £10 Scots fine was imposed on those found keeping grinding querns privately.[166]

Bondages, customs and multures were abolished unsystematically and over a lengthy period. Improved roads meant that farmers could carry their unmilled grain to distant markets rather than having it all ground locally. Specifically, this caused the number of meal mills in Udny and Methlick to fall from sixteen to four, over a fifty-year period. By 1842 in Turriff, thirlage and bondage had both entirely ceased, but knaveships lingered on at a reduced rate of three per cent. The process of abolition had already begun in the eighteenth century. At a time when multures and mill services were still called 'heavy' and 'oppressive' in Grange,[167] Rothiemay's multures at one-thirteenth were converted to less onerous cash fees, 3s 6d per £1 of the annual rental of the farm. Rents-in-kind there were also converted into money, and labour rents abolished altogether. However, the miller of Rothiemay was still paid one-eighteenth of the grain milled. 'Would it be any disadvantage to society,' James Simmie asked, if everyone were 'at liberty to choose his miller, as well as his smith, his carpenter, or any other mechanic?'[168] Over the next few decades many people, including some of the most prominent landowners, agreed. In effect, the payment of an income tax from the peasantry to the gentry ceased to make sense once the crown, and not the gentry, became chiefly responsible for national defence, bridging, local policing and the administration of justice generally; but here, it was only in the mid-nineteenth century that this process could be called truly complete.

It is a truism that in early-modern Europe townspeople had more freedom than people working the land, but this is far from clear in our case. Town councils and toun guards could represent an extra layer of bureaucracy between kirk and laird, with their own range of powers to levy taxes, admonish, inflict corporal punishment and even decree banishment (*Lost crimes and punishments*, p. 68). Each council, moreover, was a 'self-perpetuating oligarchy': 'whenever the time came to appoint a new town council, the only people allowed to vote were the members of the old town council.'[169] Moreover, only these same councillors could vote for towns' MPs, and before 1832, when Peterhead was added, the only towns in the area that *had* an MP – whom they shared with each other and with Elgin – were Banff, Cullen, Inverurie and Kintore.

## LOST WORLD OF THE PLOUGHMEN

It was fashionable for scholars in the mid-twentieth century, following on from the work of British anthropologist Margaret Murray (1863–1963), to assert that one or another rural custom was a pagan survival dating back to Roman times or earlier. One of the most absurd such claims was made on behalf of the Society of the Horseman's Word. Writing in the academic journal *Folklore* in 1967, H.A. Beecham supposed that the society 'had been extinct for too many centuries to yield more than an occasional trace-memory', and was amazed to discover that it still existed 'in remote places such as north-east Scotland'. Beecham went on enthusiastically to endorse the Horseman's Word as an 'ancient' survival of the worship of a pre-Christian 'horned god'.[170] What it actually did is fairly well attested:

> The Horseman's Word initiated youthful ploughmen into the world of men, at least until World War II . . . Initiations were usually at Martinmas, 11 November. The initiate had to appear at the barn, between 11 p.m. and 1 a.m. . . . taking with him a candle, a loaf of bread, and a bottle of whisky. At the door he was blindfolded and led before the secret court – an older ploughman, a master of ceremonies, at an altar made by inverting a bushel measure over a sack of corn. The youth was then subjected to questioning and made to repeat a certain form of words [sometimes including Bible passages read backwards]. At the climax of initiation he got a shake of the Devil's hand – usually a stick covered with a hairy skin. He was then given the Word – 'Both in One,' meaning complete harmony between man and beast – which conferred power over horses, making them stand still when no one else could move them, or come to their handler from a distance. This power was sexual too, and represented power over women. Until the initiation, the young man would have problems with his horses, caused by older ploughmen tainting the horse collar with pig dung, or a tack embedded in the collar.[171]

The Society was particularly associated with Aberdeenshire and Orkney.

*Poses and gestures: natural or laden with hidden meanings?*

*A hard land inhabited by survivors.*

*Modern man, medieval transport. (All photos these pages courtesy of the estate of Eric Ellington)*

My own scepticism about the ancientness of the Horseman's Word began as soon as I heard of it, for the simple reason that ploughing using teams of two horses was virtually unknown in this area before 1770. From Keith in the 1790s, Alexander Humphrey wrote that

> agriculture is here just in its infancy; the long drawing team of 8 or 10 oxen in yokes, sometimes preceded by a couple of horses, is yet often to be seen creeping along, dragging after them an immense log of a clumsy Scotch plough; when 2, or at most 4 good horses, or even good oxen in collars, with the modern light plough . . . would perform the same work, equally well, in a much shorter time.[172]

Mixed teams of horses and cows were still used at the same date in Rathven, Inveraven and Strathdon, where horse-only teams seem to have been the preserve of the well-to-do. The reverse was the case in Rayne, where two-animal teams were used only by crofters, while the eight- or ten-ox plough was used on large farms only. In Cabrach, where there were no gentlemen, the ploughs in use at the same date were of the 'old Scotch' type, drawn by teams of six to ten oxen, 'or cows and oxen, or horses and oxen together'.[173] In Auchindoir, similarly mixed horse-and-ox and oxen-only teams were the only two types in use – both with the old type of plough.[174] In Mortlach, mixed teams 'of a very indifferent kind' made up the majority, though some ten-ox, four-horse and two-horse ploughs were known.[175] In Grange, a quarter of the 167 ploughs were of the old eight- to ten-ox variety, and less than three per cent were drawn by two animals (of any type). The great majority of ploughs there used '4 or more horses each, or horses and cattle yoked together, as those who have small possessions can afford.'[176]

In Udny and Fyvie, meanwhile, virtually every variation *except* the two-horse plough was seen. Only oxen were used in Old Deer in 1793, but by 1840 these had given way to mixed teams of one horse and one ox, or even a horse and a cow, among those farmers who could not afford a second horse. Cullen, Auchterless, Gartly and King Edward were highly unusual in that ploughing with horses was already the norm as the nineteenth century dawned.

Generally, histories of this area speak of a clear-cut development, centred around 1800, in which the twelve-ox teams of the Middle Ages were suddenly replaced by small teams of (large) horses; but the reality was much more complex. First, as the sharp-eyed reader will have already noticed, no one was still using as many as *twelve* oxen in Banff and Buchan in the late 1700s, ten or fewer having become usual. (A ten-ox team was achieved by eliminating the

A 'mixed team' in action near Peterhead.

The Ploughmen's Society Hall, Old Rayne, built c.1830 with financial help from the Leith of Freefield family.

'mid-throcks' i.e., the two oxen forming the fourth row from the front.[177]) Secondly, there might be a simultaneous use of ox- and horse-drawn ploughs on a given estate, or even by the same individual. In Forglen, for instance, horses or oxen were used in ploughing 'according to the nature of the ground'.[178] In Lonmay in 1800, horse teams of six or even eight 'dwarfish small-boned beasts'

*Carpenter's apprentices in upland Aberdeenshire, with masonic symbols (composed of actual tools) in the shop window behind them, c.1905.*

were commonplace, but a generation later, teams of four oxen were still used to pull the new plough for some purposes.[179] These purposes might include 'very stony ground' (as in Fyvie) and bad weather (as in Meldrum). Around Fraserburgh in the 1790s, the use of oxen was actually on the rise, and in eighteenth-century Turriff – far from being a sign of backwardness – the use of oxen in ploughing was 'an indication that the owner was a person of substance', especially if he had a hired *gadesman* 'whistling by their side'.[180] Finally, references to ploughs being horse-drawn do not necessarily imply that the implements themselves were modern. The old wooden 'Scotch pleugh' was pulled by four or six *horses* in mid-eighteenth-century St Fergus, where later in the same century, the new Berwickshire plough was sometimes drawn by four to six *oxen*.

The Society of the Horseman's Word is no less interesting for having been a proto-trade union of the Improvement period. It is now believed to have evolved, via the similar society of the Miller's Word, from Freemasonry of the more usual type. None of the three can readily be traced to before 1700. Its own claims about Alexander the Great notwithstanding, the Grand Lodge of England is beginning to get very excited about the impending three hundredth anniversary of its foundation in 1717.[181] Scottish Rite Freemasonry was first heard of in 1733, and attempts to establish its origin as far back as the reign of King Charles II (d. 1685) have met with failure.

## THE 'EGYPTIANS'

People today are rightly shocked by the severity with which our ancestors treated the unemployed and anyone else who did not occupy a clear-cut societal role. Conversely, the men and women of the Stuart and Georgian eras would no doubt be equally horrified by our post-industrial society's tendency to disconnect us from our native places, and from a sense of place in general. Whether or not they were actually Romany – and at this distance in time it is nearly impossible to tell – wanderers in Banff and Buchan were denigrated as 'Egyptians' by their more settled neighbours. The famous song 'Macpherson's Lament', associated with Robert Burns but printed fifty-eight years before Burns was born, commemorates an actual incident in Banff in which a well-known fiddle player and others were sentenced to death for being, among other things, 'Egyptians and vagabonds'.[182] The fiddler, James Macpherson, who could not have been born much before 1675, is usually and perhaps wilfully confused with Sheumas an Tuim, James [Grant] of the Hill, a famous outlaw of the 1630s who had hideouts in Kirkmichael, Inveraven and Knockando.

Desperate, hungry people 'swarmed the country' during the famine of the 1690s, and the toun guard of Banff was increased to forty-four men, specifically to 'secure the boundaries' and keep them out.[183] In 1742, Old Meldrum had thirty-nine beggars under the age of fifteen, and by 1752, 'vagrants and randies' were a big enough problem that Meldrum kirk session appointed a constable, Charles Benzie, answerable directly to the minister.[184] Rathen 'could, with ease, support its own poor, but is harrassed with vagrants', William Cumine complained in 1793.[185] At the same date, Clatt was 'exceedingly pestered with beggars and vagrants . . . many of whom are great impostors',[186] and Rayne was visited by half a dozen new beggars from the Highlands each day during the summer. In Glenbuchat, where battles raged between the Corgarff Castle army garrison and Highland Banffshire whisky smugglers on their way south to Perth and Dundee, the local 'tinkers' appear to have played both ends against the middle.[187]

Townspeople of Banff, including four ministers, all the medical doctors and all the landowners, founded an Establishment for the Suppression of Begging, a 'mighty edifice of civic unity' which operated with great seriousness from 1828.[188] Grange, William Duff wrote in 1842, 'has long been infested with cairds, tinkers, and sturdy-beggars; but it may be hoped that the evil will soon be removed by the county police.'[189] Similar hopes were expressed in Auchindoir and Kearn, and were realised in Turriff, where the newly instituted Aberdeenshire constabulary succeeded in reducing by about ninety per cent the 'overwhelming concourse of vagrants' for whom Turriff had long been a 'favourite haunt'.[190] As police activity increased, vagrancy ceased to be a problem of the older towns, and instead became associated with the remotest rural spots. A particular cove near the parish boundary of Slains and Cruden 'was often used as a place of concealment in the days of smuggling, and has since been occasionally occupied by gypsy vagrants', John Pratt noted in 1858.[191] At around the same time, at Aldunie in the wild uplands of Cabrach, a 'Tribe of Wandering Gypsies', ten in number and all surnamed Stuart, 'lodged in an outhouse'.[192]

In March 2011, Aberdeen City and Shire received £157,000 of Holyrood funding to 'to tackle the problems of unauthorised traveller camps'.[193] The city council helpfully enumerates these problems as 'poor health, low literacy skills, isolation, mental health, living with fear of constant eviction, experience of not being listened to, bullying and harassment in schools, and discrimination from the settled community'.[194] Amid such negative publicity constantly being generated by government and others – including a city council worker recently convicted of threatening to come after travellers with bats and petrol bombs – the positive contributions that have been made by travelling folk to the culture of the North-east, particularly in music, are rapidly being swept under the rug.

## LOST CRIMES AND PUNISHMENTS

One of the most unusual features of Scottish life before 1747 was the parcelling out of the justice system to private individuals, as their heritable property. England had its pockets of territory where the king's writ did not run, such as County Durham under its prince-bishops, but around half of Scotland by area was in a similar situation. Barons' courts and burghs of barony could try all crimes except murder, arson, robbery, rape and treason, while regality courts and burghs of regality (including, from 1601, Fraserburgh) could try any crime but treason. In the sixteenth century, there were almost as many Scots barons as there were parishes. Moreover, as of 1600, all but two of the king's sheriffs were hereditary peers or lairds, so Scottish justice as a whole could fairly be described as in the pocket of the nobility. Royal burghs and the Kirk also had wide-ranging powers to punish a variety of crimes.

Many punishments of the old time were harsh, but it would be a mistake to assume they were comprehensively *more* harsh than punishments of today. For one thing, imprisonment 'for any period of time' was 'too expensive', even for the larger towns.[195] So taken as a whole, the system relied principally upon fines, banishment and public humiliation. Banff relied heavily on banishment – sometimes to a set distance of twenty-four miles – to deal with what would now be misdemeanours, including prostitution, petty theft and begging without permission. But banishment was also used to punish acts no longer considered crimes at all, such as extramarital sex and long-term unemployment. Breaking a decree of banishment resulted in much harsher penalties including branding on the face, or even death. On the other hand, crimes of violence short of murder were dealt with much more lightly than now, with modest fines and financial compensation to the victim being the usual result.

Even murder charges could frequently be avoided through prompt payment to the victim's family and an apology. Sir George Ogilvy of Carnousie and Ardgrain admitted to killing his own cousin, James Ogilvy, in 1628, but got off with a fine. The following year, his second wife alleged that he had tried, on different occasions, to beat her to death and to starve her to death; but on both these charges he was acquitted. The next year, Ogilvy 'was not prosecuted for his involvement in the killing of William Gordon of Rothiemay . . . as he had had a commission to arrest him'.[196] He later became a JP and Sheriff of Banff-shire before leading royalist forces to victory in the famous Trot of Turriff (13 May 1639), in partnership with George Gordon of Haddo, ancestor of the lords Aberdeen. In the years following the moderates' defeat in the second Civil War of 1648, Ogilvy was persecuted by the Cromwellian military occupation forces, but nevertheless was appointed a JP again, by Cromwell, in 1656! After the restoration of the monarchy in 1660, he was investigated for a third killing, but apparently got off again, since he later took his seat in parliament as Lord Banff.[197] Many historians today are at pains to deny that early-modern Scotland was in a state of anarchy; but a justice system operated by (and largely for) men and women steeped in a culture of violent family feuds, duelling and private warfare certainly had some anarchic features.

An interesting window on the law-and-order situation in general is provided by the case of Jean Gordon, illegitimate daughter of a tenant farmer in Bank of Cabrach. Jean was accused of stealing twenty-six sheep, belonging to her uncle John Gordon and his son, in Cabrach in 1841. The defence argued that,

> notwithstanding the great amount of civilization and education now prevalent, there were in some remote parts of the country, such as the Cabrach, very loose notions still existing concerning the way and manner in which people might lay hold of property to which they conceived they had a right.

Jean was let go with a caution – but was charged separately with breaking out of Banff gaol by setting fire to the door! She was convicted of the fire-raising and got four months.[198] The gaol in question predated the one demolished in the 1950s; it was probably the structure of 1796 that was condemned in 1836 due to overcrowding and escapes 'by deception and by tunnelling', but which was not rebuilt until 1844.[199] It is a turret from this later structure that survives in Reidhaven Street.

Metal 'jougs' were sometimes affixed to the market cross, as at Old Rayne (they had disappeared by 1900). These were chains for exhibiting a minor offender to passers-by for a set period of time. The Kirk specialised in similar punishments by ritual humilation, including especially sitting on the 'stool of repentance' during sermon time for a set number of weeks. 'Crimes' involving speech, such as rudeness, slander and nagging, could be punished with the scold's bridle: a metal full-head helmet with integral tongue depressor. It would certainly rate as torture today, but it proved very popular with burgh authorities and quickly spread from its Scottish places of origin to England, Germany and the New World. Witch burnings were rarer here than in the south-east of Scotland or Germany, but they still did occur, as when John Philp was burned at the stake in Banff in 1630 for 'charming and washing sick people' at the Lady Well of Ordiquhill.[200] If Philp's actions sound less than wicked, we must remember that the law made no distinction between the commissioning of witchcraft and its actual practice, and also criminalised counter-magic; so three groups – witchcraft patrons, witchcraft practitioners, and *victims* of witchcraft attempting to protect themselves using magical means – were considered equally guilty.[201] But criminalisation did not stop anti-witchcraft jewellery, mostly for newborns and fishermen's wives, being fashioned continuously in Aberdeenshire into the mid-nineteenth century.

Witches in Kirkmichael were, unusually, believed to ride broomsticks, and were thought to dance on the surface of the Aven on 12 May each year.

## DISSENTERS

One of this part of Scotland's most distinctive features is its religious diversity amid a surprising lack of inter-confessional animosity. Persecution of Catholics and Protestant Dissenters by the central government and Established Church certainly occurred. In Banff, the Kirk minister himself regretted the 'forfeitures, penalties and disabilities' under which Episcopalians laboured until 1792.[202] But such persecution was not usually abetted by locals, or inflamed by local jealousies. It is telling, perhaps, that the last Roman Catholic parish priest of Belhelvie became the first Protestant minister there. Likewise, Patrick Innes served as parish minister of Banff for ten years before, and ten years after, the overthrow of the Episcopate in 1689. In Kirkmichael in the 1790s, where Catholics made up a third of the population, Presbyterian minister John Grant allowed a Catholic priest

> to use every liberty, as if toleration had extended to this country . . . to marry and baptize, impose penalties, and exact them among his own people, in the same manner as if he were of the Established Church[.][203]

The enlightened Grant defended the wisdom of this policy to his superiors, in forceful terms. At the same date in Peterhead, probably the most religiously diverse community in the region (then or now), it was said that there was less conflict over religion than in any other large prosperous town in the country. A few years earlier, Richard Pococke reported from Banff – whose 600 Episcopalians represented perhaps a quarter of the population – that harmony prevailed: 'the wife often going one way and the husband another: So that there is no sort of animosity in the Town upon the account of Religion'.[204] Despite a

*Panel showing the Crucifixion in Kinkell. Similar pre-Reformation stonework, notably at Clatt, was intentionally destroyed. Unusually, the item depicted was saved by being built into the new Protestant parish church of 1772, itself now a ruin.*

growing proportion of Episcopalians and other Dissenters, the people of early nineteenth-century Ellon also expressed their religious differences 'without animosity'.[205] Even on the eve of the Great Disruption, the people of Turriff were said to live 'in the utmost harmony with those who differ from them, and have hitherto been able, amid much contention, "to preserve the unity of spirit in the bond of peace."'[206]

Despite vague modern notions linking them to English immigration, the Episcopalians were Scots who favoured keeping the practices of the Church of Scotland as they had been before 1689. There were English Anglican (and Scandinavian Lutheran) influences, but these were fairly distant. According to Rev. Marshall Lang, sometime minister of Meldrum, the *Book of Common Prayer* published in England during the reign of King Edward VI was in general use in Formartine as late as 1574, and Presbyterianism *per se* did not even exist in north-east Aberdeenshire before the reign of William II and III in the 1690s.[207]

William Wedderburn, regent of Marischal College and a man of prodigious intellect, was deposed by the General Assembly in 1644. He was reinstated and deposed again in 1646, after which he moved to Strathdon where he was minister by 1651. The reasons for this are not even suggested by Lang, except by saying that the only member of the Garioch Presbytery ever to sign the National Covenant was Wedderburn's 1647 successor, Rev. George Leith, the rest of the Garioch and the county generally exhibiting 'Stout resistance'; even Leith was accused of 'time-serving' and signing the Covenant for careerist reasons 'rather than in the light of his own conscience'.[208] Ellon Presbytery was so Episcopalian in 1696 that it was 'temporarily defunct, or rather . . . still-born as a Presbyterian Presbytery', and its just two more-or-less Presbyterian parishes, Tarves and Slains, were detached and given over to the presbyteries of Garioch and Deer, respectively.[209] William Urquhart, Leith's successor as minister of Bethelnie, was such a staunch Episcopalian that, for nine years after the 1688 Revolution established Presbyterianism once and for all, he continued to conduct Episcopal services with no salary – leaving at his death no personal belongings and a debt (to the kirk session, no less) of £8 6s 8d. The Aberdeen Synod was composed partially of such Episcopalian diehards until at least 1708. But even within the avowedly Presbyterian churches in the 1690s, 'the order of Service was not fixed . . . each Church being left to itself "to worship with a liturgy or without a liturgy, the minister with a surplice or without a surplice"'.[210]

Change was slower to arrive in some areas than others: Episcopalian and/or Jacobite clergy continued to occupy Kirk posts and/or buildings until 1716 in Banff and Pitsligo, 1717 in Fraserburgh, 1718 in Alvah, and 1727 in Botriphnie. Monquhitter parish did not get its first Presbyterian minister until 1727 – five

*While serving as a Royal Navy surgeon in the 1750s, Fraserburgh-born James Ramsay (1733–1789) was shocked by the way slaves were treated. He later became an Anglican clergyman and returned to the West Indies, where he continued to practise medicine, at no charge, and ministered to a mixed-race congregation. His Abolitionist publications, beginning in 1784, were highly influential, especially among churchmen. Ramsay's fellow Abolitionist, the Quaker William Dickson, 'found eager audiences in towns such as Fordyce, Huntly and Turriff' in 1792.[211]*

months after the death of King George I, and three complete reigns since Presbyterianism was ostensibly established. Rural Formartine in general had long been a haven for ministers who found the notoriously royalist and Episcopalian city of Aberdeen not royalist or Episcopalian *enough*. The first-ever parish minister of Forglen, which was detached from Alvah *c.*1640, was Alexander Scroggie, who had been ejected from King's College for opposing the National Covenant. Sir James Strachan of Thornton was minister of Keith until 1690 when he was ejected as an Episcopalian, after which there was virtually no preaching in the parish for ten years. Perhaps no one dared. In Strathdon in the Queen Anne period, the Episcopalian minister John Robertson was so popular that when he was replaced by a Presbyterian, Mr Macsween, the people set upon him and tried to forcibly smother him. Macsween saved himself through his 'considerable bodily strength'.[212] Such attacks were common enough to acquire a particular name, 'rabblings', the goal of which was generally not murder but to keep control of the church building and maintain Episcopal services. Wholly peaceful tactics were also used, as when Alexander Lunan gave his church in Daviot two valuable silver communion cups inscribed '*For the use only of Episcopal ministers 1705*'. The Episcopal clergy and their many supporters often prevailed for years rather than weeks – eleven years, in Rev. Lunan's case. In Deer, the Presbyterian minister who was eventually intruded in 1719 preached 'with a sword on the pulpit cushion'.[213]

St Andrew's Chapel in Banff, which had 'probably the only organ north of Aberdeen', was unroofed and burned with most of its contents by Hanoverian troops during the '45.[214] The Episcopal meeting house of Ellon, which eventually became the church of St Mary's on the Rock, was burned down by the government twice in the space of thirty-one years. Its patrons included the local lairds Gordon of Esslemont, Fullerton of Dudwick and Turner of Turnerhall – extreme Jacobites who were exempted by name from the amnesty of 1746.[215] According to legend, only one inhabitant of the town, Alexander Lendrum, helped with the destruction – and his puritanical rantings sat so ill with the English soldiery that they ended the business by beating him almost to death with 'a stick from the demolished chapel'.[216] The thatch-roofed Episcopal chapel in Udny was also burned after Culloden, but by a local hireling of the Established Church minister. By 1768, however, the number of meeting houses in the two parishes had doubled, with the rebuilding of the original two, and the construction of two more – one on the lands of Esslemont and one on the lands of Dudwick. The minister of all four was John Skinner, son of the renowned minister/poet of the same name. This energetic young man later became bishop of Aberdeen, in which office he was 'instrumental in the repeal of the penal laws

in 1792'.[217] The Udny of Udny family also 'afforded asylum to the two congregations [i.e. Ellon and Udny] in the trublous times'.[218]

Turriff's Episcopal chapel – on the site of the Victorian post office – was
gutted of internal woodwork by government troops during the '45, but the
structure itself was saved by the intercession of the Established Church minister,
Andrew Ker. In 1794 it was serving as the village schoolhouse. Most such structures were of unknown, but probably humble appearance. Fortunately, very
exact drawings of the Episcopal chapel of Arradoul in Rathven survive. Extant
in 1782, Arradoul's was a simple one-storey, two-bay structure with twenty-four
pews; from the outside it could easily have been mistaken for a cottage. It was
demolished in 1837.

The Plymouth Brethren is an umbrella term for a very loosely organised
conservative evangelical movement that arose within Anglicanism, initially in
Dublin in 1827. It spread to Britain via Plymouth beginning in 1831, but it was
along the coasts of Buchan that it scored some of its most enduring successes.
The Brethren also form the largest group dissenting from Lutheranism in the
Faeroe Islands. Officially anti-denominational, i.e. just Christian, the self-
evidently Protestant movement has itself divided into at least four major sub-
groups, and a number of smaller groups, at least one of which is perceived as a
cult even among members of other Brethren congregations. Much of the
theology and discipline of present-day Brethren churches would seem familiar
to English Puritans of the Civil War period.

The Quakers, a new sect *actually* from the 1640s, established themselves
in Kingswells near Aberdeen before 1673, creating a burial ground there. Their
thriving community at Kinmuck, which became the largest in Scotland 'with
cobblers, tailors, blacksmiths and a wool mill', was established by Patrick
Livingstone from Montrose in 1681.[219] It lasted until 1946, and until 1807 included
the oldest Quaker school in Scotland (illustrated p. 98).

Moving northward from the Don, the number of Quakers tended to
decrease as the number of Congregationalists increased. In early nineteenth-
century Old Deer, an increasing number of Congregationalists displaced a
declining population of Episcopalians – a mirror image of the trend in New
England at the same date. The Congregationalist chapel in High Street,
Inverurie was demolished before 2003. There were also Baptist chapels in
Aberchirder, and on the site of the Milton Cottages, Kemnay.

John Barclay was born in Lorraine in 1582. His mother was French and his
father a Scottish law professor who had roots in Turriff, and who fled to Pont-
à-Mousson when King's College Aberdeen was Protestantised in 1569. Though
considered French by the English, 'Barclay seems to have been proud of his

*A rare but rather unfortunate engraving of John Barclay, lost literary master, who did not in fact suffer from macrocephaly.*

Scottish ancestry and to have valued his allegiance to James VI and I'.[220] His first publication, at age nineteen, 'was the beginning of a distinguished literary career, which would bring him fame all over western Europe'.[221] His first purely fictional work, the *Satyricon*, deals humorously with a visitor from another world called Euphormio, and was published to immediate acclaim in 1605 (the same year as *Don Quixote*). Thinly disguised as the god Neptune, King James was positively portrayed in the book, which ran to five editions in the author's lifetime. This may have led to Barclay's success as a courtier in London beginning in 1606; the king gave him a pension of £200 a year, presumably for his help in editing and distributing the monarch's own literary efforts. But by 1615, Barclay had fled to Rome.

The Barclays were Catholics, but hardly fanatical ones: John's father had even written a book arguing that the pope should be stripped of his temporal powers, which was published in four Latin, two French and two English editions. The official reason John Barclay gave for leaving England was that he wanted his three children to be able to remain Catholics, but Britain 'may have become less welcoming to Roman Catholics during the 1610s'.[222] It was in Rome that Barclay composed his most famous work, *Argenis*, whose title character is a princess 'with three suitors, one good, one bad, and one who is finally recognized as her long-lost brother'.[223] Arguably the first novel by a British person (*Quixote* is usually considered the first novel by a European), *Argenis* met with immediate and immense popularity, and the price of a copy – already quite high at 5s sterling – nearly tripled due to demand over the course of May 1622. Sadly,

Barclay had already died, not yet forty years old, and *Argenis*'s two sequels were written by other people. Ben Jonson was commanded by the king to translate *Argenis* into English, but if he did, the translation has been lost. Barclay's reputation has also faded away, since he wrote only in Latin, no longer a language read for pleasure by Europe's middle classes. Worst of all, from a strictly Turra point of view, some scholars believe his ancestors were from Gartly – or even from Collairnie in Fife!

In contemplating great artists like Barclay, and great business leaders like *The lost tycoons* (below, p. 159), it is impossible to avoid a sense of the tragic loss of manpower and brainpower suffered by this region over many decades – caused, as often as not, by official intolerance in matters of religion.

## LOST SCHOOLS

In eighteenth-century Corgarff, the children were 'not only at a great distance from their own parochial school, but . . . quite out of the reach of every other school, at any season'.[224] In Grange at around the same time, the people were accused of being 'backward' in sending their children to school.[225] In Forbes, there had never been any sort of school when the minister, Benjamin Mercer, tried and failed to establish one in 1789. Mercer supposed that his predecessors had 'kept a boy for educating their own children'.[226] A few years later in Alvah, there were four private schools in addition to the parish school, but the minister there criticised their fees as being 'much too high'.[227]

However, such complaints – whether about the number and location of schools, the cost of attendance, or popular apathy toward them – were actually quite rare. Scotland's extremely advanced attitude toward the provision of primary education in the two or three centuries before the 1872 Education Act is frequently remarked upon, and with good reason. But praise for the Scottish system tends to focus on the parish schools, and to ignore the enormous number of other schools that existed. Private, but serving members of all social classes, the quality of these schools varied widely. Some had financial endowments, while others depended solely on the fees they charged. The latter group were termed 'adventure' schools, not because of any adventurousness in the curriculum, but because the teacher/owners succeeded or failed 'at their own adventure'. Widespread religious non-conformity may serve to explain why Banff and Buchan became so particularly well served by these small, often short-lived, and sometimes excellent schools.

In Glenlivet, there were no fewer than seven: three for Protestant boys, two for Catholic girls, one for Protestant girls and one for Catholic boys. Longside had (in addition to three parish schools) six private schools and five Sunday schools, including one specifically for Episcopalians. A similar situation prevailed in Ellon, where private schools occupied the Feu House and part of the Tolbooth into the 1830s. In Glenbuchat, a 'winter and spring' adventure school 'on the celebrated classical spot where John of Badenyon lived' was found to be 'small but useful'.[228] The adventure school at Collieston of Slains had twenty-five pupils, and the charity school at Foggieloan had twice as many pupils as the parish school. People in Greens of Monquhitter and Balquholly complained that their areas were too far from their (excellent) private school, at three to five miles, but such distances would have been considered a doddle in south-western Aberdeenshire at the same date. Banff had no parish school at all in 1798, only a public academy run by the town council and as many private schools, including two boarding schools for ladies. Here, as on Deeside, the early boarding schools attracted pupils from throughout the British Atlantic world – including, in Banff's case, at least two 'Indian chiefs' who arrived in 1797.[229]

Two private schools in Forglen were not thought of very highly. In 1790s Peterhead, there were at least a dozen private schools, but none of them were particularly good: the rate of university placements from the parish was extremely low, with an average of just one admission (to any university) every four years. Half a century later, the overall number had dropped to nine, but

*Netherton Free Church School, seen here, was built in 1865 (clearly at considerable expense), but closed shortly afterward and became a private house. One of Fordyce village's four schools was converted into a rectory in 1882.*

the quality seems to have improved; two Peterhead schools dedicated to 'the higher branches of female education, such as Music, French, Drawing, &c' were said to be 'taught by experienced and well qualified instructors'.[230] One school in Cabrach closed its doors as early as 1779, but three had grown up to replace it by the early 1840s, at which time there were also private girls' schools in Aberlour and Botriphnie. In Lonmay in the three decades after 1812, the number of schools and school places sextupled, but these 'were no sooner opened than they were filled with scholars'.[231] In Botriphnie in particular, demand for private schooling may have been fuelled by the unenlightened attitude of the parish authorities: while it was 'the fashion formerly' to teach the boys Latin and send them to the university, they wrote, this benefited only these few individuals. So, out of a warped sense of democracy, or laziness – or both – the revamped parish school taught nothing but English and accounting.[232]

ABOVE. *Now a garage, this elegant building housed the Banff Grammar School in 1787 and was later the* Banffshire Journal *newspaper office.*

OVERLEAF. *Buchan teachers, 1890s. James Dick (1743–1828), a Forres-born West India merchant, left his enormous fortune to primary education in Banffshire, Aberdeenshire and 'Elginshire' (as Moray was then known). In practice, it meant that schoolmasters who applied to the fund and demonstrated their proficiency in classics, maths and science would have their salaries doubled. The fund still exists, but due to inflation the strong competitive advantage it once gave the North-east has dwindled into insignificance.*

Public/private distinctions could also become hopelessly blurred, as in eighteenth-century Udny, where a quarter to a third of the parish school pupils were gentlemen-boarders paying thirteen gold guineas a year each (£13 13s). This situation persisted for fifty years, the boarding population growing from eleven to thirty, and their fees more than doubling. Similar hybrid parish/boarding schools are known to have arisen in eighteenth-century Meldrum and nineteenth-century Kemnay, and there may have been others. From Fyvie in 1793, it was reported that the parish schoolmaster had been poached from 'one of the best academies in the neighbourhood of London'.[233] And charity schools, established from the time of Queen Anne (r. 1702–1714), were conceived by 'private gentlemen' operating in their 'private capacity', but built with Kirk money and sited on the basis of a Kirk survey.[234]

Schools were only as good as their teachers, but in this respect the region was especially lucky. The Jacobite academic William Meston, ejected from Marischal College in 1715, founded an academy in Turriff 'for instructing young gentlemen in such sciences as were then taught in the universities'.[235] (His career as a poet and fugitive is touched on in my book *Lost Deeside* in this series.) Meston's school was closed following a duel between two of its pupils, John Grant (who survived to become absentee laird of Dunlugas and a Prussian major-general) and Gordon of Embo. Before taking up his post at the university, Meston had also taught the future Prussian field marshal James Keith (*The lost generals*, p. 166).

Meston was following in the footseps of Turriff-born Thomas Ogston, who having been ejected from King's College in 1568 taught at the excellent grammar school in his native village. Established in 1546, the grammar already had a 'considerable reputation' when he arrived. The Ogston/Meston tradition was carried on in Turriff, if not systematically. In the 1830s, to satisfy local parents' 'anxious desire' that their childen be properly educated, there were at least seven private schools, one with seventy pupils and a university-educated head.[236]

Dr George Chapman, printer and author of the *Treatise on Education*, was born to a farming family at Little Blacktown, Alvah, in 1723. He taught school in Banff (among other places) before moving to Dumfries. In later life he returned to Banffshire and appears to have established and/or taught in three different schools: a private grammar in Inchdrewer Castle, a non-parochial public school in the town of Banff, and a third school particularly aimed at the children of the poor. The exact chronology of this is far from clear. In any case, Chapman did believe that schools should support the existing system of social classes while at the same time allowing a safety valve for the highly intelligent but poor scholar to move up in the world – essentially prefiguring the grammar school

*Episcopal school pupils in 1926.*

system of the mid-twentieth century. The *Treatise on Education* ran to five editions within nineteen years of its first publication in 1773.

In Aberdour, the parish schoolhouse was 'quite ruinous', but in one of the two private schools, Jean Lesly persisted in the role of schoolmistress with great success despite being over ninety years of age.[237] Most spectacularly perhaps, Gavin Greig, schoolmaster of Whitehill in New Deer, became simultaneously a successful novelist, playwright and leading scholarly collector of ballads.

As a rule, adventure schools had only one teacher apiece, and the ones that took only girls were invariably taught by women. In places with many different adventure schools, the proportion of male to female teachers might be roughly even (as at Fraserburgh) or heavily weighted to the female side (as at Peterhead and Pitsligo).

Life could be hard for teachers here, 'adventure' or no. In 1721, the schoolmaster's stipend of Logie-Buchan was divided in two, with the idea that two masters would be hired, one to serve the children on each side of the river. However, until 1803, the result was that there was no schoolmaster in the parish at all, 'the encouragement being so small, that no person qualified for teaching, can accept of it'.[238] (Shades of modern academia there, indeed!) Late eighteenth-century Cullen's parish schoolmaster taught Latin as well as the more usual subjects to fifty boys, despite his salary being 'very small'.[239] In early nineteenth-century Meldrum there were three private schools, one of them for girls; 'but the want of salary renders the continuance of these . . . uncertain'.[240] The single, unendowed, private school in early nineteenth-century St Fergus was run by a man who had trained as a clerk, but who was prevented 'by disease' from pursuing that occupation. As an 'adventure' teacher he earned £20 a year, compared to the parish schoolmater's £34. An endowed school at Cullen for children aged two to seven paid a salary of slightly under £15 per year, plus free rent of a house and the school building itself. Its teacher also kept the school fees which, at a penny per week per child, would have been somewhere north of £12 per year.

None of this is to suggest that having their schools endowed guaranteed the teachers a comfortable living. Three wealthy Ellon farmers – George Ledingham in Nether Ardgrain, George Connon in Commonty and John Wilken in Broomfield – endowed a private school in about 1850. Located in Commonty, it was for children 'too small to go to Ellon' – some as young as three. It was taught at first by Margaret Johnston, then by James Cheyne, and lastly by William Johnstone, and lasted into the 1880s. After the school closed, the impoverished Mr Johnstone lived in the parish poorhouse and was employed as the local truant officer.[241]

Schoolmasters could, of course, be commanding figures regardless of their material circumstances. In the parish of Ordiquhill in the 1760s, it was said there were only three hats and three watches – belonging to the laird, the minister and the schoolmaster. Jane Montgomery, the imposing woman who kept a school at Logierieve from 1806 to 1846, was still remembered half a century later for 'her tall figure . . . and her terrible tawse!'[242] In Cabrach, numerous tales are told of masters' personal generosity to the poor, successful efforts to bridge streams, and so forth, in addition to various efforts to shield the community's distillers from the eyes of the law. All of these activities were conducted by the masters seemingly without any concern for their personal safety, and Bodiebae-born Thomas Robertson (schoolmaster 1865–1909) narrowly escaped prosecution for the manslaughter of an Excise officer.[243]

With important exceptions including the Townhouse of Peterhead (the first floor of which was 'occupied for school-rooms' in the 1830s) and Inchdrewer Castle (restored from ruins in 1971), many dozens of early schools have left no traces. The so-called Old Schoolhouse of Corsindae, though a genuinely eighteenth-century building, was actually an inn until 1861. Like the houses of ordinary folk which they most likely resembled, most early schools have been remodelled beyond recognition or dismantled for parts. Jane Montgomery's aforementioned school at Logierieve had ceased operation by 1894 and was 'occupied as a servants' house'.[244]

Nowadays, it is the council-run village schools that are constantly threatened with closure, as our population ages and contracts. Too many Aberdeen-shire children now travel ludicrous distances each school day. As for independent schools in rural Aberdeenshire? You can now count them on one hand: a decline of ninety-eight per cent or more as compared to two centuries ago.

## THE LOST UNIVERSITY

The number of universities in England and Wales before the nineteenth century was two. Even if universities and colleges in English North America are included, this number rises only to eleven at most. It is surprising enough that, as of 1600, Scotland had three times as many universities as England, serving a population one-eighth the size of England's, but even more surprising that half of these institutions were in Aberdeenshire. In the 1580s and '90s, the wave of new university foundations that included Trinity College, Dublin and the University of Edinburgh gave us Marischal College in Aberdeen – and the University of Fraserburgh.

The first mystery is why Fraserburgh was chosen at all, given that the founding brief of Aberdeen's King's College a hundred years earlier was to serve a rather loosely defined north of Scotland that perhaps included even Orkney, Shetland and the Outer Hebrides. Students from as far away as Harris and Coll certainly did attend King's. Yet, it was observed in the seventeenth century that 'youths from the Shires of Caithnes [sic], Inverness, Murray and Ross' attended Aberdeen only 'with difficultys'; and that Fraserburgh itself was 'a place remote from education very much'.[245] Others have located the Fraserburgh project in a rivalry between Buchan's two great town-making families, the Keiths who founded Peterhead (and Marischal College) and the Fraserburgh Frasers. In this view, Marischal's foundation in 1593 was first and foremost a tit-for-tat response to the chartering of Fraserburgh University the previous year.

Both Marischal and Fraserburgh were consciously modelled on Edinburgh University, founded in 1582 and Scotland's first specifically Protestant university. Fraserburgh's first principal, Charles Ferme, was a Protestant minister. He was one of Edinburgh's early graduates, and taught Hebrew and Theology there as late as July 1597. Despite the charter date of 1592, Fraserburgh obtained its first funding (other than for building work) in December 1597. Specifically, this was in the form of tithes generated by the four parishes of Tyrie, Crimond, Philorth – renamed Fraserburgh in 1613 – and Rathen. A similar system, also implicating Rathen, was long used to support Aberdeen's St Machar Cathedral, and was naturally unpopular in the parishes concerned, which it tended to deprive of essential services. Ironically, in light of Fraserburgh University's fairly militant Protestant outlook, the diversion of tithes to non-religious purposes had been one of the grievances that led to the Protestant Reformation across Europe.

Principal Ferme arrived in Fraserburgh in 1598, and got into trouble almost immediately, objecting to the creation of the first Protestant bishop of Aberdeen in 1600. Involvement in a series of protests against episcopacy led to his imprisonment in Doune Castle in October 1605 'at his own expense'. He escaped, was re-imprisoned (again at Doune) in 1607, escaped again, and was exiled to the Isle of Bute, where he 'suffered much privation' until *c*.1610. Ferme's nineteenth-century biographer Alexander Gordon believed that Ferme then returned to Fraserburgh, where 'the university maintained an existence till his death . . . on 24 Sept. 1617, aged 51'.[246] Gordon's version of these events seems well documented, or at least better documented than the popular version which has the university actually open for business in 1595, or even as early as 1592, and shut for good in 1605. A scholarly theory that the university never 'actually operated as such' is also thoroughly outmoded, as evidence of five years' worth of teaching has been uncovered.[247]

Whether it closed in 1605 or 1617 or some intermediate date will probably never be known. But the University of Fraserburgh's three-storey, 'quadrangular' building was intact enough to house the students and staff of King's during a plague outbreak in 1647, and it may also have housed the town's early-seventeenth-century grammar school.[249] Much confusion has been caused by a 1791 account of the town written by Rev. Alexander Simpson, whose references to

*The lost University of Fraserburgh likely resembled the Cromwell Tower of King's College, Aberdeen (centre right). As late as January 1840, it stood in the High Street just to the east of Barrasgate Road, where its 'vaulted cellars now filled with concrete survive beneath the tarmac'.*[248]

the remains of a College of Fraserburgh might be either to the university, or to a pre-Reformation collegiate church – some outpost of the Abbey of Deer. Simpson's successor John Cumming rather thought it was the latter; and contrary to popular belief, the street called College Bounds provides no real clue, since it was given this name only in the mid-1870s. A surviving Jacobean carving of Moses and the Ten Commandments, sometimes claimed as coming from the university's chapel, might in fact be from 'some civic structure' associated with the Common Good Fund.[250] No greater certainty attends the structure of the university as a whole, some historians choosing to interpret the description 'quadrangular' to mean 'square or rectangular' merely, as opposed to containing a quadrangle, as at King's.[251]

Amid a tragic lack of interest in Ferme and his pioneering institution, losses of artefacts have been ongoing. In the words of a March 2007 archaeological report:

> On the north side of College Bounds, the fire-damaged Alexandra Hotel has been completely demolished [since 2003] . . . A condition of the permission to demolish was for the recovery of the sculptured stonework reported in Pratt *Buchan* and Henderson *Aberdeenshire Inscriptions* . . . but nothing was found when the internal plaster was removed in the relevant area. The inscriptions were said to have come from the University buildings and were believed to constitute one of the few physical survivals of that short-lived institution. It appears that no detailed survey of the hotel was undertaken prior to demolition to determine if any portions of earlier structures were incorporated into its fabric.[252]

Ferme is also known to have written two books. *Analysis Logica* was published in 1651, but his *Lectiones in Esterem* was either not published at all, or all copies of it have been destroyed.

In many respects, Fraserburgh may rank as the 'most lost' place in the region. The arrival of the railway 'changed Fraserburgh's situation from core to periphery in terms of economic activity', which 'paradoxically increased its economic reliance on shipping'. In terms of the road network, meanwhile, Fraserburgh was 'not "on the way to" anywhere else, and . . . few eighteenth- and nineteenth-century travel writers came to it.'[253] As late as the 1790s there was no direct postal service between Fraserburgh, Peterhead and Banff. Letters sent between these places all had to travel first to Aberdeen and then back northward.

# CHAPTER 3

# 'DING IT DOON UTTERLY'

## THE PICTS AND BEFORE

Major Pictish headland forts were located at Green Castle (Portknockie), Cullykhan (Troup) and Dundarg, while places with names beginning Pit- were also of some importance in Pictish times. Perhaps because Pictish artefacts were once so numerous, regard for them here was low. In the Georgian era, indeed, the various parts of this region seemed to be vying with one another in a 'race to the bottom' when it came to respect for Pictish remains, or earlier remains of any sort. Auchterless was one of just a few places where 'Superstition still spares them, though stones are so scarce.'[254] Another was St Fergus, which in the early-Victorian period still 'teemed with superstitions', according to Alex McAldowie, who spent his boyhood summers there.

> My uncle informed me that his father had ploughed up what, judging from the multitude of neolithic flint implements found in the field, I think must have been the remains of a tumulus or stone circle. None of the farm servants dared plough over it, and some people collected on a neighbouring hill expecting to see the earth open and swallow up both horses and ploughman.[255]

Despite such fears, several 'Druidical temples' in Tullynessle and 700 yards of an equally ancient paved road, six yards wide, were destroyed between the 1760s and 1790s.[256] At least twelve stone circles and a whole 'druid' city of fifty or sixty buildings on the north-east side of Parkhouse Hill in Old Deer were obliterated at around the same date, and a standing stone with 'hieroglyphical characters' in Rhynie was reported as 'lately broken'.[257] An ancient circular structure in Clatt with a floor three feet thick was destroyed between 1800 and 1840.

Marnoch kirk was built in the middle of a 'Druidical circle' of which only two stones remained by 1842.[258] The minister's manse of New Deer and the parish church of Culsalmond were both built directly over Pictish stone circles. Another such ancient monument in New Deer 'is not yet all removed', Rev. Hugh Taylor commented sanguinely in 1793. Ancient funerary urns were also found there 'but mouldered at a touch'.[259] Another tomb, on top of the Meethill of Peterhead, remained 'for ages untouched' but was gone by 1837; the contents of the tomb were 'exhibited to the public, at one shilling a head', and the funds used to build a monument to Earl Grey 'and his political principles' on the site.[260]

A mile and a half west of the kirk of Cruden, the property called Stones commemorates a Pictish stone circle 'removed by the tenant in 1831 to make room for "improvements"'.[261] Half a mile nearer the church, near the Moot Hill of Cruden, another such circle 'with other fragments of antiquity . . . disappeared during the present century', John Pratt wrote in 1858.[262] A stone circle near Ballindalloch had 'most of the stones . . . taken away' before 1800.[263] Two in Keith were 'mostly demolished', also before 1800.[264] There were 'two or three' stone circles, one of them 'very large and very entire', in Belhelvie until about 1810; but by 1840 there was 'not a vestige of any of them'.[265] A large one on the farm called Newtown of Montblairy, Alvah, was entirely destroyed in or about 1842, and a small one north of Turriff became a Victorian croquet lawn.

A cairn erected on the spot where Sir Patrick Gordon of Auchindown was killed in 1594 was two-thirds washed away by floodwaters in 1829, but usually it was humans who were to blame for such losses. The famous Cairn of Memsie, up until robberies of the 1780s or '90s, was actually one of a trio. Writing from early-Victorian Inveraven, William Asher told a familiar tale of 'cairns removed

The Standing Stones of Dyce by James Logan (1794–1872).

to make way for the plough', and ancient coins 'the size of half crowns' which 'cannot now be particularly described' since they were sold privately to a silver-smith who subsequently emigrated. On the farms of North and South Ythsie in Tarves, several large cairns containing 'a quantity of gigantic human bones' were dismantled for fence-building stone '[n]ot many years ago', according to a report of 1842.[266] Burial cairns on Mill-hill, Gartly, thought to date back to the Harlaw campaign of 1411, 'were cleared away' in or about 1801.[267] St John's Well farm, Fyvie, was the site of the cairn of Cairnchedly, which was rapidly diminishing by the late 1830s, 'most of the cottages in the neighbourhood having been built out of it'.[268]

On the lands of Rannes, the local minister (in his own words) 'obtained permission to ransack' an ancient burial chamber in the 1760s; sadly, his description of what he found while ransacking provides no major clues as to its age or culture of origin.[269] On the farm called Bethelnie near Old Meldrum, the remains of a supposedly Roman encampment existed 'until lately', George Garioch wrote in 1840; it has 'now been levelled and the ground is ploughed'.[270] Two sides of another Roman camp, on the farms of Buss and Logie-Newton in Auchterless, remained undamaged in 1840, but half a century earlier there had been three sides. Now, it is discernible only from the air.

It was quite unusual that the famous Boar's Head Carnyx, an ancient bronze war-trumpet discovered at a depth of six feet on the farm of Liechestown, Deskford, in 1816 was given to a museum rather than to a private collector. It was more typical that an unidentified ancient complex on the nearby farm of Inalterie was 'filled up with rubbish' and covered over by a kailyard at about the same time.[271] In or by 1842, the cairn of Cairnelpie in Alvah and a carved monument found nearby were broken up for building material '[w]ith true antiquarian taste and feeling', as Andrew Todd reported sourly;[272] and Letterfourie House was built, in part, from pieces of the 'remarkable' stone circle called Core Stanes that previously stood on the heights of Corridown.[273]

## PRE-REFORMATION RELIGIOUS STRUCTURES

Unlike Deeside, where church sites traceable back to the dark ages are still occupied in many cases by later medieval ruins, Banff and Buchan have experi-enced a more complete erasure of medieval religious buildings, amid a stronger survival of early-modern ones. There is no parallel on Deeside, for instance, for the parish churches of Meldrum and Glenbuchat, in continuous use as such since the 1680s; or the remarkable laird's loft of the Forbes family in Rosehearty, dating to 1634; or the sixteenth- and seventeenth-century monuments and woodwork of Cullen's Auld Kirk. But convents, monasteries, collegiate churches, bede-houses, well-chapels and the like, though more common here, were less likely to survive: perhaps because Catholicism was considered a stronger and more immediate threat to the Established Church's authority. A remarkably complete pre-Reformation church in Clatt had a freestone carving of the crucifixion, decorated with 'vermillion, azure, and gold leaf' – until during repairs in the later eighteenth century, the 'officious zeal of the workmen broke and defaced the tablet, before it could be rescued from their hands'.[274] Likewise, only anxiety could readily explain why Fyvie kirk, described in the 1790s by its own minister as 'one of the best and most commodious old churches in the county', complete with a 'still quite fresh and sound' desk dated 1502, was swept away and replaced wholesale in 1808.

St Congan's hospital, Turriff, founded in 1272, had its lands taken away in 1497; its ruins are thought by some to lie deep beneath St Ninian's Manse. Even less is known about a similar hospital founded at Monkshome, Newburgh in 1261 and completely built over by 1970. Cullen's bede-house was 'taken down' a little before 1800.[275] Richard Pococke, Anglican bishop of Ossory in Ireland, reported from Banff in July 1760 that the Carmelite convent of St Mary, first established on St Leonard's Hill in 1321, was 'entirely destroyed'.[276] Forty years later, however, two of its monastic cells were 'still to be seen . . . in a pretty entire state'.[277] It is probable that two different sites, both formerly belonging to the Carmelites, were meant; in any case, the major destruction had been the result of arson at the time of the Reformation. One theory places the principal ruins under Duff House's extant 'gothick' mausoleum of 1791. During the mausoleum's construction, 'many human remains were found on the site and placed in a large urn, since lost'.[278]

Mortlach was home to a lost bishopric, which had been second in precedence only to St Andrews from 1010 to 1139; the supposed foundations of the bishop's palace were still visible on the banks of the Dullan a little way downstream of the church in 1791. Fraserburgh's pre-Reformation collegiate church, said by some to be the original home of the town's Moses carving usually associated with the lost university, has already been mentioned. Arndilly House was built directly on top of the ruined medieval parish church of the former parish of Arndilly or Ardendol, and before 1850, no traces remained of former Christian churches and chapels at Phona, Nevie and Deskie.[279] A holy well and 'remains' of a chapel of Our Lady lay one mile east of the church of Auchterless in 1840.[280] The manse of Tyrie was built directly over a pre-Reformation religious community. There was an old chapel in Inveraven called Chapel Christ, with a burying ground on the east side of the Livet, but it was washed away by floods (probably in 1829); Chapelton of Kilmaichlie in the same parish was visible only as outlines on the ground by the early-Victorian era. The church of Forvie, which John Pratt seems to be alone in supposing was buried 'about the year 1688',[281] was probably lost during the Europe-wide hurricane-force winds of August, 1413.

Before 1800, St Michael's Well in Kirkmichael lay 'neglected, choked with weeds, unhonoured, and unfrequented'.[282] In an alder-overgrown swamp on the farm called Bog of Montblairie in Alvah, there was a ruined chapel, a fragmentary castle said to have been built by the earl of Buchan and a holy well, where many people still living in the 1790s recalled

> boughs adorned with rags of linen and woollen garments, and the cistern enriched with farthings and boddles [the tiny copper coins worth 2d Scots], the offerings and testimonies of grateful votaries, who came from afar to this fountain of health.[283]

Its iron ladle had only recently disappeared. But fifty years later, the castle was 'levelled with the ground, and the swamp on which it stood has become a fruitful field'.[284] A different holy well, associated with St Columba, was located on the Hill of Alvah. Precocious nineteenth-century efforts to preserve the 1540s chapel of St John, Deskford, did not extend to its holy well, which was drained by 1884 and could not be located at all in 1961. In Foveran, portions of the pre-1474 Chapel of the Holy Rood stood in the kirkyard until about 1890, when 'a man was commissioned to level out the cemetery and the remains of the chapel were removed'.[285]

A pre-Reformation chapel, associated with another miraculous well, stood in the Brae of Laithers but 'was some years ago removed by the plough'.[286] An old chapel in Glenbuchat met a similar fate within living memory of 1795. At the same date in the Braes of Gartly, there were only 'vestiges' of four Catholic chapels, at Heatheryhillock, Brawlinknows, Tillythrowie and Kirkney.[287] A medieval Catholic chapel in the parish of Glass was still in use as such in the mid-eighteenth century, but it had ceased operation by the 1840s. 'At a place called Chapelden . . . on a haugh opposite the Toar of Troup' the ruined walls of a Roman Catholic chapel were still 'held sacred by the husbandmen' in 1835, but such consideration by that date was rare indeed.[288]

Folla Rule near Turriff takes its name from the chapel of St Rule at Follach, founded in 1376. Reduced to 'vestiges' by the 1720s, it had by 1840 entirely vanished. Traces of two other chapels could still, however, be seen by St Paul's

*The remains of Banff's Bede House, demolished in 1903. In Cullen, the sixteen bede-men and bede-women wore blue uniforms, and were interviewed twice a year by a herald sent from Edinburgh, who mediated in any disputes between the inmates and the patrons.*

Well, Eastertown, and on the farm of Fetterletter, Gight. The existence of another can be presumed from the farm name St John's Well in Minnonie, Fyvie parish. The twelfth- or thirteenth-century priory of St Mary, Fyvie, 'consisted of a large chapel within a courtyard of buildings, of which the last traces vanished in the eighteenth century'.[289] It was located on the north bank of the Ythan about one mile below Fyvie Castle. 'In this parish, indeed, the external machinery for the support of the Roman Catholic faith, appears to have been very complete'.[290]

Some identifications of Catholic sites are erroneous, or at best mysterious. On the Leask estate in Slains, a chapel dedicated to St Adamnán (who died in the early eighth century) was long supposed to date from the saint's lifetime, despite it having been built in the 'arched Gothic' style of the twelfth century and later.[291] In Forglen in the 1790s, the parish minister Robert Ballingall identified remains of a supposedly pre-Reformation chapel 're-edified by George Ogilvie, Master of Banff' in the seventeenth century. But in the 1960s the same site, complete with inscribed stone regarding Ogilvie's restoration work, was identified by the Ordnance Survey as *Ballingall's own parish church*, which was replaced but left standing as ruins in 1806. It is possible that the Ogilvie plaque was moved, but both versions of the story cannot be correct.

Often, as with the aforementioned St John's Well farm, field and farm names provide the only substantial evidence for the sites of lost Catholic institutions. The place-names Chapeltown and Chapelpark reflected the presence of two different pre-Reformation chapels in Methlick, ploughed under as recently as 1792. The sheep farm called North Chapelhouses, Meldrum, commemorates a Catholic chapel of Our Lady. The place in Marnoch called Chapelton was, by the nineteenth century, the only surviving clue that a chapel had once been there. The same principle extends to towns: Banff still has its Carmelite Street, and Newburgh its Monkshome, while in and near the village of Turriff, places called Temple-brae, Temple-feu, Abbey-land and Monks-land all suggested the placement of long-vanished religious foundations.

## PARISH CHURCHES AND MANSES

We should not assume, simply because they were new, that the new Protestant churches of the sixteenth to the eighteenth centuries were uniformly well constructed. Both in comparison to the Catholic Church and in absolute terms, the early Protestant Church was desperately poor. Stephen Masoun, who was simultaneously minister of Bethelnie, Bourtie, Fyvie, Tarves and Rayne from 1574 to 1612, had a stipend of less than £9 sterling a year. 'Forced to live by some method very many of the early Reformed ministers took to selling ale, either privately or at a tavern, and in this ignominious fashion between "beer and the Bible" they managed to eke out a livelihood.'[292]

As a rule, post-Reformation churches here were built as quickly and cheaply as possible, to fill an immediate need for a certain quantity of seating – a quantity which demand frequently outpaced, as the region's population rapidly grew. The churches of Lonmay, Strichen, Botriphnie and Ordiquhill were all built between 1608 and 1627, and all 'taken down' by 1820.[293] The 1764 church of Monquhitter was shoddily built and 'in considerable disrepair' less than eighty years afterwards; and in a similar (if extreme) case, a church in Glass was built in 1782 and rebuilt in 1791. Crimond's 1812 kirk, built to replace one from 1576, was considered '[u]nlike most country churches' in being provided with a steeple, a bell and a clock.[294] Marnoch's early nineteenth-century church replaced a 'very old . . . ruinous one', but had itself to be rebuilt before 1842, due to its original 'insufficiency'. 'It is one of those old-fashioned barn-looking

LEFT. *J.W. Whymper's rather sinister Victorian engraving of the 1723-dated west gable of Boyndie parish church, abandoned in 1773.*

BELOW. *So many early kirks survive only as roofless ruins or single gables that it is refreshing to find a picture of one substantially intact and unaltered. This is the church of Dyce, probably built in 1544, as it looked c.1820. Not long before, its roof had been of thatch. Abandoned in 1872 and unroofed twenty years later, its replacement church was in turn abandoned and unroofed between 1925 and 1932.*

Balnakettle's Seat

Tilliegrig.

Rosebank.

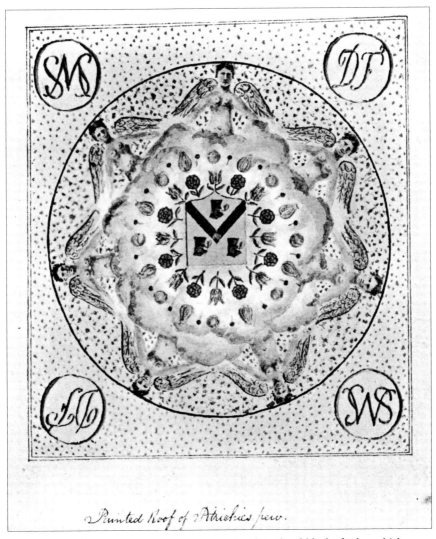

*Painted Roof of Pitrichies pew.*

OPPOSITE. *Elaborate seventeenth-century woodwork in the old kirk of Udny, which was demolished and its contents scattered in 1821.*

ABOVE. *Painted ceiling of the Pitrichie pew, Udny old kirk. It is unusual for even a picture of pre-1800 church furnishings to survive in this region.*

houses, which are now very properly disappearing', the minister commented.[295] The church of Gartly, meanwhile, was 'substantially repaired' so often by 1824 that only the steeple could be called truly original.[296] And Trinity Church, Whitehills, was '[r]elocated here stone by stone from Banff in 1925'.[297]

The manse of New Deer, whose construction in the 1770s was considered a fine excuse for destroying a Pictish monument many centuries old, was itself replaced as early as 1832. Manses in general were especially short-lived, and I know of no substantially original seventeenth-century examples north of Stirlingshire. Part of the blame for this lies with the Scottish parliament, which decreed in 1663 that the budget for building or rebuilding any manse be fixed at £1,000 Scots (about £83 sterling at the time). Despite inflation in the price of labour – latterly severe – this law was not amended or repealed throughout the eighteenth century. Construction methods were also problematic. 'So late as 1714 part of the Manse of Foveran consisted of what was called "the Mudd Hall," the walls of which were of wrought clay only, mixed with straw.'[298] The 1766 manse of Tarves, Francis Knox wrote in 1842, 'though still inhabited, is in a very crazy condition, and fast hastening to decay'.[299] Most manses of similar date were already gone by then. Ministers everywhere, Rev. Walter Chalmers wrote from eighteenth-century Deskford, 'must daily feel the grievance of inhabiting houses that will not defend wind and rain'. So bad was the usual standard of manse-building, Chalmers even suggested no manse should be paid for unless it was able to stand for a full year. Yet, those who complained about their manses were often met with 'illiberal abuse' from the landowners (many of whom were not even themselves members of the Church of Scotland) who paid to erect these sizeable houses again and again.[300] The 1748 manse of Strichen was called

*The Quaker school of Kinmuck, claimed as the oldest in Scotland, as it would have looked when newly opened in 1681. Manses of the same date were probably of similar design, though less solidly built.*

'very old' in 1840,[301] and at eighty-one years old, the manse of Tullynessle would also have been thought exceptionally long in the tooth when it was pulled down in 1805. It was even more unusual that the manses of Forglen and Meldrum, built in 1683 and 1710 respectively, had received no serious complaints about their construction or condition a century later. They may, indeed, have been the only pre-Georgian manses in the whole region that were still in use by 1806. In any case, both were remodelled beyond recognition by the end of the 1820s.

Isolated documentary references make it appear likely that most eighteenth-century and earlier manses had thatched roofs. The oldest surviving house of this type in the country, Larbert Old Manse in Stirlingshire, has a pantiled roof today; but houses with such roofs 'were rare prior to the 1850s unless as an inexpensive substitute for thatch. The use of pantiles for houses is a late nineteenth-century feature and . . . caused considerable controversy.'[302] Banffshire and Aberdeenshire houses of various types often had 'a roof of straw so heavily impregnated with a moist clay mixture that no roping was necessary.' This was about nine inches deep and expected to last forty or fifty years, as compared to the not more than twenty-year lifespan of thatch alone.[303] This fifty-year maximum life of the roof could explain why so many manses in this region, newly built in the period 1750–1780, were deemed fit only for demolition by 1800–1830. The first generation of slate-roofed manses, however, are among the most sought-after residential properties here today.

## MOOT HILLS, SPAS AND OTHER PUBLIC GATHERING PLACES

Inalterie's lost ancient compound was associated with a motte or cairn called the Law Hillock, which was demolished for building stone in or by the mid-1830s. The name reflects a widespread belief that certain specially designated hills, some of them man-made, served as courts of law in a distant era when justice in Scotland was mostly administered by barons. Georgian schoolmaster Alexander Simpson believed Turriff had been the site one of these 'moot hills', and the villagers of his day still referred to the end of town between the kirkyard and the market cross as 'the Castlehill'.[304] Ellon's moot hill, located eighty or ninety yards downstream of the north end of the bridge, was used for important public ceremonies, perhaps including trials, between at least 1206 and 1615. Its demolition c.1710 to make room for an inn has already been mentioned, but this first inn was itself 'pulled down in 1853 . . . far gone in decay'.[305] ('Ellon is now so essentially modern in appearance that it is difficult to realise that it is a place

*Artist's impression of the Bass of Inverurie in its heyday, with wooden superstructure intact.*

of great antiquity', the burgh council commented in 1952.[306]) The moot hill on Mains of Ardiffery in Cruden was 'an open-air seat of justice . . . removed when the land was reclaimed'.[307] In Tyrie there was a similar 'Moat' hill 'in the immediate vicinity of the church' until the early nineteenth century, but who demolished it or why has gone unrecorded. In eighteenth-century Strathdon, the Doune of Invernochty – with part of its bailey still standing, and a moat fed by the Bardock burn still functional – was considered 'the largest and most complete of any thing of the kind'.[308] Fifty years later, wall fragments on top were still present, but the water had stopped flowing, and other ancient buildings round about it had 'been long since obliterated by the plough'.[309] Oddly, the generation who plundered the site speculated only that it might have been of Roman, ancient British, or Pictish origin. The truth – that it was the product of Norman feudalism – was not considered at all.

Despite such recent disrespect, more mottes per square mile seem to have been built in Buchan than in Mar. Existing or demolished examples (not otherwise mentioned in this chapter) have been noted at Moathillock and Castlehill, both in Auchindoir; Moathead of Auchterless; the Meethill estate, Peterhead; the Law of Melrose in Gamrie; the Law of Crovie; Castle Point, Gardenstown; Castleton of King Edward; Ruthven, between Huntly and Keith; Milltown of Boyndlie; Tullynessle; Rathen; the Bass of Insch; the Bass of Inverurie; Kinnairdy Castle and Castlehill Farm, both in Marnoch; the Ha' Hillock in Alvah; Ha' Hill of Minnonie; Mount Carmel a.k.a. Colenard in Banff; Clola in Old Deer; Netherton of Lonmay; Gallowhill of Grange; and Hangman's Hill of Inverugie. Though not a hill, the Earl's Loch on the farm of Scotstown in Forglen ('mostly drained up' before 1800) might reveal a similar history.[310] Most of these sites have never been the subject of serious archaeological examination, and much of the scanty information about them has come from ploughmen and well-diggers.

Places founded as burghs, as well as villages that attained burgh status later, had the right to erect market crosses and inevitably did so. Rarely 'crosses' in

*The motte and now-demolished castle of King Edward, as seen by Banff artist Charles Cordiner in 1782.*

RIGHT. *More than half of the region's mercat crosses have vanished, some without explanation. The three most elaborate that survive – at Banff (below left), Cullen, and Fraserburgh – all have tangled histories. Opinions differ sharply as to whether Cullen's cross shaft is a seventeenth-century survivor of the demolition of the old burgh, or a Victorian copy. All three crosses were moved at least once, Banff's to the top of Sandyhills Doocot (right) before coming back into the town centre. The cross has been lovingly restored, but the doocot is now on the 'At Risk' register.*

BELOW RIGHT. *By 1858, Fraserburgh's tolbooth had been pulled down, and its mercat cross had lost its gaol cell. Only the 1736-dated shaft of the cross remained; but an authentic-looking replacement head (bearing the royal arms as used 1603–1714) has since been attached. The modern explanatory plaque reads like a description of the Ship of Theseus or 'Trigger's Broom'. Can an object, all of whose parts have been replaced since 1603, still be 'from' 1546?*

ABOVE LEFT. *Turriff's old cross, reputedly the ugliest in Scotland, was removed in 1865.*

ABOVE RIGHT. *Typically, the region's least messed-about mercat cross, in Old Rayne, is also its least well-known.*

LEFT. *Peterhead still maintained a Town Cryer when this photograph was taken in 1931.*

'any conventional sense', these could contain traders' booths, sundials, drinking-water pumps, speakers' platforms, and (as at Fraserburgh) small gaols – alone or in various combinations.[311] With or without such useful gadgetry, the erection or re-erection of a market cross was a commonplace act of civic pride beginning about 1440; and this was very far from being a North Country and Scottish phenomenon, as is now widely believed. Nearly every town in Britain had a market cross between 1500 and 1640; Liverpool had two, Bristol three, and some other places in western England, four or five. Of the 109 Scottish market crosses still standing in 1900, just one-fifth definitely dated to before 1650. It is the continued interest in market crosses, and especially the creation of new ones *after* 1650, that sets Scotland apart in this respect.

Here, such crosses now exist only in Banff, Macduff, Cullen, Fraserburgh, Fyvie, Old Rayne and Turriff, begging the question of what happened to them in Clatt, Peterhead, Inverurie, Old Meldrum, Newburgh, Ellon, Rosehearty, Aberlour and Cornhill of Ordiquhill. Fyvie's current cross, like Turriff's, is Victorian but Fyvie would have been entitled to two different crosses at different periods in its history. A royal burgh existed at Woodhead of Fyvie in the fourteenth century, but it was clearly defunct by 1673, when Peterswell of Fyvie was made a burgh of barony – partly on the grounds that the nearest royal burgh was twelve miles away. Cornhill, like Woodhead of Fyvie, may be accounted a failure, so the destruction of its civic symbols should not be surprising. At the other end of the spectrum, Aberlour did not become a burgh of barony until 1812, when cross-making – and baronial jurisdictions – could be considered well past their prime.

Clatt's cross, dating from 1501, would seem to have fallen down by the early nineteenth century: the oldest inhabitants in 1866 remembered 'having seen it lying about' but by then it was gone for good.[312] Newburgh's, extant in 1558, 'was broken by a cart'.[313] Inverurie's cross, dating from 1671, was twice moved before being broken up. A stone from it was built into a wall of the Kintore Arms Hotel, but '[i]t is not now visible, and may have been removed when a doorway was made in the wall c.1954'.[314] And Peterhead's and Ellon's lost crosses could have been swept away along with the burgh tolbooths, which disappeared (both aged about 130) in the 1790s and 1830s, respectively. But the absence of early-modern market crosses from Portsoy, Rosehearty and Old Meldrum – all more or less thriving communities, and all chartered between 1550 and 1681, well within the market cross's heyday – remains a mystery.

In the Restoration period (1660–1688), idle gossip around the market cross tended to move indoors: to coffee houses where the new newspapers were read and caffeine-fuelled political debates raged. This region boasts a perfectly astonishing survival of one of these famous coffee houses, in Market Square, Old Meldrum. Now called Morris's Hotel (illustrated on p. 173), it was built in 1673. The coffee-house tradition, or something like it, continued into Georgian times here, with public 'News-Rooms' established at Old Aberdeen, Peterhead, and a place called Cortebrae near Strichen.

Not all gathering places were quite so formal, of course. In Victorian Fraserburgh, local shipwright John Webster owned

> a substantial yard for storing imported wood at the head of the North Pier. The yard, referred to locally as 'The Logs', was a well-known meeting-place and unofficial playground until it was swept away in the redevelopment of this part of the harbour towards the end of the [nineteenth] century.[315]

The region also boasted four wells – in Peterhead, Fraserburgh, Tarlair and Inverboyndie – whose healing properties were endorsed by eighteenth-century medical men, and as such should not necessarily be lumped together with the Catholic Church's miraculous healing wells already mentioned. The Red Well of Inverboyndie never saw any ambitious developments themed around it, beyond a 'beehive-shaped enclosure',[316] but Fraserburgh and Peterhead both

*Rare image of Tarlair before the swimming complex and tea pavilion were erected. The pool is not only the best preserved, but the oldest of its type in Scotland, designed in 1929 and completed in 1931. Similar complexes at Arbroath, North Berwick and Prestwick were substantially destroyed.*

made serious runs at becoming spa towns on the English or German model. In a much later period, Tarlair (whose original well house survives, albeit in an unappealing condition) became the site of a large and rather magnificent art deco public swimming pool.

A mineral spring on the south-east side of Fraserburgh was being marketed as a tourist destination by 1791. Two open-air pools, cut into the rock below Kinnaird's Head, were added soon afterwards, and by 1808 the complex was completed by the addition of a pump room, bathing machine, and 'long, low two-storey building' with 'projecting pavilions'.[317] It was still in use in 1822, but the Fraserburgh seafront became steadily less attractive to pleasure-seekers in inverse proportion to the success of the local herring fishery, which commenced in 1815.

A similar sequence of events occurred in Peterhead, where an even more successful spa was ruined by the success of the even smellier whale-blubber-boiling industry (p. 31). The town's Wine Well, from which issued healing waters with a flavour like cherry brandy, was discovered in 1592 and originally called St Peter's Well. However, the well water only developed as a major attraction around 1760, when Richard Pococke described it as stronger than that of Tunbridge Wells, 'but not so strong as the German'.[318] Land values in that part of town soon shot up to an alarming £1,150 per acre, and a fine hotel was built in 1773, followed twenty years later by a 'hydropathic pavilion' above the well itself.[319] The well pavilion was demolished in 1936.

At the time of writing, it is barely possible to find an operational cinema anywhere between the Don and the Spey. This was not always the case. Former cinemas dating from the interwar period in Bridge Street, Banff and Church Street, Dufftown have been placed on the 'At Risk' register in recent years. The former was built into an eighteenth-century house – itself of some quality – while the latter is reputed to be exceptionally well stocked with original fittings and equipment. Another in Marischal Street, Peterhead has recently been in use as a bingo hall. The cinema that operated near the market cross of Turriff is all but forgotten.

## HUMBLER HOUSES AND SHOPS

Like manses, the houses of ordinary people were exceptionally short-lived. In 1629, the town council of Banff ordered the houses of 'idle persons' banished from the burgh to be knocked down – suggesting that such houses had no intrinsic value at the time.[320] Thatch was prevalent: the first new house built in the 1815 new town section of Ellon was described as a 'one-storey thatched cottage' occupied by a veterinary surgeon, Mr Hay.[321] Thirty years later, the row of six shops on the north side of Ellon Square – grocer, saddler, baker, carpenter, tailor and druggist, 'all with gable ends to the street' – were 'of one storey and thatched' with the sole exception of Rae the grocer's.[322]

The shop of Ellon's Victorian shoemaker John McLean was long, low, one-

*Balgrennie Cottage prior to its comprehensive reconstruction as a 'modern' building in 1907.*

*A typical eighteenth-century upland Aberdeenshire estate cottage with a stone chimney at one end and a 'timmer lum' at the other.*

storey and thatched, 'wi' a long timmer lum, wippet wi' strae rape'; while the small candy factory of his neighbour 'Candy John' Johnston was entirely of wood and called 'The Ark'.[323] Both had been built over by 1921. The old New Inn, run by the Cowie family for several generations, 'had the look of belonging to the early eighteenth century, with its massive chimney stacks, rather flattened roof . . . frowning eaves and comparatively small windows'.[324] A presumably similar business in Old Meldrum flourished in the mid seventeenth century '[b]efore the town was built'. All that remained of it by Victorian times, however, was the 'singular and striking' Tree of Parcock: a 200-year-old ash, thought to have been planted to guide travellers to the inn of the same name. The Commercial Hotel in New Aberdour, when newly built in 1798, seems to have had a thatched roof.

The overall number of public houses noted as existing in the first half of the nineteenth century seems roughly the same as at present; but as with most

LEFT. *Banff's original post office in Castle Street, photographed c.1890.*

BELOW. *A particularly grand general merchant's shop in Glenbuchat, c.1905–10. It appears to have had more employees than the entire glen now has residents.*

ABOVE. *Banff Bowling Club, 1903–81, seen here shortly after it opened.*

LEFT. *Pantiled roofs, associated with smiths' shops in inland areas, were unexceptional in coastal towns.*

other building types, existing pubs are almost exclusively of the late nineteenth century or later. The same applies to banks, which by 1842 had been established in Keith (where there were three), Cullen (two), Marnoch, Forglen, Old Machar, Meldrum, Belhelvie, Peterhead, Longside, St Fergus, Strichen, Fraserburgh, King Edward, Turriff, Ellon, New Deer, Methlick, Fyvie and Monquhitter. But to the best of my knowledge, only one purpose-built bank from before 1842 – at 49–57 Low Street in Banff – survives anywhere in northern Aberdeenshire or Banffshire. Given that even post offices were often low, haphazardly-built buildings comparable to McLean's cobbler's shop, it is quite possible that the early banks' premises were of a primitive and essentially temporary character.

In 1748 in Banff, 'most of the useful articles of merchandise might be procured in the same shop'; fifty years later, specialisation ruled, with separate grocers, ironmongers, haberdashers and confectioners all established.[325] Yet, for most of the region, permanent retail premises of *any* sort were still relatively rare in 1840, when it was calculated that forty open-air fairs were held within a ten-mile radius of the parish church of Fyvie, and twenty more within another three miles. One of the few 'crimes' that regularly resulted in imprisonment in seventeenth-century Banff was trading from a private house rather than at the market cross. This suggests that shops *per se* were not yet seen – though in 1699 the town had three, or possibly four excellent silversmiths, who were unlikely to have worked in the open air. The Aikey Fair in Aikey Brae, originally a horse

*Thatched cottages in North Street, Peterhead, 1870. Tile roofs and clay walls were more common in coastal than inland areas, but this is a generalisation. In 1840s Turriff, the larger farmhouses were mostly of mortared stone, but the cottages were 'in general built of mud, ill-constructed, ill-ventilated, and ill-roofed'.[326]*

fair, attracted 30,000 people in 1952, and the popular fair now known as the Turriff Show has been held at Lammastide for 501 years; its success probably ruined the Rounie Law cattle fair in neighbouring Forglen.

Between 1800 and 1840, the number of annual fairs held in the parish of Turriff fell from nine to eight, and the burgh's weekly market was also ended within that period, not because of economic decline, but because shops had become plentiful. The transition from fairs to fixed premises was accelerated (though not caused) by the arrival of the railway. Even so, the tradition of fairs was so strong that a new one first made possible by the railway, the Maud Mart, lasted for 99 years down to 2003, with around 6,000 animals 'from across Scotland' being sold there every Wednesday.[327]

Eighteenth-century Tomintoul consisted almost entirely of 'turf-thatched hovels',[328] and farm buildings in Monquhitter were 'mostly thatched with straw or heather' as late as the 1840s.[329] Unlike straw thatch, Aberdeenshire heather thatch was laid in horizontal courses from gable to gable, and from the bottom up; for best results, the plants were pulled up by the roots rather than scythed down. In coastal areas, even including the large, prosperous town of Fraserburgh, thatched roofs made of a sea grass called *bent* or *agrostis* were seen alongside slates and pantiles, and many walls were of *clay bool*, a mixture of field stones and clay.

Of Easter Auchleuchries, now a modern five-bedroomed house, Robert Smith remembered:

> Grandfather Murdoch had a box-bed with doors that closed and shut out the world. He had a big open fire with pots bubbling on the swey. He had a porch with hens clucking about the doorway and steading behind the house. But all that was a long time ago – now the past had been wiped out.[330]

Yes and no. Thatch was placed over slate roofs simply for insulation at Glendronach and elsewhere as late as the 1950s, and some cottages near Troup, though 'modernised', were observed to still have 'walls of straw and dung' in 1990.[331]

## CASTLES AND TOWERS

Across Europe by the end of the sixteenth century, gunpowder artillery had become powerful enough, and mobile enough, that fortifications of fifteenth-

*Old Slains. The shop made from a boat hull may post-date the lost village of Oldcastle of Slains, which was abandoned after its entire fishing fleet was wrecked in a storm on 15 February 1900. Despite what certain experts have claimed, the superficially similar ruined walls of Dunnideer are actually two centuries older – and moreover, 'partly built from the remains of the prehistoric vitrified fort in which it stands'.[334]*

Brucklay Castle

TOP. *The 'star fort' built around Corgarff Castle by its Hanoverian army garrison, useful as it may have been against the occasional musket ball, was little better than a parody of the mighty ramparts of Berwick-on-Tweed or Luxembourg.*

BOTTOM. *Brucklay Castle, long the home of the famous Dingwall-Fordyce family of naval officers and politicians, was built in the sixteenth century and extended five times between 1600 and 1850. Its lake was man-made 'using only spades and buckets' and, perhaps unsurprisingly, took twelve man-years.[335] Seen here in its Victorian heyday, it was later used as a prisoner-of-war camp. Intentionally unroofed as a tax dodge in 1951, its contents were auctioned off the following year. By 2008, Brucklay was a windowless ruin with broken floors and ivy growing in the drawing room.*

century and earlier type, including tower houses, were essentially obsolete. Scotland's relative poverty, however, meant that large siege artillery remained the preserve of the monarchy alone, while bad roads and widespread royalism ensured that Banff and Buchan were rarely targeted by it. The 'modern' angle-bastioned earthwork artillery fortress, as exemplified by pre-1850 Geneva, the lost castle of Roxburgh, and the town of Berwick-upon-Tweed, never made it much north of the Borders. The 'star fort' built around Corgarff Castle was little more than a parody of such designs, and it is highly unusual (not to say contentious) that the fifteenth-century Castle of Esslemont was transformed from an ordinary L-plan tower house into 'a five-sided artillery castle' prior to its demolition in 1769.[332] Family feuds, clan battles and cattle raids, gruesome though they could be, were seldom conducted with weapons more powerful than swords and pistols, so the old tower houses remained highly effective protection. Even during wars, fifteenth-century tower houses could do sterling service, as when Jacobite-held Fedderate Castle, built c.1480, held out for three weeks against Gen. Hugh Mackay's Williamite forces in 1690. It *was* eventually blown up, but only because it had proved 'an impediment to agriculture'.[333] A major exception to this general situation was the destruction of Old Slains Castle

*Waterton House, Ellon, in 1770. The Forbeses of Waterton were in constant financial trouble of one sort or another, culminating in the loss of all their lands in the Ellon area before the end of the eighteenth century. In 1711 Thomas Forbes II sued the earl of Aberdeen, his uncle, alleging that he had defrauded him of 8,000 merks. John, son of Thomas Forbes III, was a junior officer in the Scots Dutch Regiment, who died at Osterhout in 1748, of a fever that had lasted forty-two days. His doctor declined a fee but did ask for 'a dozine of fine Aberdeen pairs of stockings'.[336]*

by royal artillery, during a 1594 rebellion led by its owner Francis Hay, ninth earl of Errol.

The most elaborate castles in Buchan, described somewhat hyperbolically by Charles McKean as 'palaces', included Inverugie, Philorth and Pitsligo. The ruins of Bognie Castle, clearly visible from the A97 between Aberchirder and Huntly, are also wider – and with more, larger, more regularly spaced windows – than the term 'tower house' would typically encompass. Boyn, also cited by McKean, was even more genuinely palatial, and though it was described merely as a mansion house, so was Auchnagatt. Belonging to the Strachans of Glenkindie, who were Covenanters, Auchnagatt was destroyed by the royalists. As befitted such a large estate – it had 7,200 acres of shooting in the 1890s – the house was also enormous, containing, for instance, twenty-eight fully furnished beds and fifteen dozen plates. Not merely its contents, but Auchnagatt itself has vanished so thoroughly that its precise former site is a matter of pure speculation.

The sixteenth-century castle of Cullen-of-Buchan, still prominent as ruins in 1807, was demolished by the end of the same century. It was survived by the clay-built farmhouse of the home farm, which incorporated 'a great variety of pieces of architectural masonry of varying dates'.[338] This farmhouse's 1574 date-

*The same site as opposite, cleared completely, in 1840. As a final indignity to this once powerful family, the* Daily Advertiser *reported in 1788 that a daughter of the last laird had died four days out of Antigua and 'was preserved by her affectionate son in a hogshead of rum for three weeks, till the vessel arrived' in New York.[337]*

*The Castle of Boyn in the late nineteenth century. The ancient royal forest of Boyn extended from Gamrie to Portsoy and inland almost to Turriff.*

*Huntly Castle, completed in 1606 by Scotland's wealthiest family, would certainly fit the description 'palace', with its delicate French-inspired oriel windows, superb fireplaces, and astonishing multi-storey armorial over the main entrance, the finest thing of its kind in the United Kingdom.*

stone was missing by 1963, and the whole structure burned beyond repair in 2001.

An ecclesiastical palace of the Middle Ages, Fetternear, was replaced by a mansion of 1566, and extended in 1693. Its sham-castle appearance dates, like Hatton's, only from the early 1800s. It burned down in 1919 and remains a shell.

The Tower of Deskford was pulled down in the early nineteenth century specifically to stop it falling and crushing the adjoining St John's Chapel, but as we have seen, such regard for pre-Reformation remains was exceptional. Of a motte-and-bailey castle in Grange that was a frequent residence of the abbots of Kinloss, by the late eighteenth century there remained 'nothing but a heap of rubbish; being entirely destroyed for the sake of the stones, which are very scarce in this corner, for building houses'.[339] Wooden internal elements of various castles also found their way into commercial buildings of the Improvement period: for instance, roof timbers and panelling from Auchmedden Castle were seen twenty years ago in 64 High Street, New Pitsligo, and

The Palace of Boyn, drawn by Charles Cordiner, 1782. It, and not English sham-castles such as Lulworth in Dorset, was probably the model for local sham-castles like Hatton (1814). However, Scottish architect James Adam's unexecuted 1767 design for a grandiose neo-castle at Lowther in Cumbria could also have played a part.

Formerly known as Philorth Castle, Cairnbulg received its current name soon after it was sold by Sir Alexander Fraser of Philorth to the Frasers of Durris in 1613. The name of Philorth was, at the same date, transferred to one of Sir Alexander's houses one mile to the west. This new Philorth (pictured) was completed in 1666 and completely destroyed by fire in 1915.

This 1616-dated armorial stone is seemingly all that remains of the c.1600 tower house of Keith Inch, a.k.a. the Queenzie, Peterhead. Oddly, the arms depicted are not those of the Keith family, so the stone may represent an heiress-wife, or be an artefact from somewhere else altogether. (Photo by Barry Robertson)

Tolquhon Castle, c.1400 with major additions of 1584–89, was 'fast sinking into shapeless heaps of stones and rubbish' when these pictures were created in the 1840s.[340] The 'witch's hat' roofs have since been lost, and the fifteenth-century Preston tower reduced from four storeys to one; but the rest of the structure appears surprisingly sound.

in the same village, panelling from the castles of Pittullie and Pitsligo found their way into several houses in Low Street.

Many smaller castles have been lost along with the reasons for their destruction. The so-called Wallace Castle, a thirteenth-century fortification located on the Ha' Hill of Minnonie, was described in 1913 as having walls eighteen feet high and ten feet thick, with a gothic archway. It disappeared without trace or explanation by 1965.

It should be remembered, of course, that for every castle left to collapse, another has been lovingly maintained or artfully restored.

## TOWNHOUSES OF THE ARISTOCRACY, GENTRY AND MERCHANTS

When travel by the aristocracy was fraught with danger but their resources were practically limitless, they readily built second, third, fourth and fifth houses: not for conspicuous display, but as centres for the management of their widely-dispersed lands, towns and jurisdictions. The fourth earl Marischal, who died in 1581, had so many houses that it was said he could travel from Caithness to the English border, and along the way sleep every night in one of his own beds. The selling of various commodities was mostly restricted to towns, which meant that buying largely was, too. This ensured that most of the Scots peerage and the better-off lairds tended to have at least one urban dwelling in addition to their principal country seat. These lairds' townhouses were not especially ornate or fortified, and frequently differed from merchants' houses only in that their occupants had another home somewhere else.

Banff's uniquely well-preserved early-modern townscape boasts a continuous row of three merchant houses dating from 1585 to 1740, facing the graveyard, as well as other isolated examples throughout the burgh. Such survivals are rare indeed, with multiple early-modern examples knocked down – and none surviving – in Turriff and Peterhead alone. Even in Banff, at least two venerable gentry townhouses, one belonging to a grandmother of Lord Byron, were demolished between 1870 and 1902. Earlier losses in the town included the magnificent House of Airlie, inhabited in 1759, abandoned by 1779, and long gone (except for its external steps) by 1868. Likewise,

A few old persons at the end of the last century [i.e. c.1800] had in remembrance seeing some large massy ruins standing on the space now occupied by the Town House and Plainstones, called the Towers,

*Little Fillacap, a probably early-eighteenth-century house in Low Street, Banff. It was owned by relatives of the poet Lord Byron, who paid it several extended visits. Occupying the highest rank of 'English' poets, Byron was raised in Aberdeenshire, and his mother Catherine was thirteenth laird of Gight. The house was pulled down in or by 1871, to make room for James Matthews's rather less elegant court-house and county hall.*

*This house, known as The Turrets, was removed in 1902 to make space for the Banff Library and Museum.*

remains of the residence of the Lords of Banff. In some old writings, this mansion is styled a Palace, a distinction it is supposed to have acquired in consequence of having been the temporary abode of certain of the Scottish Kings, who, as appears from the date of some old charters, had visited the town, most probably on their hunting expeditions to the Royal Forest of the Boyn. This fine old mansion was demolished by General Munro, in August 1640[.][341]

For good measure, Munro's troops hewed down every fruit tree belonging to the Towers and uprooted every hedge. 'All the wonder heer is,' an eyewitness reported, that 'using Banfes house so ill, they should have spared the earle of Airlyes lodging, which is distant and separate from Banfes house only by the

*Fraserburgh's oldest and finest surviving gentry townhouse, Warld's End, was built c.1700 for the future Jacobite general John Gordon of Glenbuchat. It was confiscated after the '45, tastefully remodelled in 1767, and barely touched since. Within living memory it was, to the best of my knowledge, the only gentry townhouse in Buchan with a corrugated tin roof; by summer 2008 slates had returned. As remodelled, it is oddly similar to two country houses in distant Strathdon: Bellabeg and Inverernan.*

*Errol's Lodging, a sixteenth-century townhouse of the earls of Errol with minor later additions, stood near Turriff's market cross, and housed William Meston's grammar school. It was knocked down in 1974 after being deemed a problem for road traffic. It should not be confused with its neighbour 'Castle Rainy', a somewhat humbler townhouse of the seventeenth century, pulled down in 1845 'having become ruinous'. Rumours that Castle Rainy was 'erected by the Knights Hospitallers, probably as a sort of hotel' in the early 1500s appear to be unfounded; it more likely 'belonged . . . to a family named Rainie' or Rennie.[343] Errol's Lodging may have been an inspiration for Archibald Simpson's now demolished 1815 wing of Druminnor.*

lenthe of the formentioned garden.'[342] The final above-ground remains seem to have been pulled down in or about August 1746, because falling masonry had nearly crushed a child.

As late as 1860, Ythan Terrace in Ellon consisted of townhouses of the local gentry, but half a century later it was harshly criticised as a haunt of juvenile delinquents.

*The earl Marischal's townhouse in Port Henry Lane, Peterhead, demolished in 1962. Its reputed construction date of 1599 would appear to be plausible, based on this and other photographs.*

*Seventeenth-century house in Seagate, Peterhead, probably built for a merchant.*

*One of the best-preserved gentry townhouses in the region is so-called Fordyce Castle, built in the centre of Fordyce village in 1592 by Thomas Menzies of Durn. (Photo by David Walker)*

## SCOTLAND'S 'MOST LOST' BUILDING TYPE?
## THE SMALL COUNTRY HOUSE, 1664–1678

While medieval castles and Georgian country houses 'are familiar to all students of Scottish architecture,' John Dunbar wrote in 1966, 'very little attention' has ever been paid to the Lowland lairds' houses of the late sixteenth, seventeenth and early eighteenth centuries.[344] These dwellings had no single dominant style, and 'as often as not' became farmhouses in the mid-to-late eighteenth century, when across the country, small estates were absorbed or combined into larger ones.[345] The century from the Reformation to the end of the Civil Wars was a time of transition, from quasi-medieval-style tower houses to 'modern' mansions such as Memsie in Rathen.

Houses from the transitional period 'combine castellated and domestic features in very variable proportions'. Defensive grilles called *yetts*, placed over doors, were outlawed in 1606, and gun-loops were considered extremely old-fashioned by 1608.[346] The transitional period was also characterised by 1) 'a general increase in the size of window openings, and the more frequent use of

*Mains of Drummuir, a late-transitional seventeenth-century laird's house in the parish of Botriphnie. It was fortunate indeed to escape destruction at the time Thomas Mackenzie built his sham castle of Drummuir in 1846. Photograph by Anne Burgess.[349]*

glass'; 2) greater symmetry in the placement of windows and their size; and 3) the disappearance of defensive parapet walkways and turrets.[347] Most importantly, in a tower house, an expansion of living quarters 'could take place only by means of a fundamental change of plan-form', and new lairds' houses ceased altogether to be towers after 1661, with Leslie Castle, near Insch, being the last of its kind.[348] Charming local examples of late-transitional lairds' houses are provided by Mounie Castle, Daviot (1641) and Mains of Drummuir, south-west of Keith, probably 1650s.

Dunbar assigned to 'the years immediately preceding the [1707] Act of Union' the emergence of 'a new type of medium-sized domestic residence, which owed nothing to the tower house', with 'windows . . . almost always regularly disposed about a central entrance-doorway'. Though Dunbar must have been aware that the nation's hundreds of lairds must have built *something* in the two decades after 1661, the earliest full-blown examples of this new style that he was able – or willing – to identify were Dalnair Manse, Stirlingshire (1682); Old Mains of Rattray, Perthshire (1694); and an unexecuted design published in John Reid's *The Scots Gard'ner* (1683).

Dunbar was clearly in the grip of an ideological model of development, in which pre-Union houses had to demonstrate their 'conservatism and retrospection', whereas Georgian ones must exhibit 'advanced standards of design'.[350]

*Dated 1664, when the property was owned by John Moir (later of Stoneywood), Nether Ardgrain near Ellon is probably the oldest extant house of its type in the country. Presumably similar houses at Blelack, Monaltrie, Campfield, Inverenzie, Inverey, Auchinhove and Auchendryne are all known to have been destroyed during the Jacobite wars. The Hall of Tolophin and Old Hall of Lochan have been reduced to footings by causes unknown, and Avochie is little better; while Frendraught, Leith Hall and Mains of Brux been modified almost beyond recognition. The 1693 House of Byth was replaced by a 'more fashionable version' in 1932.[351] Photograph courtesy of Rae Younger.*

*Balnacraig House, Deeside, as it looked in 1921. The central block dates to 1673, and the wings were added in the 1720s or '30s. It is similar enough to Ellon's Nether Ardgrain – even in the way it was expanded – that a shared model and/or a shared team of craftsmen should not be ruled out. MacGibbon and Ross dismissed Balnacraig as 'almost destitute of ornament',[352] but after two centuries of pseudo-baronial claptrap elsewhere, simplicity is its great strength.*

*Old Rubislaw House, built in 1675 and demolished in 1886. It was of a similar design to Old Stoneywood, built in or before 1674. Rubislaw was built by the Forbeses, but quickly acquired by the Skene family of Wester Fintray and Zamoski, Poland, who held it for eight generations beginning in 1687. The estate in Ellon formerly known as Hilton or Rosehill was renamed Turnerhall after 1683 by another rich Poland merchant, John Turner. The house Turner created was rebuilt in 1861 and demolished in 1933.*

The idea that a radically advanced style actually emerged naturally in Aberdeen-shire's Nether Ardgrain (1664); Balnacraig (1673); Stoneywood (c.1674, demolished); Old Rubislaw (1675, demolished); and Craigmyle (1676, demolished) did not fit his preconceptions.

Absurdly, if half-heartedly, Dunbar chalked up any examples of the style's emergence pre-1707 to the English influence of the occupying army of Oliver Cromwell, and/or to degenerate rural copying of the designs of Scottish architect Sir William Bruce. The first idea is absurd because none of the houses in question look English; and the second, because Bruce did no known architectural work before 1670, and merely dabbled until 1679. If anything, the fashionable but anonymous new-style lairds' houses of the 1660s and '70s inspired Sir William's designs (such as the masterful Auchindinny, Midlothian, c.1702), not the other way round. Yet, Dunbar chose to accept Nether Ardgrain's extension date of 1731 as the date of construction of the entire house, ignoring its 1664 date-stone and other features linking the house stylistically to Balnacraig (of which he seems to have been wholly unaware) and even to Larbert Old Manse (1635), which – though not built for a laird – is arguably the oldest surviving house of comparable style in the entire country.[353]

Dunbar was not alone in his views. Sheila Forman claimed that, by the time Sir William Bruce died in 1710, 'the purely Scottish idiom had been all but abandoned'.[354] Dunbar and Forman's contemporary George Scott-Moncreiff defended Scottish architecture of the pre-1710 period, but as 'the architecture of the Renaissance . . . rustically misconceived'.[355] Drumlanrig, designed by Tarbat-born James Smith and finished in 1690, could scarcely be described at all: Forman called it 'most nearly related' to Baronial; 'traditionally Scottish [but] . . . a new departure'; 'medieval', 'Baroque'; 'Renaissance'; and 'Scottish Gothic merged with the classical' – all in the space of two paragraphs.[356]

Now that the mock-baronial style of houses like Nethermuir has finally fallen from favour, one would expect to encounter defenders of Nether Ardgrain's unnamed and apparently un-nameable Scottish style. Yet, it is still commonplace to suppose that the very remarkable period 1660–1700 in Scottish architecture did not really happen. Its buildings have recently been called a hangover of the English Palladianism of a hundred years earlier; a precocious forerunner of Scottish Georgian; and even the beginning of a Romantic style which, in the event, failed to appear. Since the mid-1980s, also, there has been a strong tendency to regard the whole of 1660–1800 as a single period in Scottish architecture, albeit with no agreement on what that period should be called. James Macaulay adopts this periodisation, only to admit immediately that 'stylistic unity was fracturing' by 1745.[357] With a sudden urgency, I feel we must re-examine post-Civil War but pre-Adam style as a thing unto itself. Perhaps because Dunbar failed to consider Balnacraig, while David McGibbon and Thomas Ross failed to consider Nether Ardgrain, the possibility that these two Aberdeenshire houses might be related – stylistically or otherwise – has not to my knowledge been suggested before.

Interestingly, both these incredible survivors were built by townsmen, and I suspect that the new country house style was in some degree merely a transfer of an urban style to a rural setting. Obvious similarities can be seen between Ardgrain and Balnacraig, on the one hand, and two Fraserburgh houses: Gill's Lodging, now demolished, and the house called Warld's End. Historic Scotland calls the former 'c.1700' and the latter 'early eighteenth century (or earlier?)',[358] but on the whole I would propose a date of c.1670 for Gill's and only somewhat later for Warld's End. Mounie 'Castle', built in rural Daviot in 1641 by Robert Farquhar, Provost of Aberdeen, may well be the missing link between the true castle and the true country house.

*Gill's Lodging, Fraserburgh, as depicted by David MacGibbon and Thomas Ross before its demolition.*

*Mounie Castle, Daviot (1641). (Photo by David Walker)*

Even the great 'baronialists' MacGibbon and Ross did not suppose that Balnacraig's supposed lack of Scottish features made it seem English (or Dutch or French or Swedish either). If anything, Nether Ardgrain, Balnacraig, Birkhall, Craigmyle, Memsie and 25 North High Street in Portsoy now seem *more* distinctively Scottish than the pseudo-baronial horrors that circle the Earth from Alberta to the Antipodes, damned by their very ubiquity, leftovers of an exhausted empire. Our ignorance of the older style is all the more tragic, since Restoration-era Scottish buildings – and even revivals like Sir Robert Lorimer's marvellous Rhu-Na-Haven (completed 1911) – are better suited to modern tastes and ways of life than the medieval, Georgian, and other buildings by which they are surrounded.

## NEOCLASSICAL COUNTRY HOUSES

Outside of Ireland, where in any case many of them have been restored, it is unusual to see grand houses of the eighteenth and nineteenth centuries standing windowless and open to the sky. But here, one may do so in several places, including Tillery House (1788, burned 1950s); Aden (completed by 1832, intentionally unroofed); Fetternear (mostly 1693–1850, burned 1919); House of Leask (1827, burned 1927); and Old Ellon Castle (thoroughly modernised between 1706 and 1785, only to be abandoned in 1801). Glassaugh House, an exquisite Georgian mansion begun in the 1770s, was latterly used to house cows on the ground floor, pigs on the first floor, and chickens above the pigs. Houses of similar magnificence that have been completely lost include Pitfour, the 'Blenheim of Buchan' (*c.*1700, extended 1809) and New Ellon Castle (1851); both were demolished in 1927. Strichen House (1818–1821) became a hydropathic hotel from 1926 to 1929. Its golf course closed with the hotel, and during the Second World War it was a barracks for British, Polish and Norwegian servicemen. In 1954 it was 'gutted'.[359] Mountblairy House (1791) was extended in 1825 and gone before 1960.

The mansions of Buchan were 'all made to last', Robert Smith concluded, but '[n]ot many did'.[360] Such losses are all the more tragic as they may mask earlier losses, as at Boyndlie House, a 'typical Georgian mansion' dated 1814, which was built directly over a 1660 house, which in turn may have erased another house extant in 1547.[361] Strichen House also obliterated a seventeenth-century 'palace'.[362] As soon as defensibility was removed from the equation, houses were judged as fashionable or unfashionable, on which standard, constant change was required. Almost invariably full of praise for the landlords anyway, it is interesting how often the ministers of the early-Victorian period

*Aden House today. A photo album of the Russell of Aden family, which included a picture of Sidney Russell's 1922 wedding – with future Home Secretary Willie Whitelaw as a three-year-old page boy – was lost for many years until found on a village green in Hampshire in 1988. A policeman there figured out where it belonged and it was returned for the cost of postage. (Photo by David Walker)*

noted with approval that their patrons had built, or rebuilt their houses in the latest style. Such rebuilding was not always enough to save them, of course, and Rothie House – an eighteenth-century mansion 'baronialised' *à la mode* in 1862, had been abandoned less than a hundred years later. With so many older and stylistically purer structures also at risk, a recent plea that Rothie's 'ruined shell' be the subject of 'works to consolidate and protect it from structural collapse' are likely to fall on deaf ears.[363]

John Adam's Old Troup House of *c*.1760, essentially a larger version of the current Banff Castle, was superseded by a 'baronial' design in 1897. Among other lost buildings in this category, it is worth mentioning the various designs by the famous Adam family that were produced, but never executed. These included William Adam's original wings of Duff House; Robert or James Adam's house for Lady Innes, probably intended for Banff; and Robert Adam's 'grandiloquent castellated palace' that 'never materialised' on the former site of Findlater Castle.[364] William Adam's interiors for Carnousie Castle apparently *were* produced, but later removed; and his wings for Craigston Castle were also executed, 'but not as picturesquely as drawings show'.[365]

## LOST PROPERTY EMPIRE: THE GORDONS OF LESMOIR

In the late Middle Ages the area called the Cabrach (also spelled Cabroch, Cabrauche, Cabragh and Cabraugh) was considerably larger than the current civil parish. For instance, until 1472 it included the estate and now parish of Glenbuchat. Since time out of mind, the king's highway now called the A941 has traversed the greater Cabrach, connecting the pre-feudal religious community at Mortlach with the village of Rhynie. The main castle guarding this important route, which ultimately linked the ancient provinces of Moray and Mar, was Lesmoir in Essie, a lost parish which straddled Cabrach's present border with the parish of Rhynie. Mains of Lesmoir, Lesmoir Castle and Essie Kirk, founded together as a Norman manor, were clustered together about two miles east of the current Cabrach/Rhynie parish boundary, and formed a place of considerable strength, moated and also taking full advantage of natural water obstacles.

The semi-legendary early fifteenth-century builder of Lesmoir was Jock Gordon of Scurdarg:

> Jock of Scurdarg had houses grand
> In Bogie, Mar, and Buchanland,
> Straloch, Pitlurg, and Auchindoir,
> Cairnbarrow, Buckie, and Lesmoir.

Lesmoir became a distinct lairdship in or before 1537, when James Gordon was identified as its first laird.[366] He was still there in 1544, by which time a castle or ha'-hoose had been completed on the site. He could not write, but this was not particularly unusual even in high society at the time. The house was then rebuilt in a 'sumptuous' fashion by Alexander Gordon, third laird of Lesmoir, between 1591 and 1600. The Lesmoir family's social rank is further indicated by the fact that Alexander's daughter Katherine married (in or by 1594) the same Alexander Burnett of Leys who completed Crathes Castle in 1596.

The fourth Gordon laird of Lesmoir, also James Gordon, was created one of the country's first baronets by Charles I, in 1625, and given lands then known as 'New Lesmoir' in Nova Scotia.

> Although they were, inevitably, more or less mixed up in the civil and religious commotions of the sixteenth and seventeenth centuries, the Lesmoir Gordons never played a prominent part in the national, nor even to any great extent in the local, affairs of their day. On the

contrary, they seem to have set their affections upon the acquisition of land; with so successful a result that . . . at the time of their greatest prosperity they had a fortune of 30,000 marks a year.[367]

This prosperity ended partly because the Gordons of Lesmoir remained steadfast royalists. Douglas Simpson further asserts that they were Catholics, but I see no particular reason to believe or disbelieve this. Curious as some of their religious beliefs may have been, various members of the family married Protestants in the 1590s, were buried in the parish church of Essie in the 1630s, and accepted the Protestant church's jurisdiction in the 1650s:

> [I]n the Presbytery Records of Strathbogie, under date 13th August 1651 . . . it appears that at Milton [of Lesmoir] the old Scottish superstition was followed of reserving a part of the farmland unploughed for the use of the 'Goodman,' that is, the Devil: it being hoped thus to placate his Satanic Majesty and avert his unwelcome attentions from the rest of the farm. Taken to task on the subject by the Presbytery, Sir William Gordon of Lesmoir admitted that part of the Mains [of Lesmoir] was [also] thus 'given away (as is commonly said) to the Goodman,' and had not been ploughed, but stated that 'he had a mynd, be the assistance of God, to cause labour the samen.'[368]

None of this stopped Rev. Thomas Gordon, great-grandson of the third baronet of Lesmoir, from being ordained minister of Cabrach on 25 June 1740.[369]

In the Civil War, Lesmoir Castle was held for the king by John Leith of Harthill who (or whose ancestor of the same name) had rented Denscheill farm in the Cabrach about 1600.[370] The castle was sufficiently strong and remote that Lady Grant of Grant sought refuge there shortly after Christmas, 1644, when the Covenanters stole all her jewellery and drove her from Place of Elchies.[371] Then, on 27 March 1647, Lesmoir was captured by the Covenanting general David Leslie. The assault and its aftermath are surprisingly well documented, including Leslie's admission that he decided who among the royalist soldiers was 'Irish' – i.e. a Highlander – and summarily hanged all twenty-seven that he thus identified.[372] The village located immediately around the castle was also burned to the ground, though whether intentionally or as 'collateral damage' from combat is not clear. From Gen. Leslie's correspondence with his superiors in the Covenanting state, he was clearly concerned, not that he had committed any error by this mass execution, but rather that he had exceeded his authority by sparing the lives of three Lowland soldiers and the two officers! He also asked if he could destroy Lesmoir entirely, but the Committee of Estates apparently did not let him, as the castle was still inhabitable a century later.

In 1725, Lesmoir was described as 'a pretty house with seven clusters of chimneys'.[373] But even before the last hurrah of Jacobitism, the Gordons of Lesmoir were forced to sell off their lands – and finally, Lesmoir Castle itself, in 1743. At first, the new owners were the Gordons of Wardhouse, who allowed Sir William Gordon, sixth baronet, to continue living in the house until he died. The Wardhouse family sold the estate to Alexander Garioch of Kinstair, who in 1759 advertised it for sale, calling it 'very improvable', 'well-grassed' and with 'inexhaustible moss'.[374]

The new owner of Lesmoir was John Grant of Rothmaise, who began demolishing the house for building stone. He in turn went bust in 1779. Pieces of the castle found in the surrounding area suggest it was structurally similar to the castles of Towie-Barclay and Delgaty, both near Turriff. One or more fireplaces from Lesmoir were later seen at Blackmiddens farmstead and Terpersie Castle.

## FORTS, BATTERIES AND AIRFIELDS

Military remains in Banff and Buchan also seem to have been accorded no value once their practical utility had ebbed – though in modern times, low land prices and lack of money for demolition work have sometimes ensured their survival, where prosperity would have seen them erased. A fort built in the southern reaches of Kirkmichael, Banffshire in 1715 was abandoned and in ruins before the end of the eighteenth century. In the same period, Boddam Castle's artillery battery was reduced to a single cannon by persons unknown; the fate of the last cannon is in turn unknown, and the entire Boddam site has never been the subject of an archaeological investigation. (Even John Pratt, an early adopter of preservationist values, called it of 'no particular interest, either as a place of strength or as a specimen of architecture'.[375]) The shore batteries of Peterhead had a more tangled history:

> In 1588, an Armada warship, the *St Michael* [sic for *Santa Caterina*?[376]], was wrecked on the coast. Its armament of seven brass cannon were removed to a small fort erected on Keith Inch where the old or meikle battery was later built . . . [W]itnesses in 1741 claimed that at the time of the Dutch wars in 1666, a Danish ship ran aground, and six iron cannon and two brass cannon were seized. These were delivered to

the inhabitants of the town and subsequently mounted on a battery erected on the bay at Keith Inch. This battery protected the south harbour of Peterhead until 1715, when the brass cannon were mounted on the Tolbooth Green by town inhabitants with Jacobite sympathies. As a result, the batteries were dismantled in 1717, and the Spanish cannon sent to London. Moir's plan of 1739 indicated two sites where a battery was drawn up, as he puts it, in 'the late war with France' (probably the War of the Spanish Succession 1702–13) but no structural remains are indicated . . . In 1780, in response to the threat of privateer raids during the American War of Independence, cannon were returned and the Meikle battery was erected in the form of a half moon surrounded by a palisade, with a guard house, about 1780, on the site of the earlier battery. It is shown on Ainslie's plan of 1805. After the peace with France . . . the battery was partially dismantled [in 1817], but the guard house was untouched. All traces were finally removed between 1876 and 1880.[377]

In Banff from 1781 to 1815, there was another 'half-moon' battery, built at least partly of turf, with eight guns, storehouse, powder magazine, guard room and officer's apartment. Intended to discourage lone privateers – such as the *Tartar* of Boston, Massachusetts, which had taken the *Janet* of Irvine in Banff Bay, and the *Anne* of Banff, both in 1777 – the effectiveness of such 'thinly scattered' fortifications in the event of a full-scale invasion was 'a point somewhat problematical'.[378]

The French privateers who raided this coast in the eighteenth century sailed from the Norwegian ports of Bergen, Stavanger and Egersund. The pattern would be repeated in the Second World War, with most of the German ships, aircraft and submarines that posed a direct threat to this area being based in Norway. It was also specifically to counter a German invasion via Norway that Buchan's beach defences were built.

Apparent siege-works near the Bullers of Buchan were 'much defaced' between the late 1830s and the late 1850s.[379] In Fyvie, rival entrenchments of 1644 were 'still distinctly to be seen', and still went by the names of Montrose Camp and the Camp-fold, in 1838. By 1973, the former had 'suffered from afforestation' and was 'in poor condition'.[380] The latter 'was levelled and trenched over' entirely by 1871.[381]

The First World War saw Peterhead used as a coaling station for minesweepers, and a Royal Navy seaplane slipway could still be viewed from Peterhead prison in 1999; but on the whole the Great War left few material traces here. Recently revealed following the felling of a Forestry Commission conifer plantation, there are only scant remaining ruins of RNAS Longside (Lenabo), which 'was seemingly built to last for eternity' with brick houses, a cinema, and 'a main entrance adorned with pseudo classical pillars', all long gone.[382] The naval seaplane base at the south-eastern end of the Loch of Strathbeg was 'used as a cattle shed for many years' and had been demolished by 1999.[383] In the Second World War, however, extensive beach defences were built, including an anti-tank stop line between the Loch of Strathbeg and the sea, which was rated 'well preserved' by the Royal Commission on the Ancient and Historical Monuments of Scotland (RCAHMS) in 2005. In all, at least fifty-five wartime pillboxes have been recorded within the former Banff and Buchan district council area (which is of course considerably smaller than the area covered by this book). Ostensibly to counter an invasion from Norway, these measures were probably more to reinforce morale: Buchan was 'so extensive and so open and had so many roads' that the army did not actually plan to defend it, but only contain the invaders to the north of Stonehaven.[384] Churchill's famous phrase might as well be modified to 'We shall fight them on the beaches (except in Banff and Buchan)'. The morale-boosting effort, such as it was, tragically backfired in Fraserburgh when a young girl was killed by a 'friendly' beach mine.

With Englishmen George Dean and Bert Nutter(!), two Buchan emigrants to the US named John Scott and George Morrice returned home to build an aeroplane at Invernorth, Rathen in 1911. They hoped to win a £1,000 prize, offered by the *Daily Mail*, for the first Scottish-made aircraft to fly between Glasgow and Edinburgh. The plane was about half done when Mr Dean fled, on hearing that his jilted wife was hot on his tail. With no other entries, the prize was cancelled.

It is very often, in writing about what has been 'lost' in Aberdeenshire that the 'loss' is down to lack of diffusion of knowledge. We remember Sir Jack Alcock and Sir Teddie Brown, the first men to fly across the Atlantic; Amelia Earhart, the first woman to fly solo across the Atlantic; and so forth. We are not so good at remembering Tryggve Gran, the first man to fly across the North Sea, starting from Cruden Bay. An incredible feat, his flight was *twenty-five times longer* than the Channel flight made – barely – by Louis Bleriot in the same type of plane.

As a Norwegian, Gran was barred from joining the Royal Flying Corps but did so anyway, taking on the identity of a fictional Canadian officer, 'Teddy Grant'. Memorials to Earhart worldwide, plus a minor planet named after her in 1995, are too numerous to list; but all Gran seems to have got is a lone plaque in Cruden which looks like a reused part of an old printing press.

*Airships C7, C10 and NS11 were part of a Longside-based fleet during the First World War that numbered up to twelve such craft at a time. All were cold, loud and generally uncomfortable. Their kill rate of enemy submarines was also miserably low, though by their very existence they may have acted as a deterrent.*

'Mutt' (John Moe) and 'Jeff' (Tor Glad) were Norwegian spies and saboteurs, though Moe's mother was from Lancashire. Initially recruited by the Nazis, they turned themselves in and began working for MI5 soon after landing at Crovie in April 1941. Their deception work 'did indeed influence the Germans in some way because the bombing in the Buchan area stopped for a whole year' after they arrived, George Dey remembers.[385]

The air-raid warning system at Fraserburgh was very slack, often giving the alarm only after an attack had finished, or no alarm at all. The inefficiency of the sirens was matched only by the unreliability of the German ordnance, which regularly failed to detonate. During one raid, in September 1941, eight bombs were dropped of which not one exploded. Even small-bore cannon rounds were sometimes found unexploded in the streets of the town. In the worst single incident to affect Fraserburgh during the war, on Bonfire Night 1940, a rare *timely* air-raid warning was ignored by the people in the Commercial Bar, Kirk Brae, where a darts tournament was underway. A direct hit on the pub killed thirty-four and wounded fifty-two.

In stark contrast to the Blitz image of large fleets of high-level bombers, German aircraft attacked Buchan in ones and twos, flying at what would be called 'treetop level' elsewhere, but here known as 'mast height'. Though officially they were targeting the Rolls-Royce Merlin engine plant and another factory (Maconochies) that made food rations for the army, it became horribly personal. In addition to dropping incendiary devices and high-explosive bombs weighing up to 1,000 pounds, the Germans regularly shot at the inhabitants with their machineguns. Even an unexploded bomb could do severe damage, as when one landed in the kitchen area at Maconochies in April 1941. Fearing, under-standably, that it might go off at any second, many of the workers were injured (particularly by window glass) in the general rush to escape. Twenty-one

*Peterhead's predominantly female firefighters, 1943.*

required surgery. Similar so-called 'nuisance' attacks on Peterhead destroyed fifty-eight houses and killed thirty-eight people. In the First World War, the only notable local building to be bombed by a Zeppelin was Craig Castle, near Rhynie.

Duff House, mistaken for an army headquarters rather than the prisoner-of-war camp that it was, was bombed by a lone Heinkel in July 1940. Six German prisoners and two British soldier/cooks were killed in the attack, which also cost the house its east wing, housing the kitchen and heating plant. Some of the same Germans who had been bombed by their own side were subsequently torpedoed by their own side while en route to a new camp in Canada. The Heinkel was shot down on its way home by Spitfires from Dyce. Thirteen months later, the Banff Distillery warehouse was bombed and strafed; 'To prevent further fire and explosions . . . whisky was tipped into the Boyndie Burn causing some disorientation among the cattle and poultry'.[386]

These threats from the air were countered by RAF Peterhead (four miles west of the town), home to British- and Polish-crewed squadrons of Spitfire, Seafire and Mustang fighters and – when Lossiemouth was closed by snow – Stirling heavy bombers, including the famous *MacRobert's Reply*. RAF Fraser-burgh, immediately to the south of Cairnbulg, concentrated on photo-reconais-sance pilot training and air-sea rescue. The Royal Navy also built a new, exceptionally well-equipped 900-acre air base on the south shore of the Loch of Strathbeg, centred about one mile west of the old one, flying mostly small single-engined Barracuda torpedo bombers. There was so little darkness in the summer months that to practise night flying, pilots blacked out their goggles.

With a few exceptions, including three rather odd masonry pillboxes, the wartime buildings of RAF Peterhead had mostly fallen into ruin by 1975, when the site returned to use as a civilian helicopter airfield, known confusingly as Longside. By the late 1980s, the only above-ground remains at RAF Fraserburgh were of the parachute store, 'and the runways are now blocked by poultry houses'. Some say that when the naval station at Crimond closed, the aircraft themselves were 'broken up and bull dozed into the ground'.[387] RAF Buchan, a radar station near Peterhead established after the war, ceased manned operations in 2004. Five years later its officers' mess reopened as a four-star hotel.

The RAF Coastal Command base at Boyndie (known as RAF Banff) and its satellite station at Dallachy conducted a war-within-the-war, as thrilling in its own way as the siege of Malta. Eight squadrons known as the Banff Strike Wing were led by Max Aitken, an ace with sixteen kills and Montreal-born son of cabinet minister Lord Beaverbrook. Ironically, in light of Beaverbrook's famous campaigns for the collection of scrap metal, the Banff Wing's super-fast Mosquito fighter-bombers were made almost entirely of wood. Mosquito armament at its height included rockets, machineguns and a six-pounder anti-tank gun, giving each squadron the 'strike potential equivalent of a destroyer.'[388] As well as Canada, the aircrews and ground crews came from throughout the Commonwealth, Britain and Norway. Their story is, not least, a lost opportunity for a great film. The Boyndie site is now a co-operative wind farm and go-karting track; Dallachy's lies in picturesque ruins.

Small cast sizes in low-budget war films and television programmes have significantly obscured how many people actually were needed to run an air base. RAF Peterhead alone was home to 1,576 men and 389 women, and HMS *Merganser* (the name eventually assigned to the naval air base at Crimond) could house 2,287 male and 637 female personnel. All told, the air-war-related population increase in Banff and Buchan must have been the equivalent of a second Fraserburgh. When the war ended and the bases closed, the sudden loss of their spending power would have been a bitter pill indeed.

## INDUSTRIAL ARCHITECTURE

As previously mentioned, the late-eighteenth-century linen boom left only a handful of architectural traces. We are luckier to have at least seven late-eighteenth-century windmills, albeit all lacking their sails. The best preserved one, mechanically speaking, is probably the Savoch mill in Lonmay. It was used in 1791 in a certain Mr Sellar's thoroughly unsuccessful attempt to drain the Loch of Strathbeg (the second in half a century). The Inverugie Distillery, west of Peterhead prison, used a similar but taller windmill, also for pumping water, for about a century ending in the 1880s. Peterhead in the 1830s also had a wind-powered sawmill about which little is known. Sandend windmill, probably the most ruinous of the survivors, was built in 1760 on the site of – and possibly out of – an ancient burial cairn. The original purpose of the prominent windmill off Albert Street in Fraserburgh (aptly named Windmill Street until 1900) is not so clear; after it ceased operating as such, it was used by the herring-curers who came to dominate the town's nineteenth-century economy.

As in many other parts of the world, windmills were also used for grinding grain. One such, in Peterhead's own Windmill Street, was demolished in the middle 1930s. Its products in 1795 had included malt and pearl barley. An extant stone-built example on the Turnerhall estate in Ellon, tentatively dated to 1787, had its sails

blown off on 28 December 1879 in the same storm which did for the Tay Bridge; this led to the capping of the windmill and the installation of a three-horse gin in front of the tower to power the adjacent

*A horse-drawn sledge was used to haul paraffin barrels to and from these characterful but now demolished timber warehouses at Sunnybrae, Glenbuchat.*

threshing barn . . . This itself was replaced by a stationary engine in the base of the tower which caused a fire which destroyed the original timber-work and fittings of the windmill.[389]

Less attractive examples also exist at Montbletton, south of Macduff, and Northfield, Crovie.

Horse-powered grain mills, virtually unknown in southern Aberdeenshire, were commonplace here in the early nineteenth century. Pitsligo in 1840 had seven, alongside six that were water-powered and one that was wind-powered. At the same date, there were seven in Alvah, at least one in Strathdon, and a great many in Methlick and Oyne, as well as a six-horse-powered bonemeal mill in Newburgh. However, animal-powered stationary equipment – like ploughing with horses rather than oxen – was quintessentially of the Improvement period. In eighteenth-century St Fergus, the only farmer to have any animal-powered machinery was James Clarke in Netherhill, a leading Improver who introduced the use of shells as fertiliser; but even Clarke's equipment was ox-powered, not horse-powered. Locally, only Turriff and Auchterless appear to have had horse-powered grain mills before 1800, and complete examples do not exist, though well-preserved remains were seen at Lower Hillside, Cairnie, in 1990. More

*Turnerhall's Georgian windmill base is probably the most attractive, architecturally speaking, of half a dozen such survivors in the region, including the stumpier version at Northfield Farm, Crovie. (Photo by David Walker)*

fragmentary ruins of these 'horse engine houses' exist at Backhill of Easterton (Fyvie), Protston (Gamrie), as well as at Badnabein, Ordachoy, West Tornahaish, West Dunandhu and Ordachoinachan, all in Strathdon, where horse-power enjoyed either an exceptionally long life, or a post steam-engine renaissance. Of course, anyone who had to power his mill by non-magical means would have envied the initiates of the Miller's Word, by saying which 'a mill could be set to work and corn ground without human assistance.'[390]

The high sea cliffs of eighteenth-century Aberdour were home to two nationally important millstone quarries, to which the workmen descended via stairs cut into the rock face, or where this proved impossible, by ladders. The finished millstones were then dropped onto the beach below – presumably at high tide – and carried to market by boat. Both sites were owned by the earl of Aberdeen. By 1840, the Coburty operation had closed, and the one at Pennan employed only four or five men where twelve had worked before.

More than one ruined castle became the home of an early business enterprise. A Mr Sellar – the same man who tried and failed to drain Strathbeg? – operated a beer and porter brewery within the ruins of fourteenth-century Inverugie Castle in the 1790s. James Ferguson added floors and a roof to the same ruins so that he could use it as an observatory, but his successor

*The Invernettie Brickworks opened a mile south of Peterhead in 1797 and supplied 'tiles and bricks of excellent quality, from a bed of clay worked to a great depth' of up to forty feet.[391] The bricks were exported, chiefly to places farther north within Scotland, from Invernettie's own harbour. By 1979, the site had been cleared. Two similar sites were functioning near Banff in 1798, and bricks were also made at Claypots and other places around the Loch of Fingask.*

RIGHT. *Inverugie Castle about 1920; it has since been reduced to about half this height – less in some places – and is totally inaccessible to the public. Its ornamented gateway, dated 1670, was recorded in 1887 but gone by 1968 along with much else. A different castle, also called Inverugie and considerably older, was located 'immediately to seaward of Peterhead Golf pavilion' and visible as ruins until 1895.*[392]

BELOW. *Inverugie Castle today. (Photo by Barry Robertson)*

'dismantled it of these modernizings, and allowed ruin to reassume her empire'.[393] And reassume it she did with a vengeance: the height of Inverugie's walls has been reduced by perhaps half, just since the First World War. Rattray Castle, badly damaged in 1308 and later buried in drifting sand along with its moat, seems to have housed 'industrial kilns' at an unknown date, probably before the removal of foundation stones in the 1730s.[394]

## THE RAILWAYS

Not everyone welcomed the railway to this part of Scotland. It was feared that grouse would be frightened off, timber-floaters and fishermen would lose their livelihoods, and people of different classes would be brought together in 'objectionable variety'.[395] Such protests were all eventually overcome. However many jobs the railway may have cost us in the long run, the building of the Keith-to-Dufftown line alone employed 700 men working twelve hours a day; and it has been suggested that the canning industries of Peterhead and Fraserburgh would not have been founded if the railways had not come. The new-found ease of tourist access in the later Victorian period also led, among other things, to 'an unprecedented boom in hotel construction'.[396]

As on Deeside, some towns 'boomed' because they were near railway stations, while others, bypassed by the system, were all but forgotten. Some winners of this particular game were Dyce, Inverurie and Maud, to say nothing of the city of Aberdeen itself. The losers included Old Meldrum – a railway dead-end in comparison to its rival, Inverurie – and Rosehearty, New Aberdour, Mossat, Lumsden and Methlick, which were never connected to the network at all. There were plans to join Newburgh to the railway system in 1845, 1856 and 1898, but these never got off the ground; into the twentieth century, people took the 'horse bus' or bicycled or even walked.[397] Iron-rich Tomintoul likewise was expected to become 'A Scotch Merthyr Tydfil' as soon as the railway arrived, but arrive it did not.[398]

The present-day existence of a railway line from Aberdeen to Keith via Dyce, Inverurie, Insch and Huntly, and a tourist line from Keith to Dufftown, obscures the fact that more than seventy other stations in this region were built between 1856 and 1903, and closed between 1915 and 1979. In terms of sheer numbers this sounds rather intense. Far from being a London Underground of the north, however, the network – like most previous systems of transport and communication in the area – concentrated on a handful of nearly parallel north-to-south routes. Modern observers remark simply that it 'remained incomplete' and that we had too many prosperous small villages for one transport network to serve all of them adequately.[399] But weird local rivalries and meanness amounting almost to insanity played their usual part. A person wanting to go from Brucklay to Turriff – ten miles west as the crow flies – would have had to go twenty miles south, then twenty miles north again, using several different trains. An east-west connection from Turriff to Maud was once proposed, but this led to nothing. It is indeed 'curious' that after an unsuccessful experiment which ended in 1872, the Banff line was never again extended to Macduff, a brisk twenty-minute walk to the east.[400] Using the most efficient connections in 1910, a rail journey between these two neighbouring ports was seventy-five miles long and lasted three hours and fifteen minutes. Fraserburgh to Portsoy, thirty-one miles west by road and slightly less by sea, would probably have taken all day.

| Line (opened) | Closed to passengers/freight |
| --- | --- |
| Inverurie–Lethenty–Old Meldrum (1856) | 1931/1966 |
| Inveramsay–Wartle–Rothienorman–Fyvie–Auchterless– Turriff (1857) | 1951/1966 |
| Grange–Knock–Glenbarry–Cornhill–Tillynaught– Portsoy (1859)[401] | 1968/1968 |
| Tillynaught–Ladysbridge–Banff (1859) | 1964/1968 |
| Turriff–Plaidy–King Edward–Banff Bridge–Macduff (1860)[402] | 1951/1961 |
| Dyce-Newmachar–Udny–Logierieve–Esslemont–Ellon–Arnage– Auchnagatt–Maud (1861) | 1965/1979 |
| Maud–Mintlaw (1861) | 1965/1970 |
| Mintlaw–Longside–Newseat–Inverugie–Peterhead (1862) | 1965/1970 |
| Dufftown–Craigellachie (1863) | 1968/1971 |
| Craigellachie–Aberlour (1863) | 1965/1971 |
| Maud–Brucklay–Strichen–Mormond–Lonmay–Rathen–Philorth– Fraserburgh (1865) | 1965/1979 |
| Portsoy–Glassaugh–Tochineal (1884) | 1968/1968 |
| Keith–Aultmore–Enzie–Rathven–Buckie–Portessie (1884) | 1915/1915 |
| Garmouth–Portgordon–Buckpool–Portessie–Findochty– Portknockie–Cullen–Tochineal (1886) | 1968/1968 |
| Grange South–Grange North (1886) | 1960/1960 |
| Ellon–Auchmacoy–Pitlurg–Hatton–Cruden Bay–Longhaven– Boddam (1896) | 1932/1948 |
| Fraserburgh–Philorth–Cairnbulg–St Combs (1903) | 1965/1965 |

Former stations not mentioned in the table included Pitcaple, Oyne, Kennethmont, Gartly, Rothiemay, Buchanstone, Kinaldie, Wardhouse, Millagen and Ordens.

Peterhead also boasted nineteenth-century Britain's only government-owned line, sometimes called the 'British State Railway'. As of 1900 it was two and a half miles long and used four olive-green locomotives: the *Victoria* (1892), *Prince of Wales* (1892), *Alexandra* (1892), and *Duke of York* (1896). Its purpose was to bring prisoners from HMP Peterhead, who were working on the National Harbour of Refuge, between and among the harbour, the prison, and Stirlinghill Quarry. The prison had in turn been built to ensure a ready supply of convict labour for the harbour project which provided an exceptionally strong haven in which British vessels could find shelter during severe storms. Unsurprisingly, windows were not provided, but members of the public were sometimes allowed to ride in an open wagon pushed in front of the engine.

A second, somewhat more comfortable state-owned railway connected the public station at Longside to an Admiralty-owned station serving the Lenabo anti-submarine airship base. Built in 1916 at the height of the First World War, the Lenabo line was abandoned in 1920 and dismantled in 1923. In the next war, a Warwick air-sea rescue aircraft based at Cairnbulg crashed into Dyce station, destroying a train there and killing two.

Though some convicts no doubt used them too, much of the traffic on the commercial lines consisted of fish. Paradoxically, this could be carried to market

Alexandra, *one of the locomotives built by the Hunslet Engine Company of Leeds and used on Peterhead's convict railway in 1900.*

*The original Banff and Macduff Station, intended to serve both towns, was inconvenient for both and closed in 1872. After it was replaced by Macduff Station (pictured) and Banff Bridge Station, the only rail route between the two towns was seventy-five miles long. No one episode better illustrates that the rail network was not designed for the convenience of passengers, but rather to funnel fish and agricultural products south into Aberdeen as quickly as possible. Freight services in Buchan and Banffshire outlived passenger services by an average of seven and a half years per line.*

in London more quickly from Aberdeen than from Grimsby and Hull, since the English ports were a full day further, by sea, from the fishing grounds which their boats shared with the Scots. As a sop to the fishing industry, 'the first train on each branch usually ran to rather than from Aberdeen'.[403] Fishwives travelling inland on business were also given third-class returns for the price of a single. Prior to the failure of the whale fishery, whale and seal oil produced in Peterhead was also sent by rail to Dundee, where it was used extensively by the jute industry. Rail freight traffic also increased at the expense of coastal shipping during the First World War, when the latter became excessively dangerous. (Even fishing boats were commonly sunk by enemy action until late in 1915.) In the immediate aftermath of the war, however, the railways went into steep and, in the event, terminal decline due to competition from both motor buses and 'a copious supply of army lorries which could be purchased cheaply and used in peacetime for new road haulage businesses'.[404]

The Great North of Scotland Railway (GNSR), an idiosyncratic but generally well-liked local monopoly operating north from Aberdeen and as far west as Ballater, Keith and Cullen until after the First World War, was nearly stillborn. David Chalmers, powerful and unscrupulous publisher of the *Aberdeen Journal*, talked it down in an effort to promote his own rival scheme, the Aberdeen, Banff and Elgin Railway (ABER). ABER was vanquished when it was revealed that Chalmers had used 'questionable methods to procure distinguished names for the company's prospectus'[405] – a shady tactic which continues in Aberdeen to this day, as singers Annie Lennox and Shane MacGowan, both victims of similar hoaxes, will attest.[406]

The Aberdeen–Huntly section alone, as envisaged in 1846, was the longest stretch of railway ever proposed in Scotland up to that time, and the undercapitalised, inexperienced company approached its construction with considerable doubt – even fear. In contrast to the Deeside railway, whose stock was comically oversubscribed, the Huntly line raised only £400,000 of its authorised £1.1 million. Construction, delayed by six years, began at Oyne and saved time by building the track directly over the Aberdeen–Port Elphinstone Canal. The canal, which had been completed less than fifty years earlier at a cost of nearly £40,000, was drained for the purpose – twice in fact, as at the first attempt, several vessels were left stranded in the mud.

The station at Gartly was in use as a Forestry Commission office by 1978, and Maud Junction, one of the better-preserved examples, houses a railway museum that is open by request. Numerous partial remains of overbridges and embankments can still be seen from the A947 between Aberdeen and Turriff, and in other places throughout the region.

# CHAPTER 4

# 'AN' JUST THE CONTERMASHOUS KIN' THAT LIKES A FECHT FOR FUN'

## PICTS, ROMANS AND 'DANES'

The Picts, who ruled eastern Scotland from Fife to Shetland between the third and ninth centuries AD 'have been the subject of myth and misconception' since at least Roman times. They have been accused of practising free love, of being no bigger than elves, of covering themselves in tattoos, of living underground 'through fear', and of coming to Scotland only because they were refused entry into Ireland.[407] Modern opinions have been less condemnatory but no less diverse, and there is 'apparently no limit to to the theories that may be devised by those who delight in making bricks without straw'.[408] It is now widely believed that the Picts were monogamous, of normal stature, not tattooed, surface-dwelling, and indigenous to Britain; but the more we learn about them the more they seem to qualify as Britain's, or even Europe's, 'most lost' people. No written documents definitely ascribable to the Picts have survived, and of their language, we know only that it was different enough from Gaelic that they needed interpreters. The idea, suggested in the 1830s, that it was a more ancient form of Gaelic was soon dismissed as 'wild'; the theory that it was similar to Welsh is more plausible but unproved, and 'we do not know their own name for themselves'. 'An extreme form of an extreme argument', meanwhile, 'declares that the Picts never existed' outside the Roman imagination.[409]

Known for their beautiful carvings of horses, hounds, hinds, wild boar, wolves, other animals and people, as well as abstract designs, the Picts pursued the usual range of rural occupations 'but above all they were warriors'.[410] The most powerful local tradition concerning the Picts in Banff and Buchan is that they repeatedly fought off huge armies of Danes. Amateur local etymologists of the Enlightenment period assigned a bogus 'Danish' origin to nearly every place ending -den, including Cruden. This seems to me about as logical as naming every bomb site in Fraserburgh 'Germany Street', but the tradition is too powerful to dismiss out of hand. Did Vikings, despite their well-known preferences for areas with sea-lochs and navigable rivers, actually attempt to wrest the North-east from Pictish control – and lose? Certainly, the Pictish fortress at Burghead was 'violently destroyed' before the year 1000, but 'whether this was Pict against Scot, or both against the Norsemen, neither archaeology nor history can tell'.[411] Alexander Simpson, minister in eighteenth-century Fraserburgh, was particularly muddled: '[R]uins of Danish, or Pictish houses, as they are called ... though insignificant in themselves, serve to demonstrate that the inhabitants of Buchan were, at one time, of Scandinavian origin.' Simpson ascribed the use of the word 'Pictish' to ignorant 'country people' who were sadly unaware of their own supposed Danishness.[412] The fantasy of Danish settlement in Cruden (or 'Crudane') was so strong that one observer claimed to have seen ruins of a Danish castle there in 1806.

The Picts were certainly tough customers, who once took on the defenders of Hadrian's Wall from the rear, in an early example of amphibious warfare; they also decisively defeated the Northumbrians in Angus in 685. The Vikings never settled in Banff and Buchan – despite what Rev. Simpson and others believed – and 'all, or nearly all, of the 130 or so "pagan" Scandinavian burials' in Scotland date from the century *after* the Pictish state definitively collapsed.[413] But the defeat, or non-appearance, of the Norsemen on our shores did not stop the Scots taking over Pictland in the ninth century. Dr Alex Woolf believes that 'ceaseless Scandinavian attacks on the heartland of the [Pictish] kingdom' did occur, and weakened it so much that its takeover by the Scots was inevitable, or at any rate fairly easy.[414] Whatever the case, the Picts and their foes retain an 'aura of mystery' that will probably never be dispelled.[415] Not for nothing are the Dark Ages called dark.

## THE GUN-MAKERS

In Turriff, Fraserburgh and elsewhere I have been frequently drawn into discussions on the merits of various rifles and rifle calibres with people in all walks of life. Cabrach schoolmaster Thomas Robertson escaped prosecution for the shooting to death of an Excise officer in the 1880s (he was aiming at the horse), and kept his post as schoolmaster until he died in 1909. In Auchindoir, wasps' nests were 'usually destroyed, by cutting the nest at night and letting it drop into hot water, or by blowing it to pieces by a large charge of gunpowder'.[416] In the Garioch as on Deeside, gunpowder was also commonly used for clearing field stones. One of the most popular organised games in Cullen was cannon-ball-throwing; after it was banned (a man had been killed), target-shooting matches took its place. In the seventeenth and eighteenth centuries, sometimes directed by retired sailors, groups of Peterhead civilians routinely fought off French privateer attacks using the town's cannon. A naval gun of slightly later date, used for generations as pub car park decor here, was recently examined on a lark by some officers of the Royal Artillery and found to be not only in full working order, but still loaded. It did not surprise me much, therefore, to learn that two of the most important firearms innovators, in the history of Britain or anywhere, came from this area.

Alexander John Forsyth, son of the minister of Belhelvie and future minister of Belhelvie himself, was born in 1768 and graduated from King's College Aberdeen in 1786. Like many forward-looking young men of his time he was interested as much in science as in theology, and in his case, mechanical engineering and chemistry – though he also put a toe in the water of the Buchan/Formartine controversy, claiming (perhaps uniquely) that Formartine was limited to 'lands on the sea coast'.[47] In whatever time was left to him, he particularly enjoyed shooting ducks and geese on the foreshore. The sporting guns of the time were mostly flintlocks, which gave off the proverbial 'flash in the pan', and the wilier birds were frequently scared away by the flash and puff of smoke before the bullet had even left the barrel. The good reverend bent his mind to this problem, first trying to hide the flash from the birds using a sort of hood over the mechanism.

By the time Forsyth was ordained, the French Revolution had begun, igniting a quarter century of war between Britain and France. The demand for gunpowder was immense. Hearing that the enemy were experimenting with various gunpowder substitutes, Forsyth began to do the same, nearly blowing himself up in the process – that is, until he discovered that one of the new compounds could be ignited not only by fire, but by rapidly applied pressure from a hammer. Forsyth completed his first 'percussion' fowling piece in 1805. It worked so well that the young minister was invited to London to show it to the Master-General of the Ordnance, a powerful figure in overall command of the nation's artillery and military engineers. By 1806 Forsyth was based at the Tower of London, making experiments full-time; the Ordnance Department paid off the presbytery to find another minister during his absence. The work remained hazardous, and at one point the workmen assigned to help Forsyth took fright at the dangers involved, but in the end he successfully produced a short musket as well as a small cannon that worked on the percussion principle.

But Forsyth was a better inventor than he was a businessman, and the

Master-General of the Ordnance duped him into accepting compensation that was a proportion of the government's savings in gunpowder over the following two years. In other words, the Master-General could get the invention for nothing simply by not deploying Forsyth's designs in the field until 1809 – a decision which was his alone to make. He also managed to convince Forsyth not to patent his designs, for patriotic reasons. Forsyth agreed, and the next month was told to take a hike.

Finally realising what was going on, Forsyth patented his invention in the spring of 1807, with help from James Watt. The Forsyth Patent Gun Company was formed to exploit the patent after it was granted the following year. Though he had long since returned to his parish work in Belhelvie, Forsyth was involved with the running of the company – via correspondence with a cousin – for more than ten years. 'An entire generation of gunmakers revelled in the glory of Forsyth's creation',[418] but the money they earned from it stayed overwhelmingly in their own pockets; and it took an astonishing thirty-five years for Forsyth to get a mere £200 out of the Ordnance Department, despite them using a version of his mechanism in muskets deployed in front-line service. A further £1,000 was later authorised, but it arrived in Belhelvie only after the inventor had died of old age.

Farther up the coast in 'proper' Buchan lies the Pitfour estate, now a shadow of its former glory, when lairds collected alligators, built temples, follies, canals and even a racecourse with a crenellated tower for the spectators. At its height their empire covered fifty square miles; in the early-Victorian period it was described as having 'a colony of tame swans' among other recent improvements costing nearly £80,000. It was the family seat of the dynamic Ferguson family, whose most dynamic member, Patrick Ferguson, has been characterised as 'one of Scotland's most courageous and dashing, yet least famous, military heroes'.[419] His central claim to fame is the invention of the world's first practical breech-loading military rifle. This is a remarkable enough thing by itself, but I was stunned to find that he accomplished it in 1775, in time in fact to carry the weapon into action himself, against the rebelled colonists in America. Cowboy author Louis L'Amour, in his 1973 novel *The Ferguson Rifle*, called Ferguson 'a much hated man . . . known for his harsh opinions of the colonists', but 'a fine gentleman' with 'a good face'. L'Amour called his invention 'the most efficient weapon of the [eighteenth] century' – and one which might have won the Revolutionary war for Britain 'in a matter of months' had it not been for the short-sightedness or treachery of English generals. L'Amour claimed further that the rifle could be shot eight times a minute.[420] Maj. Ferguson himself claimed only five shots per minute for the prototype and seven shots per minute

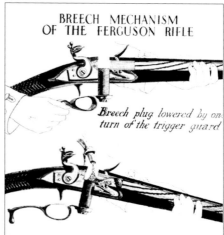

*Patrick Ferguson.*  *The Ferguson rifle.*

for the production model. But he could also hit a bullseye from a hundred yards while lying upside down, and sustain a rate of fire of four shots per minute even when walking quickly. Graeme Rimer, Head of Collections at the Royal Armouries in Leeds, has said that '[i]n the history of British military firearms very few are of such rarity or have stimulated such interest'.[421] The Royal Armouries themselves had no example until an auction sale in November 2000, when they acquired one that had lain unloved somewhere in Buchan until the 1960s.

Patrick Ferguson's father, the second laird of Pitfour of his surname, was dogged by Jacobite rumours. Though they lived mostly in Edinburgh, the family were full of the *joie de vivre* for which Buchan Episcopalians have always been famous. Patrick's younger sister Jeanie, at the age of sixteen, hunted, shot, spoke Latin, played chess and danced the hornpipe excellently. Patrick was commissioned in the Scots Greys at age fifteen, but (unusually in that age of amateurs) spent the next two years studying at Woolwich. During the Seven Years' War he developed synovial tuberculosis, and as a convalescent in Pitfour, he 'fell in love with Buchan and its people' – and thirteen of its young ladies in particular.[422] In 1766 he visited Dunkirk where, even at that date, the British expat community was 'largely Jacobite'.[423] Over a period of twenty-four hours, he waded thirty-six miles through deep snow to visit the Jacobite Lord Ogilvy, a cousin by marriage. He was with the Greys on anti-smuggling patrol in Sussex not long afterwards, and around this time he may have become acquainted with the real person upon whom Robert Louis Stevenson's character Allan Breck Stuart was based.

The rifle Ferguson invented after serving in the Caribbean was of smaller calibre, lighter, and shorter than either the standard-issue Brown Bess musket, or the later Baker rifle; and according to its inventor it also used a quarter as much powder as a Brown Bess. A hundred rifles were made in 1776 by four Birmingham firms (Barker & Whately; Galton; Grice; and Willets), and pirated versions were being sold to the East India Company by the following year. The original batch were first deployed with Ferguson's company at the Battle of Brandywine, where (in an incident that is still hotly debated) Ferguson chose not to snipe a senior rebel officer. Ferguson claimed there were two men, one in green and blue, and a supposedly French officer in hussar uniform. Most Americans who know the story believe that one of them was George Washington. Capt. John De Lancey, Ferguson's second in command, said many years later that the man Ferguson spared was not George Washington but Kasimierz Pulaski. Historian M.M. Gilchrist points out that all of this was hearsay and that either, neither, or both of the enemy generals might have been there at the key moment.[424] (Interestingly, De Lancey's son-in-law, through whom we know his version of the story, was James Fenimore Cooper, author of *The Last of the Mohicans*.) Others 'resort to conspiracy theories' to explain why the rifle corps was disbanded after Brandywine,[425] but the losses they suffered in the battle, including Ferguson's own permanent loss of the use of one arm, are probably sufficient to explain it.

Despite his unit's disbandment, Ferguson led daring and successful raids on rebel privateer bases in Chestnut Neck and Egg Harbour, New Jersey, and wrote more than one treatise on military ethics. The fight at MacPherson's Plantation that nearly cost Ferguson his *other* arm took place on the night of 14–15 March 1780. Ferguson's troops had found the Plantation abandoned by the enemy and were still searching it when another American loyalist unit, Charles Cochrane's British Legion, attacked. It was a classic 'friendly fire' incident, made more excusable perhaps by the fact that the rank and file on both sides all had American accents. Fortunately the two sides' respective commanders, both Scots, recognised each other by their voices in the darkness and called it off; nevertheless, one attacker and two defenders died. Ferguson's loyalists later assisted the Royal Navy in the capture of Fort Moultrie, taking 200 prisoners and 45 artillery pieces. By this time, few on the British side would have denied that Ferguson – aged just thirty-six – was 'intelligent, considerate, humane, and totally dedicated to the cause of his king and country . . . one of the best officers in the army'.[426] Certainly, he had acquired a fearsome reputation among the enemy. His opponents in the American South – mostly 'Scotch-Irish' squatters on Indian land – hoped not simply to defeat but to destroy him, in what they perceived 'as a Calvinist holy war'.[427] In this they were particularly inspired by the sermons of Rev. Samuel Doak, protégé of Scots theologians who had emigrated to Princeton, New Jersey to escape from the Scottish Enlightenment – and from intelligent, joyful people like the Fergusons of Pitfour.

Patrick Ferguson's final battle took place at King's Mountain, North Carolina on 5 October 1780. After he was killed, his horse was stolen by the enemy commander Benjamin Cleveland, a corpulent sadist who left loyalist wounded on the mountain to be eaten by turkey buzzards, wolves and hogs. Those prisoners well enough to walk were 'hacked with swords' en route to prison,[428] and many were hanged on trumped-up charges a week later. Ferguson's corpse was urinated upon, and his mistress, a red-haired beauty known to history only as Virginia Sal, was also shot and killed. But this was only the tip of an iceberg of atrocities against the king's loyal American subjects, ranging from outright murder and declaring them 'legally dead' (to aid with property confiscations), to tarring and feathering, imprisonment in salt mines, and being tied naked in windowless rooms several storeys above the ground.[429]

Not just Ferguson's, but all stories of Scottish and loyalist soldiers in the War of Independence, 'have become . . . invisible'.[430] Ferguson's battlefield grave gives his rank and his regiment incorrectly, and fails to mention that Virginia Sal is buried beside him in it. He has no memorial at all in Scotland – unlike the rebel navy commander John Paul Jones, who pillaged his native Kirkcudbright and tried to burn Whitehaven in Cumbria to the ground. The war criminal and horse-thief Benjamin Cleveland, meanwhile, has two American cities named after him.

Banffshire boasts its own firearms inventor in David Gregorie (1625–1720), laird of Kinnairdy from 1664 to 1690. Principally remembered as a clinically successful self-taught medical practitioner, who treated rich and poor alike at no charge, he was a first-generation member of the famous Gregorie dynasty of scientists and scholars. Of his twenty children who lived to adulthood, three became professors of mathematics. He was also the grandfather of Enlightenment philosopher Thomas Reid. In his seventies, Gregorie

> turned his attention to the subject of gunnery. With the help of an Aberdeen watchmaker he constructed a model of an improved cannon, and prepared to take it to Flanders. Meanwhile he forwarded his model to his son David who showed it to Isaac Newton . . . Newton advocated the suppression of the invention as being destructive of the human species. As the model was never found it must be assumed that Newton's advice was followed.[431]

*The great mansion house of Pitfour probably could have been used as a calendar, having 365 windows, fifty-two rooms, twelve columns and four staircases. It was demolished in 1927, and while the open basement was visible for most of the twentieth century, by the mid-1990s 'there was nothing to show that it had ever existed'.[432]*

## THE LOST TYCOONS

It has not escaped local notice that the founder of the Glenfiddich Distillery and the founder of the Canadian Pacific Railway were schoolmates (and possibly cousins) in early-Victorian Dufftown. The flamboyant New York billionaire Malcolm Forbes (1919–1990) is fondly remembered in his ancestral homeland around the ruins of Pitsligo Castle, a Forbes stronghold from the 1420s until its near-total destruction in the Jacobite period. A superb model of this complex as it looked in 1663 has been built for the Pitsligo Castle Trust, a charity formed in 1995 to take over ownership of the castle from the Malcolm Forbes estate. Forbes gave generously to the community, and a centre for the disabled in Rosehearty is named after him. Interestingly, there is no parallel celebration of Rupert Murdoch, despite his family connection to the same place being almost as recent.

Even more obscure, due in part to conflicting information spread by the man himself, is our connection to another towering figure in the history of the global media industries. Often referred to as the father of the American mass media, James Gordon Bennett Sr worked on the *Charleston Courier* and other

American newspapers until 1835, when he founded the *New York Herald*. On his retirement in 1866, it had the highest circulation of any paper in the US. Along the way, Bennett was credited as the inventor of the newspaper interview, and with being the first editor to make advertisers pay in advance.

Bennett was born into a Roman Catholic farming family at Old Town of Newmill, Keith, probably on 1 September 1795.[433] He had three siblings named Margaret, Anne and Cosmo, and possibly others. Bennett believed their surname to be a corruption of the Norman 'Benoit', specifically, from the Benoits of Tancarville, four miles west of Quillebeuf-sur-Seine. He also cultivated a vaguely French literary and personal style that stood him in good stead in the still Francophile early US republic. In Bennett, wrote a London magazine in 1863,

> England has one of the most cordial haters that ever hated her, or any other country; and they have given their author a celebrity above most demagogues. . . . For the past thirty years he has pursued a policy – and it is nothing else than a policy – of abuse towards this country; and it is almost the only thing in which he has been consistent in his long, reckless, and inconsistent career. All such comparisons as Dr. Johnson's antipathy to the Scotch, or a Jew's hatred of pork, fall far short of Bennett's hatred of his native country.[434]

*James Gordon Bennett Sr, father of the American mass media, was born at Old Town of Newmill, Keith, in 1795.*

That 'England' could be described as the 'native country' of a man from Banffshire probably marks the high water mark of a (now lost?) homogeneous 'British' identity. Be that as it may, Bennett's account of his ancestry was sweeping and vague. Despite its grandiosity, however, we can discern in it the idea that 'his' Gordons were allies or soldiers, not direct kin, of the medieval earls of Huntly.[435] In spite of this, Bennett's biographer Isaac Clarke Pray called it 'reasonable to suppose' that Gordon was not a family name at all, and – somewhat implausibly – that Bennett's devout (Catholic) parents gave it to him as a middle name in honour of a local (Protestant) minister.[436] Matthew Hale Smith's later biography was essentially an abridged version of Pray's, but it nevertheless inflated this minister into an uncle.[437]

Bennett left the Keith area to attend a Catholic school in Aberdeen, or the Blairs Catholic seminary on lower Deeside, or perhaps both in succession. He did not in the end become a priest, but was still unmarried when he left Scotland for good in 1819. Isaac Pray did not happen to mention the names of Bennett's parents, and over time, this has hardened into the 'fact' that 'his parents' names are unknown'.[438] Yet, James Duff Law reported that Bennett's mother's grave was visible in the old kirkyard of Keith in 1903. Pray suggested that Bennett's mother, aunt, two uncles and a cousin were living on the Duff House estate in or about 1842, and others have positively stated that the family were 'well-to-do tenants of the Earl of Fife'.[439] All in all, it seems that someone could, and should, develop a much clearer picture of James Gordon Bennett Sr's life story than the murky one his many biographers have contented themselves with hitherto.

## THE LOST ARMIES

In 1632, someone with access to the Ellon kirk session book copied the following lines into it:

> My louve is on the salt sea
> And I am on the syd,
> And this would brak a young thing's hart
> Wha laitlie was a bryd –
> Wha laitlie was a comelie bryd
> Most pleasant for to see –
> The Lolands of Holands
> Hes twyned my louve and me.

This song is usually assigned to the 1650s or later, but if it was already popular in 1632, the reason is not far to seek. Scotland was neutral in the Thirty Years' War (1618–1648), but this did not stop immense numbers of her young men from enlisting in the armies of various foreign powers. By the late sixteenth century Scotland had seen 'the spread of religious dissent, significant population growth with an attendant increase in masterless men, and the decreasing need for military protection from lords'.[440] Scottish landowners' incomes were also generally too low to maintain large bodies of men-at-arms on regular wages, so 'by the 1590s the presence of significant numbers of professional soldiers in the service of individual nobles was highly unusual'.[441] Lords and chiefs positively encouraged their social inferiors to enlist in foreign armies, and for many decades before the Thirty Years' War broke out, '[t]he Scottish professional soldier, or mercenary, was . . . a familiar figure' on the continent, in Scandinavia, in Ireland and even in Russia.[442] Tens of thousands of Scots are thought to have fought in the Bohemian campaign of 1620 alone, and the war as a whole involved up to twenty per cent of Scotland's adult male population – an experience 'more intense' than anything Scottish society had undergone since the fourteenth-century wars against England.[443]

Sweden rated as a great power in the seventeenth century, and at the height of her military glory, a quarter of Sweden's armed forces were under Scottish commanders. However, it was the Danish army who received Lord Forbes's regiment of 800 men, commanded by his son, Alexander Forbes. Alexander languished as a prisoner of war for two years after the battle of Lützen in 1632, but was luckier than four of his five brothers who went to the wars and were killed. Unsurprisingly, when Britain briefly found herself at war with France in the 1620s, the king found Scotland already 'stripped bare of available fighting men'.[444] It is astonishing that this particularly rich field for both historians and writers of fiction has gone so unnoticed.

This is not to suggest that the region's 'lost armies' were exclusively military in character. There were

as many as 200,000 migrants from Scotland during the course of the seventeenth century, at a time when the population hovered around one million. That may have been the highest per-capita rate of emigration in western Europe . . . Most of that movement was directed toward the European continent. During those years, Scottish merchants and traders lived and worked extensively in the cities of France, Sweden, Denmark, and the Low Countries. Scots were especially prevalent in Poland, to which as many as 30–40,000 migrated over a period of several decades early in the seventeenth century; contemporaries believed that it represented the largest out-migration of Scots to any country during those years, exceeding even Ireland.[445]

These patterns of migration changed drastically in the eighteenth century, becoming in fact no pattern at all. During the near-famine of 1782, 'whole families' from Highland Banffshire took ship for the mainland of North America – except from Aberlour, whose only emigrants were a few well-educated 'aspiring young men', who went 'some to London, some to the West India Islands'.[446] No one at all emigrated from Marnoch during a thirty-six-year period beginning in the 1750s. At another extreme were the subtenants of Tyrie. Fed up with being evicted on six weeks' notice with no reason given, despite an entire absence of surplus housing stock, they flocked to the newly independent United States, erroneously believing that nothing of the sort could happen there. Lonmay blacksmith Andrew Presley followed suit, as demonstrated by the citizenship of his infinitely more famous descendant, Elvis Presley. Departures to the rebelled former colonies made the authorities nervous, and the Established Church minister of Monquhitter reported proudly that 'The rage of emigration never agitates the bosoms of the people, and every hovel boasts a

*On a 1937 visit, Canadian prime minister William Mackenzie King learned, very much to his surprise, that his ancestors had lived in this elegant ha' hoose, Ladysford in Tyrie. Since this picture was drawn, the house has undergone several questionable alterations, including a garage door pierced off-centre through the pavilion at right. At least it is still standing, unlike most houses of its kind.*

*Edvard Grieg, Norway's greatest composer, was the great-grandson of a Buchan Jacobite who settled at Bergen in the 1770s.*

suitable inhabitant.'[447] Meanwhile, many people fled the area without leaving Britain, with the city of Aberdeen and the 'south country' being frequent destinations.[448]

Blissfully unaware of all of this, John Craigie wrote shortly before 1800 that 'From Buchan there have never been any emigrations, and indeed there can be no reason for any'![449]

The Feu-House in Ellon (demolished *c*.1860) was long occupied by Mrs Montgomery, a great friend of the famous composer and Episcopal clergyman John Skinner. Skinner's great-grandson Marianus Cuming lived in the same house a century later, before emigrating to New Brunswick, where he edited the *St John Courier* newspaper. Cuming's son James moved in his turn to Yarraville in Australia, and became one of that country's richest men.

This rather miscellaneous emigration pattern continued into the nineteenth century, with Australia (settled from 1788) being added to the list of likely destinations. A recruiting sergeant was also stationed in Ellon down to the 1850s, and the village's four Peninsular War survivors were among the results. The pattern crystallised again around 1880, after which 'the history of emigration from the North-East region became virtually the history of emigration to the Dominion of Canada alone'.[450] Even after 1900, however, Newburgh-born James McBey remembered that about half of his fellow bank clerks 'accepted a position abroad' as soon as their banking apprenticeship was finished – sometimes as far away as Ceylon. McBey himself was offered a position on a tea plantation for £300 a year, when his salary in Scotland was £55 a year. He decided his fate by tossing an old pre-Union silver coin he'd found in Foveran kirkyard: 'if it fell showing the thistle it would indicate that I must stay on' in Scotland. Though he eventually became an American citizen and spent the last decade of his life in Morocco, '[o]n the wall of his bedroom at Tangier hung a section of the large-scale Ordnance Survey map, showing the parish of Foveran'.[451]

Even where populations have remained stable in terms of size, turnover has been immense. 'Judge of my surprise,' John Wilken wrote of Ellon in 1921, 'on returning to my native place after an absence of 40 years, to find not only a new village, with a Provost, Magistrates and Council, but with very few exceptions a new race of inhabitants'.[452] Similar complaints continue a century later, as traditional villages become dormitory communities for the oil industry. Yet, in some respects, the community spirit remains indestructible.

## THE LOST GENERALS

Every army needs a general, and Banff and Buchan were quick to supply all who were needed. Quirks of the Scottish legal system, particularly after 1587, rated hundreds, perhaps thousands of individuals as 'noble' who were not part of the titled peerage; many were not even well-off. Penniless but ambitious younger sons of minor lairds quickly discovered that they were noble *enough* to command companies and regiments anywhere in the European world – with the possible exception of their own country of birth. Here, the normal route to an army commission until 1871 was to pay a large sum for it (£1,800 to £4,800 sterling for a captaincy in the early-Victorian period). No similar system existed in Russia or Prussia. The Clan Gordon alone produced at least a dozen general officers serving in the armies of at least five foreign countries, in addition to Admiral Thomas Gordon, governor of Kronstadt, parentage unknown. John Gordon, a grandson of the obscure laird of Coldwalls near Ellon, went abroad 'in the month of June, 1700, in the 15th year of his age'.[453] By 1783, his descendant Fabian Von Coldwells-Gordon was a Prussian army colonel, and later promoted to brigadier. As the laird of Coldwalls was a first cousin of the laird of Auchleuchries, it would seem that Fabian was a distant cousin of the much more famous Ellon émigré, Patrick Gordon (1635–1699), general in the service of the Tsar of Russia. Cairnywink Cairn is supposed by old-timers to have been a monument to Patrick, but there is no proof of this. The Russian general Patrick

Gordon should not be confused with his contemporary of the same name and rank who was British colonial governor of Pennsylvania from 1726 to 1736.

It is also not clear how closely the 'Von Coldwells' or Auchleuchries Gordons were related by blood to Auchleuchries's son-in-law, the Russian major-general and sometime Jacobite commander Alexander Gordon of Auchintoul. Due to his name being incorrectly written down by the Whig authorities, Alexander retained his Scottish estates, purchased an additional estate (Durlaithers) in 1722, and was allegedly buried at home in Marnoch, albeit without a grave marker.

Thomas Buchan, the third son of James Buchan of Auchmacoy by Margaret Seton of Pitmedden, became a Jacobite major-general in 1689, having previously served in France and Holland and, since 1682, as colonel of the Earl of Mar's Regiment of Foot. Despite 'over-confidence', according to historian Paul Hopkins, 'he almost succeeded in spreading the highland rising to his native north-eastern lowlands'.[454]

James Francis Edward Keith, the Prussian field marshal whose statue ornaments Peterhead (illustrated p. 9), is said to have played a war game with Frederick the Great that involved paper cannon and up to 12,000 bowling pins. The real version was not so amusing, and Keith was mortally wounded when his army was surprised by 'overwhelming masses of Austrians' at Hochkirk in

*During the Greek War of Independence (1821–1832), in which Lord Byron the poet died while fighting for Greece, Thomas Gordon of Buthlaw became a Greek general. He began his career in the Scots Greys in 1808, but had transferred to Russian service by 1813. He survived to write extensively about his experiences and become the richest of the seven proprietors of Lonmay.*

*William Gordon of Fyvie was immortalised in Dickens's* Barnaby Rudge *for defending the House of Commons against a mob, led by his own fanatically anti-Catholic nephew, on 2 June 1780.*

1758.[455] The Jacobite son of an Episcopalian father and a Catholic mother, Keith fought in the Jacobite right wing at Sheriffmuir alongside his brother, the tenth earl Marischal. He escaped to Brittany in 1716, but returned to Scotland only to be defeated at the battle of Glenshiel in the abortive (and now mostly forgotten) Jacobite rebellion of 1719. He then served as a Spanish colonel for nine years, but as a Protestant could rise no higher. Faith was not an obstacle for the Orthodox Russians, however, who made him a general in 1728. He performed superbly in wars against the Turks and Swedes and was made governor of the Ukraine in 1740. Court intrigue caused his downfall in Russia and he moved to the Prussian service in 1747. '[A]s a soldier he was beyond question by far the greatest of all "Scots abroad"'; he was promoted to field marshal immediately, and later made governor of Berlin.[456] On his death he left everything to his considerably younger Swedish mistress, who outlived him by fifty-three years.

Another student of William Meston's grew up to be another Scoto-Prussian general. John Grant, identified in one source as 'of Dentergas',[457] was a younger brother of Patrick Grant of Dunlugas. In circumstances I have not been able to verify, John became a major of foot guards and aide-de-camp to the king of

*Prince Michael Andreas Barclay de Tolly was born into an obscure Scottish Lutheran family in Lithuania in 1761. They certainly had roots in Turriff, but claims that these Barclays were direct descendants of the author of* Argenis *(above, p. 76) appear untested. As a general in the Russian service, Barclay de Tolly orchestrated the famous 'scorched earth' policy that eventually led to the defeat of Napoleon's* Grande Armée. *He was made a field marshal after capturing Paris in 1814, and a prince of Russia the next year.*

Prussia, and served frequently as a diplomat, including on at least two missions to London. In 1759 he succeeded to the estate and title of Dunlugas, and was promoted to major-general. At the time of his death five years later, he was governor of Neisse and styled Baron Le Grant.

John Forbes of Skellater, red-haired son and grandson of Jacobite generals,[458] was educated in Glengairn and became an officer in the 103rd French Line regiment, the famous Royal Écossais, before 1763. Not a rabid Jacobite himself, and too young to have fought in the '45, he was allowed to move freely around Britain – on the condition that he did not do any recruiting. He was so offended by the anti-Scottish publications of xenophobic English MP John Wilkes that he sought a 'personal rencontre'.[459] Wilkes responded to this challenge with obvious cowardice, and the incident 'became a subject of comment in the London press, generating much sympathy for Forbes'.[460] Wilkes must have breathed a sigh of relief when Forbes was ordered to leave England. Soon after this, Forbes joined a Scottish-officered regiment in the Portuguese army and married a princess of Portugal, rising to the rank of brigadier in 1775

*The charming House of Dudwick, painted by James Giles not long before its destruction for building stone in 1865. Gen. James King, who built the house c.1636, fought in the Civil Wars as a royalist until 1644, when he entered the service of Sweden and was 'loaded with honours'.[461] The building became a farmhouse in 1786 following the death of an unrelated owner, the Scoto-Russian general Robert Fullerton. Fullerton's older brother John, an extreme Jacobite who had been exempted from pardon, used to wander around Scotland disguised as a pedlar.*

*John Forbes of Skellater, general in the Portuguese service, who as a young man challenged Scotophobic MP John Wilkes to a duel. Wilkes prudently fled.*

and field marshal in 1787. He and his troops performed especially well during a fighting retreat out of Revolutionary France in 1794. When the French invaded Portugal itself, Skellater accompanied the Portuguese royal family into exile in Rio de Janeiro, and died there, possibly of old age, in 1808.

Forbes of Skellater may have been a Catholic, but this was not the case with James Duff, who nevertheless became a general in the service of Spain. Born in Aberdeen and educated partly at the Inchdrewer Castle Grammar School founded in 1786, James was 'handsome . . . with an iron memory'.[462] He joined up as a 'distraction' after his young wife was bitten on the nose by her Newfoundland dog, dying of rabies in Edinburgh in 1805. He remained a Spanish staff officer after becoming viscount Macduff in 1809 and fourth earl Fife in 1811, fighting at Talavera and at the siege of Cadiz, where he was almost killed. He finished the Peninsular War as a lieutenant-general and was awarded the order of San Fernando. During the war he became friends with a fellow Spanish officer and Freemason, José de San Martín, who went on to liberate South America from Spanish rule and become the first president of Peru. San Martín visited the earl in Banff in 1824 and was made an honorary burgess of the town. Despite his wounds, the fourth earl lived to a ripe old age, chiefly in Duff House, but he never remarried and the earldom passed to the son of his only brother, Gen. Sir Alexander Duff of Delgaty, who had commanded the Irish 88th Foot in the same war.

With a few exceptions, including the Leith-Hay dynasty of soldier-scholar-architects and George, fifth duke of Gordon, those generals who served the

*José de San Martín, first president of Peru and honorary burgess of Banff.*

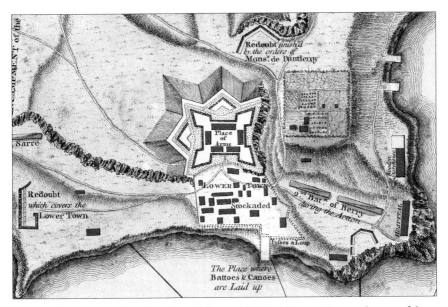

*Fort Carillon, New York, where a bungled assault by Gen. James Abercromby, son of the laird of Glassaugh, led to a decisive French victory and the loss of a thousand British lives in 1758. It was subsequently renamed Fort Ticonderoga.*

crown of their own country were somewhat less illustrious. James Grant inherited Ballindalloch Castle from a nephew in 1770 and became a major-general five years later; it was the 'high living' Grant whom George Washington surprised by his famous crossing of the Delaware, subject of innumerable American paintings and drawings.[463] Gen. James Abercromby, son of the laird of Glassaugh, was '[c]orpulent, lethargic, and unambitious . . . [but] was guaranteed a secure future in the army' due to his aristocratic connections. His idiotic frontal assault on Fort Ticonderoga in 1758 resulted in a 'bloody slaughter' which he himself conveniently survived.[464]

Keith-born Maj.-Gen. Sir James Duff, eldest illegitimate son of the second duke of Fife, played a questionable role in the suppression of the Irish rebellion of 1798; some say his actions 'embarrassed the government, and prolonged the rising'.[465] Gen. Sir Peter Stark Lumsden, who was born in Belhelvie and died in Dufftown, was remembered by Prime Minister Gladstone chiefly as a 'dunderhead' who nearly provoked a war with the Russian Empire in 1885.

Maj.-Gen. Andrew Hay, who owned Montblairy until 1801, raised a largely forgotten regiment called the Banffshire or Duke of York's Own Fencibles. Mortally wounded at the siege of Bayonne in 1814, he is commemorated by monuments in Hampshire, France and St Paul's Cathedral, but not at home.

## VOLUNTEERS

In addition to the Banffshire Fencibles, the Napoleonic Wars saw the formation of an array of voluntary armed units for home defence in case of a French invasion or French-inspired revolution. The Banff Trades were the first group north of Edinburgh to form an armed volunteer company, in 1795. Their captain was an architect, and the second-in-command a music teacher. This body merged two years later with the volunteers of Cullen, Grange, Portsoy and Macduff. By 1798, Banffshire as a whole had raised 1,218 men, of whom just over half were deployed at Banff, Macduff, Portsoy and Cullen. The idea of pro-French domestic subversion was not completely far-fetched: a 'Universal Liberty Club' was founded on Bastille Day 1791 at Portsoy by Alex Leith, distiller.

In all, Aberdeenshire and Banffshire raised fifty-three companies of volunteers between 1795 and 1802. Half a century later, after Napoleon's nephew (styling himself Napoleon III) took power in a military coup in France, the volunteer movement was revived and received an equally robust response here. Amid boundless (small 'c') conservatism and an abundant supply of firearms, what might loosely be termed the 'volunteer spirit' remains strong. I have every reason to suppose that if rioters had appeared in Turra in 2011, they would have disappeared rather quickly, and probably permanently.

*Typical Scottish volunteer soldier of the period 1794–1802.*

## SMUGGLERS BY SEA

I was initially drawn to this topic because of present-day Fraserburgh's perhaps undeservedly bad reputation for imported illegal drugs. I soon discovered that down to the nineteenth century at least, the illicit manufacturing, transport, export and import of various commodities built and sustained this part of the North-east through thick and thin to a degree that has perhaps never been fully appreciated. Not merely another hand-me-down whisky story, it is a lost history touching the economic and political life of virtually every person who lived here.

By the beginning of the eighteenth century, for reasons which have now been forgotten, Scottish skippers were considered the best smugglers in the world.[466] In 1742 alone, they are known to have trafficked illegally in 'foreign rum', tobacco, 'foreign brandy', 'foreign red wine', 'foreign white wine'; 'foreign cinamon water', 'coffee berries', 'Green Tea', 'foreign sope', 'foreign raisins', 'Irish horses', 'foreign paper', 'foreign hops', olive oil, prunes and 'foreign bone combs'.[467] Brandy, however, was key. A public statement by the justices of Banff-shire condemned

the pernicious effects of the clandestine importation and the open and excessive consumption of brandy within Scotland . . . which being run

*Not long after coffee was first drunk in Britain, people began to smuggle it in. It is hard to say if duty would have been paid at this establishment when it operated as a coffee-house in the 1670s.*

without payment of any duty is sold cheaper than spirits distilled at home can be afforded for, which proves a totall discouragement of our own manufacture, and must of consequence lessen the pryce of all grain . . . tending to the ruin of the whole country[.][468]

Certainly, people in the North-east liked their brandy. During the brief period when the York Buildings Company owned the woods of Abernethy (1730–1737), the company's 'extravagancies of every kind' included 'opening hogsheads of brandy to the country-people, by which 5 of them died in one night'.[469] Since *usquebaugh* was then still being defined as a sort of gin of the north, flavoured with coriander seed, nutmeg, sugar and saffron, it is worth wondering if the massive influx of brandy – and brandy barrels – into the North of Scotland (and particularly Banffshire) in the period immediately after 1725 had a dynamic effect on the style of *usquebaugh* that was produced: a topic to which I will return on p. 179.[470]

Thanks in large part to brandy, the typical North-east sea-smuggler of this period could begin with capital of £200 and expect to gross £200 a year.[471] In 1744, it was said,

> The *Smuggler* was the Favourite. His prohibited or high Duty Goods were run ashore by the Boats of whatever Part of the coast he came near; when ashore, they were guarded by the Country from the Customhouse-officer; if seized, they were rescued; and if any Seizure was returned and tried, the *Juries* seldom failed to find for the Defendant. These Circumstances gave the *Running* Trade the Appearance of absolute Security; and have so *thoroughly* destroyed the Revenue, that the Customs are hardly able to pay the salaries of their own Officers.[472]

For reasons that have not been firmly established, Banff did not have its own custom house until after 1790. Before it was built, written permission to land goods there had theoretically to be obtained from Aberdeen – either by post, or by personal overland journey by one of the ship's officers. This onerous and somewhat ridiculous requirement was naturally avoided where possible. The Aberdeen custom house had its hands full in any case. On 25 November 1728, the Collector of Customs wrote to the Scottish Excise Board:

> Having advice . . . [that] the Anne of Inverness burthen about 30 tons John Willison M[aste]r from Rotterdam with Dutch goods pretending

to be bound for Norway was put ashoar on the sands near Ythan mouth, I immediately Dispatched Mr Gellie the Tidesurveyor, two Tydesmen and two Boatmen (and Mr Elphinston came from Peterhead to their Assistance) to take care none of the Goods were Embar[ked.] And they Inform us that they have attended very close[ly and] prevented with much pains and fatigue, any fraud to the Revenue, the Ship having broke to pieces on the 20th. They have Secured the Goods in Cellars at the Newburgh, & a party of Soldiers are posted at the doors alongst with our Officers that they may not be Carryed off either by a mobb, or the Masters Connivance[.][473]

In a further letter on the same incident, Newburgh was described as a 'Remote Village . . . and very bad accommodation for the Shouldiers so that the officers will not Suffer their men to Remain there any Considerable time'.[474]

Mob action against Revenue officers was not limited to such country places, however. Amid the bright glare of historians' attention placed on riots in the Central Belt, it has been forgotten that in June 1730, three companies of Harrison's Regiment were ordered to march north out of Aberdeen, leaving only a sergeant and thirteen men

untill the next Regiment came up, which party were not at all Sufficient to protect the Kings warehouse here being Every night for several nights Running Insulted by a very great Mob So that the Whole party, and all of the Officers at the Port, were Oblidged to be four nights on End Out of Bed.[475]

The Collector begged that at least thirty men under a commissioned officer be sent to reinforce the custom house. Perhaps in response, the whole Customs establishment of the Aberdeenshire, Banffshire and Kincardineshire coast was given military assistance against smugglers soon afterwards. The Collector of Aberdeen replied on 16 November 1730 that 'next to Banff and Portsoy which we look upon to be very Sufficiently guarded by the Parties at the first named place and Cullen . . . Stonhive and Peterhead are the two Creeks belonging to this Port, where the greatest Smuggling Trade is carried on'.[476]

The sea-smuggling trade involved all classes, 'Proprietors . . . Tenants and Servants' alike; and so much money was sent abroad to obtain foreign smuggled goods that Scotland's coinage itself was thought to be in some danger of disappearing.[477] The 'Burgundy and Champaign &c' from the wreck of the *Anne* at Newburgh seems eventually to have found its way into the hands of the duchess

The Needle's Eye, *engraved by J.C. Nattes, shows possible smuggling activity near Troup* *in 1799.*

of Gordon.[478] '[S]o little was the feeling of disgrace attached to this demoralising traffic,' John Pratt recalled in 1858, 'that scarcely a family along the coast from the Don to the Spey, but was, more or less, embarked in it.' Political motives, Jacobite ones in particular, 'afforded a convenient colouring to this'.[479]

In a probably typical incident in 1729, Revenue officers watched the *Betty* of Montrose from a position on shore, and

> did observe for three or four hours ankers handed over the Ships side and four large fishing boats which could Easily carry fifty Ankers each load . . . and they saw these Ankers carried to a Bark belonging to Andrew Lindsay[.]

The cargo was then transferred to thirty-eight carts holding two to three barrels apiece. Sixteen carts were seized by the officers and twenty-two got away.[480] This may have been an example of a 'collusive seizure': a form of corruption much feared by the higher authorities, whereby officers would 'enter into compromises or agreements with the owner of the [smuggled] Goods, allowing him to retain a part of the Goods upon condition of the Officers not being attacked or molested in carrying away and securing the remainder'. This was still going on in 1815, when it was called 'highly improper in itself and expressly contrary to Law'.[481]

The last sea-smuggler from Collieston of Slains 'carried with him to the grave, not only the secrets of the ledger, but the clue to the many hiding-places which had so long and so completely baffled the researches of the custom-house officers'.[482] Where natural caves were not immediately available, store rooms were constructed of wood or brick and concealed inside sand dunes. These were 'capable of containing from sixty to two or three hundred tubs of gin'.[483] Their roofs had to be made at least six feet thick, 'that being the length of the excise officers' searching-spears'. Such hiding places also had to be made with a layer of dry sand on top, as a search by the authorities might occur minutes after the job of constructing one was finished, and any visibly wet sand would have been a dead giveaway.[484]

In spite of many such well-attested tales, most Scottish historians have tended to focus on land-based smuggling of home-brewed alcohol, seeing it (and by extension all smuggling) as an offshoot of subsistence agriculture, a 'secondary agricultural activity, pursued . . . when there was no harvesting or sowing to be done . . . the perfect cottage industry'.[485] The milestones of its received history are tax increases and the efforts of a desperately impoverished rural populace to evade them, for economic rather than political reasons. This sits very oddly alongside English historians' reconstruction of smuggling as a vast, hugely profitable and highly politicised species of organised crime, involving more than 50,000 Jacobites hailing from all three British kingdoms and living on both sides of the North Sea, and beyond.[486] Dunkirk in Flanders was virtually a Jacobite town, even long after 1746. James Gordon, fifth laird of Letterfourie in Banffshire was a Jacobite, 'said to have killed six men at Sheriffmuir'.[487] His successor, James, was a Madeira wine merchant from 1742 to 1760. The seventh laird of Letterfourie was Alexander, younger brother to the sixth laird and an alumnus of the Scots College, Paris. Alexander was in Charles Edward Stuart's Life Guards and took refuge with his brother in Madeira after Culloden. Francis Newton, co-founder of the still-extant drinks firm of Cossart Gordon, was also a Jacobite exile. John David Gordon, laird of Beldornie, married Maria del Carmen Beigbeider, of Jerez de la Frontera, Spain, and thereafter 'lived at that place and devoted his attention to the wine business'.[488] His eldest son married Rosa Elena Prendergast, a cousin from Cadiz. With the premature death of their only son, the title to Beldornie passed to a Scottish-resident Gordon laird of similar hybrid Spanish stock. Succeeding generations continued to marry their Spanish cousins. Similar examples could be multiplied, and one historian has argued that if Scots sea-smugglers were mostly 'perfervid Jacobites', it was only because that was the usual political outlook of the Scottish mercantile community as a whole.[489]

In this view, smuggling was political; not in the sense that the Whig state was morally against booze, but because every penny denied to the Whigs' treasury and added instead to the Jacobites' coffers was a blow struck for their war effort. At the very least, this situation would explain the half-century time lag between the first imposition of the Excise in the 1640s and the very great increase in both smuggling and anti-smuggling activity in the 1690s,[490] as well as why smuggling in southern England declined so sharply after 1749.

As is so often the case, Scottish and English historians are more insulated from each other than were the early-modern people they are writing about. In the two centuries *before* the invention of the English-language newspaper in 1643, important or sensational news tended to reach every place in the British Isles, however remote or disaffected, within ten to twenty days.[491] The world of the early eighteenth century was even more interconnected, both politically and economically. If London and the Home Counties were indeed pervaded by a pro-Stuart liquor mafia that remained economically and militarily effective for the better part of sixty years, one can be sure that Jacobites elsewhere knew something about it. There were, in all, at least thirty-three Jacobite merchant houses operating in France and Belgium, sixteen in Scandinavia and fifteen in Spain, a significant number of which were sending brandy into Britain illegally. Brandy was even used as ballast in ships running other illegal commodities.[492] During the 1715 Jacobite rebellion, moreover, the rebels were supplied with provisions by Robert Gordon, a high-level smuggler based in Bordeaux and 'deeply immersed in Jacobite conspiracy'.[493] And after 1745, Scottish Excisemen were specifically ordered to search out and inform against former Jacobite soldiers.[494]

In Ireland, the smuggling of foreign spirits into the country declined steeply after 1780, due to 'the growing competition of domestic production of spirits, licit and illicit'.[495] The situation may have been similar in Scotland, where the government estimated that it successfully detected only five per cent of the 21,000 Highland stills that were in operation in 1782.[496] Already by the mid-1780s, there was an 'impressive flow of Scottish spirits into English ports', and while this trade was mostly legal, it demonstrates that there was an established appetite in the south, as well as established sea routes, by this time.[497] One observer in 1788 noted that Scots distillers were 'uniformly deceptious', and over a single seven-month period they had sent into England 'about 183,000 Gallons of Spirits *more* than were *legally* made', on top of what they drank domestically themselves.[498] But tax increases passed in the same year made legal selling of Scottish spirits in England so uneconomical that *no landings of it whatsoever* were recorded between 5 July 1789 and 5 July 1794. Then, in 1795, all legal distilling was suspended for a year due to grain shortages. By this time, of course, the Napoleonic Wars had started, and even in times of no outright bans, legal distillation was discouraged by high wartime taxes. It is no wonder that in 1797, half the whisky being drunk was thought to have been smuggled to market.[499]

Coastal places renowned for smuggling in the eighteenth century included Newburgh, Slains, Boddam, Peterhead, Rattray Head, Cairnbulg, Fraserburgh, Rosehearty, Banff, Portsoy and Cullen.[500] This led to Customs officials being stationed at seven of those eleven places by the early 1770s.[501] The Scottish Customs fleet at this time consisted of seven cruisers and two 'hulks', and the Scottish Excise fleet, an additional four cruisers and one 'hulk', not including 'Sloops and Cutters under the Admiralty['s] direction'. However the Scottish Excise Commissioners considered this force inadequate to the task of wiping out smuggling – including, prominently, the smuggling of spirits both into and out of the North-east. The sea-smugglers, when travelling on land, were now 'well armed' – in contrast to the 1730s and '40s – but still relied upon 'artful . . . underground Concealments'. Land-based distributors of inbound smuggled goods were

> frequently met with . . . travelling in Bands of fifty, eighty, a hundred, and a hundred and fifty horses remarkably stout and fleet . . . [T]hey have the audacity to go in this formidable manner in open day, upon the public high roads, and through the Streets of such Towns and villages as they have occasion to pass.[502]

It is slightly amazing that this region, whose sea-smuggling history is no less compelling than that of the south-west of England, has been the subject of so little subsequent touristic promotion or pop-cultural depiction. A great literary opportunity still awaits some latter-day Daphne du Maurier, perhaps as yet unborn.

## WHEN WAS WHISKY?

Given the central importance of whisky-making to Banffshire's economy over the past two hundred years or more, it is surprising how little we know about precisely when, or where, whisky evolved into the delicious substance it is today. This is in part because we have grown up steeped in a bogus traditionalism – akin to certain aspects of Freemasonry, or the Horseman's Word, or even (in some areas of Buchan) slating and drystone walling – which assigns to 'ancient times' developments which in fact took place as recently as the late 1700s. Dr

Samuel Johnson tasted whisky in 1773 and said it was better than, but similar to, 'English malt brandy'.[503] At around the same time, potions *called* whisky were being made from corn, potatoes, or 'any vegetable trash that will ferment'.[504] Certainly, the British intake of legal spirits doubled between 1684 and 1700, and between 1700 and 1743 it octupled.[505] The parallel growth in consumption of tea, coffee and chocolate, all introduced in the mid-seventeenth century, was largely at the expense of beer; the mighty demand for spirits was essentially new.[506] We must confront the possibility that – far from going back to Aristotle and the Pharaohs, as most twentieth-century commentators liked to claim – Scotch whisky *as we know it* was largely the product of trial and error within the eighteenth century.

The first documentary evidence of the production in Scotland of *aquavitae*, 'strong water', is from the Exchequer Rolls and dated 1495. In that year, Friar John Cor was given eight bolls of grain to transform into spirits for use of the royal household of King James IV.[507] However, *uisci-betha* – a literal translation into Gaelic of the Latin *aquavitae*, or vice versa – is mentioned as existing as early as 1405, and 'very frequently' mentioned beginning c.1610.[508] The most observant historians, moreover, note that this early spirit was effectively a Scottish variant of gin. In 1651, John French's *usquebaugh* formula (among other recipes including 'Viper Wine', 'Essence of mans braines' and 'Spirit of Urine') contained canary sack, raisins 'not washed', dates, cinnamon, nutmeg, and licorice.[509] As late as 1725, George Smith's popular *Compleat Body of Distilling* defined *usquebaugh* as containing mace, cloves, nuts, sugar, cinnamon, ginger, coriander, licorice and saffron – and, in the case of 'Royal' *usquebaugh*, various fruits soaked 'all in a gallon of the best Brandy for seven or eight days'. Smith's other *usquebaugh* recipes called for anise and caraway, and in once case, ambergris (the nice way of saying whale vomit).[510] The transformation of the drink into its modern form might therefore plausibly be located in the middle decades of the eighteenth century, and it may be significant that the word *usquebaugh* is first definitely known to have been shortened to 'whiskie' or 'usque' between 1715 and 1730.[511] John Grant, minister of Kirkmichael in the 1790s, mentioned that birch wine, extracted yearly in March, was called *fian-na-uisg*; and '[b]y an easy metaphor, the name has been transferred to . . . that well known spirit distilled from malt'.[512]

*Aqua vitae* above proof was 'commonly called double brandy' in 1688.[513] The same wars with France that led William II and III to encourage domestic commercial distillation, led English producers to ape French styles of drink: to 'squeeze Bordeaux out of a sloe, and Champagne from an apple', as the *Spectator* put it in 1709.[514] The duke of Argyll 'switched to drinking whisky' in 1802, when and because he 'ran out of brandy'.[515] Amazingly, the question of whether any retailer of 'Spirits originally distilled from Malt, and afterwards rectified, compounded, or mixed with Fruit, Berries, or other Ingredients of Materials, so as to resemble Foreign Brandy, Rum, Geneva, &c. are subjected and liable to take out an Excise Licence' *had not yet been decided by the Court of Exchequer* as of September, 1792.[516] The flavouring of cheap whisky using 'brandy . . . herbs and other additives in the same manner as gin' persisted as late as the 1850s.[517]

The current 'blind leading the blind' approach to the history of whisky making and whisky drinking has produced an absurd narrative that requires us to hold simultaneously two opposed, and perhaps mutually exclusive views: 1) that whisky drinking percolated *downward* through society from the top, from the royal court and the abbots and bishops, to the urban merchants and professional classes, and lastly to the rural gentry and farmers, between the 1490s and the 1570s; and 2) that in or by the 1720s, whisky was a 'lower class' drink which battled its way steadily *upward* through the social scale for the next five decades, finally finding universal social acceptance only in the 1780s and since.[518] While it might be possible for some commodity to undergo this sort of 'V-shaped' development process, such a process would imply, in this case, that whisky reached its nadir of respectability in the seventeenth century. But this is not the case. The eventual lapse of a 1579 Scottish statute which had temporarily limited home distillation to persons of genteel rank, has been interpreted by academic experts as meaning that, by c.1600, 'every individual' had the right 'to make spirit for the use of his household'.[519] There are at least three references to whisky being drunk by the upper and middle classes between 1618 and 1631.[520] The involvement of all social classes in spirit-running from 1644 onward has been asserted by Steve Sillett,[521] and more than five gallons of whisky were drunk at the 1651 funeral of Sir Donald Campbell of Ardnamurchan. The laird of Glenorchy took to manufacturing whisky in 1663, while the Scots nobility seem to have drunk whatever was put in front of them in the 1670s.[522] Even English army officers stationed in Scotland in the wake of the 1715 Jacobite Rebellion were also drinking 'usky' – usually in the company of Scots styled 'gentlemen', and seemingly as a matter of routine.[523] The facts that seventeenth-century whisky would probably be unrecognisable today, and that its consumption was probably dwarfed by wine and brandy consumption, are neither here nor there. The entire idea that spirit-drinking was the preserve of the poor, as of 1730, may be a misapplication to Scotland of the situation in England during the 'Gin Age'. In the southern kingdom, in Lord Islay's famous phrase, 'the poor had run gin-mad, the rich had run anti-gin-mad'.[524] But in Scotland, just four years after Islay said this (in 1742), Prince Charles Edward Stuart himself was drinking

whisky in abundance with at least three lairds – Boisdale, Baleshare, and Kings-
burgh – and not because they, or he, could not have afforded something better.[525]
Indeed, evidence that Scottish 'usky' consumption had a class rather than a
regional basis at any time between 1618 and 1746 remains meagre at best.

As we have seen, Scottish sea-smugglers, and the domestic consumers of
their smuggled products, were disproportionately interested in brandy in the
early eighteenth century. As early as 1656, Scots were distilling their own brandy
from spoiled imported wine – making nonsense of the commonplace idea that
the domestic brandy industry was stimulated solely by William and Mary's wars
with France a generation later.[526] The Scots' strong appetite for brandy, combined
with access to brandy barrels, brandy as a known 'Royal' whisky ingredient, and
perhaps the desire to create a domestic Scottish brandy-equivalent, may be key
to understanding the transformation of the old nutmeg-laden *aquavitae* into
whisky proper. No one has ever been able to pinpoint this fundamental transition,
either in time or in space. It may be lost forever. But what we must not do is
perpetuate the error of previous observers, who have opted out of this difficult
quest by assuming, or pretending, that there was more similarity between Friar
Cor's *aquavitae* and proper whisky than ever was really the case. In seeking to
push our whisky tradition back into the 'mists of time',[527] whisky writers have
unfortunately downplayed the truly dynamic and innovative character of the
small Aberdeenshire and Banffshire distillers who broke free of both church and
state control during the seventeenth and eighteenth centuries.


## SMUGGLERS BY LAND

Writing in 1910, William Thomson called the subject of Scottish smuggling by
land 'hitherto entirely neglected',[528] which perhaps serves to explain the
excessive influence of Ian Macdonald's slim and under-researched book of four
years later.[529] Two stunts known to Thomson, but missed by Macdonald and
his many subsequent imitators, were the carrying of whisky in the knapsacks of
men impersonating soldiers, and inside the digestive tracts of dead but
unplucked geese.[530] There were also belly canteens, simulating a pregnancy,
which 'were made of sheet iron and could hold two gallons'.[531] Thomson found
that during the Napoleonic Wars, some of the larger armed bands of smugglers
'were even in some cases preceded by pipers'.[532] The immediate post-Waterloo
period, for its part, saw 'a perfect orgie of distillation and its accompaniments'.[533]
The Excise's usual interception tactics had to be supplemented by paramilitary
raid-and-wreck policies in whole districts, in the North by early 1818 and in the

Central Belt by the end of 1821 – though Cabrach remained a 'natural fortress', 'secure against all but the most determined forays'.[534] There was an inconclusive fight between smugglers and a detachment of the Black Watch in Aberdeenshire in August 1814,[535] and running battles between Cabrach smugglers and shore parties of the Royal Navy were commonplace in the 1820s.

However, actual killing by either side in these encounters was extremely rare. This makes sense, since – unusually, in tactical terms – the motivation of the larger and better-armed side was not to defeat its enemy but only to escape intact with the goods. When the notorious smuggler Philip Kennedy attacked three Excise officers in 1798 by Slains Kirk, and was mortally wounded by them, they were tried for his murder. Though the officers were acquitted, the case indicates that they were not considered 'above the law' even at that relatively early date, and that the usual rules regarding self-defence and appropriate force applied in smuggling fights as in others.

Prof. Tom Devine has contended that 'professional smugglers from outside the Highlands conveyed the whisky to market' and that '[a]fter distillation, the product was conveyed to market by "regularly trained smugglers", normally strangers from outside the district of manufacture and generally Irishmen or Lowlanders'.[536] For reasons that are not immediately apparent, this general 'business model' does not seem to have operated in Aberdeenshire, where the same Cabrach men who made the whisky carted it themselves eastward down North Donside via Kintore and Inverurie, across the river (usually at Grandholm) and onto the streets of the city of Aberdeen.

A bloody but, in the end, non-lethal battle occurred in Old Aberdeen in the summer of 1820, between the Excisemen and '15 or 16 Men . . . from the Parish of Cabrach', armed with sticks, stones and firearms. In addition to his weapons, each smuggler carried a nine-gallon anker of whisky, part of a hoard that had been concealed in the northern Aberdeen suburbs. It had been brought down from the Cabrach in six horse-drawn carts, which were then concealed at Middleton's Stables, North Street, and McHardy's Stables in Harriet Street. The Cabrach men got the better of the encounter. All but two of the Excisemen were hurt, while all but one of the smugglers escaped, the lone prisoner being John McWilliam. A £50 reward was offered for the capture of the others.[537]

Three years later, the *Caledonian Mercury* reported that the nearer the new-modelled Coast Guard came to stamping out *foreign* smuggling,

> that of the Highlanders increases, and they carry on their trade of 'Mountain Dew' in the most daring manner . . . On Thursday morning last, the 15th inst., a party belonging to that zealous officer, Lieut.

Randall R.N. from the Bridge of Don, patrolling near the toll of Tyrebagger, seized three carts and horses bringing eleven and a half ankers of whisky into town from the Cabrach, under the protection of seven men, mostly known as notorious smugglers.

A shipment of similar size from Glenbuchat was seized a mile south-west of the Aberdeen Bridge of Dee – just one hour earlier.[538]

One of the most detailed descriptions of smuggling by land comes down to us from the spectacular 1823 trial of Alexander Gordon from Largue, Cabrach. The allegations against Gordon were as follows. Firstly, on or about 4 April 1822, Lt Henry Randall RN of the Bridge of Don Coastguard Station, with Boatmen James Talbot Miles and John Rouse, 'having stationed themselves at . . . the wooden bridge across the river Don at Grandholm . . . for the purpose of intercepting smuggled Goods', spied twenty or so men including Alexander Gordon 'conveying a quantity of smuggled whisky across'.[539] The navy men 'made lawful seizure' of three and a half ankers, which were left with Mr Rouse while Mr Miles and the lieutenant gave chase to the dispersing smugglers.[540]

Gordon 'with others' then doubled back through the woods 'and did, then and there, wickedly and feloniously attack and assault' Mr Rouse, throwing him to the ground and beating him on the head, arms and back 'with bludgeons and the butt end of a pistol'. The other two officers were alerted by Rouse's cries and returned to where they had left him.[541] But this was not before the smugglers had robbed Rouse of his own pistol, cutlass and scabbard, as well as one of the seized barrels of whisky.[542] Gordon was long gone.

Secondly, the court alleged that on or about 6 July 1822, Robert Armstrong and Andrew Ritchie, both boatmen of the Peterhead Coastguard Station, 'having been placed on duty on the rising ground . . . commonly called the Heading Hill or Castle Hill of Aberdeen', were assaulted with bludgeons by the same Alexander Gordon and two accomplices who were at that moment 'engaged in conveying an anker or cask of smuggled whisky'.[543] Gordon again escaped.

He was captured in November 1822 but released, for reasons unknown, after making a sworn statement to a JP, William Kennedy.[544] Gordon robustly defended himself against the charges, and was able to sign his name, albeit in an archaic script. He declined to answer whether he had been 'employed in conveying sprits to Aberdeen'. He admitted being at Grandholm on the date of the first charge, but denied having seen any spirits seized, either from himself or from anyone else in the area. He claimed he was delivering a letter to the manager of a foundry near Grandholm, regarding the purchase of a threshing machine, but could not 'describe the situation of the foundry or the owners thereof, or the name of the person to whom [the] said letter was addressed'.[545] This, he claimed, was because before reaching the foundry, he handed his letter (which was from Alexander Watson, innkeeper at Pitcaple) to some person he met on the road.

The innkeeper was duly called as a witness, along with Gordon's various victims, two Revenue men who were not attacked,[546] Grandholm resident William Stephenson and three other residents of Aberdeen and Woodside.[547] After a trial lasting several hours, despite the judge's instruction that the case 'appeared to warrant a verdict of guilty', the jury returned a unanimous verdict of Not Proven.[548] It remains to be determined whether this Alexander Gordon was the same person as the Alexander Gordon(s) accused of deforcing officers of the Revenue at Perth on 21 April 1826, and again on 8 September 1828, and of 'assault by cutting or stabbing' on 29 April 1834.[549]

The boldness of smuggling operations around the mouth of the Don in this period was manifest, and readers are reminded of the battle between the Excisemen and John McWilliam's gang of up to sixteen smugglers from Cabrach on the streets of Old Aberdeen in 1820; and of the similar affray in Tyrebagger Woods in 1823, between seven Cabrach men and the navy. All of this suggests that a particular smugglers' route down North Donside from the Cabrach was being regularly followed. It is perhaps due to extensive local knowledge of this phenomenon, which was reported frequently in the local but rarely in the national press, that Cabrach whisky was sold in Aberdeen shops (at a large premium) under its own name; whereas in the same period, Cabrach was 'being sold as "Glenlivet whisky" in the south of Scotland'.[550] For a time – indeed, a time including the famous visit of King George IV to Edinburgh – fine single-malt Highland whisky may have suffered the fate of Kleenex and Hoover, i.e., to be known colloquially as 'Glenlivet' no matter who actually made it and regardless of where it actually came from.

Of course, not all smuggling was reported in the papers. On 2 February 1825, the famed Aberdeenshire Exciseman Malcolm Gillespie reported to his superiors that he had apprehended 'two notorious delinquents, Ebenezer Bain and Peter Bain, residenters in Powneed, Cabrach', in bed at Whiterashes with four other unknown persons on 23 December 1824. On that occasion, eight horses, six carts and 190 gallons of whisky were seized, and another thirty-five gallons destroyed. The Bains, according to the report, had 'respectable farms' and 'good circumstances' in Cabrach, 'having accumulated wealth from smuggling alone, for a number of years'.[551]

James Gordon and William Gordon, both of Cabrach, pleaded guilty in the High Court of Justiciary to 'discharging loaded fire-arms, with intent to murder, or to do grievous bodily injury . . . and more especially . . . with intent to obstruct officers of the revenue in the discharge of their duty' on 6 February 1827.[552] Their intended victims were Donald McKenzie, riding officer of Elgin, and ten men, six armed with muskets, who had landed from the Revenue cutter *Atalanta* expressly 'to make search in Cabrach'. The smugglers, who numbered between fifteen and twenty men, shouting 'Shoot them all!' (with various expletives), fired three volleys with their own muskets and appeared to have come into the field specifically to oppose the search.[553] Unsurprisingly, the Excisemen failed to locate any whisky on this occasion. McKenzie was shot through the body and in the face, but lived to give evidence. The Gordons were both sentenced to transportation for life – despite their crime being punishable by death – and their downfall did nothing to discourage 'twenty-one rounds of musketry' being fired at a drunken coming-of-age party for the earl of March, held 'in the large barn at Invercharroch' a few years later.[554]

Of course, all accounts of smuggling arrests point out the large number of smugglers who escaped. Gordon in Largue, McWilliam and the Bain brothers were exceptions proving the rule: that only a minority of smugglers caught red-handed with the goods were even detained, let alone tried and convicted. So long as the gangs outnumbered the officers of the law, and were armed with the same sort of weapons, escape for most was virtually guaranteed. The government was so embarrassed by yet another lost fight against land-smugglers in 1822 that it issued general orders to the Excise and the army, stating that Excisemen

> must be . . . explicit in their communications to the Military Officers, as nothing can be more injurious to the Public Service than His Majesty's Forces or the Officers being under the necessity of either relinquishing a Seizure, or being unable to make one, from their inferiority of force.

If in future any military officer should 'doubt the sufficiency of his whole Detachment to perform the Duties required of them, in a proper and Soldierlike Manner (without further aid), he will apply to the nearest Military Post for such aid'[.][555]

In the city of Aberdeen at least, Cabrach whisky was considered both essentially similar to, and just as good as, Glenlivet whisky throughout the 1820s and 1830s – that is to say, for many years after George IV's first alleged patronage of smuggled Glenlivet made it the more famous of the two in England. Interestingly, in the *Aberdeen Journal* for 9 August 1848, we find what must be one of the earliest artefacts of 'whisky tourism': an advertisement for the Speyside mail coach, titled 'Splendid New Country Opened to the Public'. This promised views of 'Glenlivat, so famed for its whisky'.[556]

A great deal of modern Scottish writing seems to suggest that illicit distilling was more secretive and more solitary than could possibly have been the case; even the blurbs on recent Glenlivet bottles speak of the 1820s as a period when distillers were allowed 'to come out of hiding'.[557] The Kirk ministers of Georgian times harboured no such notions that the makers of whisky were marginal figures. In common with their Irish Anglican counter-parts,[558] these clergymen frequently mentioned smuggling and in some cases did not condemn it. In the Cabrach and immediately round about, it was an almost universal fact of life. Amid the 'hovels' of 'Tammtoul' (Tomintoul), the only village in the parish of Kirkmichael, '[a]ll of them sell whisky, and all of them drink it'.[559] The village's best inn, Rev. John Grant continued, was the Sign of the Horns, kept by Mrs McKenzie, who began her career as an army whore at the age of fourteen. Despite a life spanning the battlefields of Flanders, Holland, France, Germany, Britain, Ireland and the Americas, and having had twenty-four children, she retained 'all the apparent freshness and vigour of youth', and was the village's richest and most respected inhabitant. Grant's successor Alexander Tulloch concurred that private distillation and smuggling 'prevailed universally'.[560]

James Grant, who was John Grant's contemporary minister in the neigh-bouring parish of Inveraven,[561] stated that oats were worth a guinea a boll of victual (i.e. enough oats for nine stone of prepared food) but barley sells for more, 'especially if weighty and good, and fit for malt and for the still'.[562] He went on to explain that there were two ferrymen's inns in the parish, one on the Spey and one on the Aven, both selling whisky but neither selling ale. A similar story was told by Rev. John Gordon in Strathdon, where the two so-called 'alehouses' sold 'whisky only'; and several private houses also sold it.[563] Gordon's successor Robert Meiklejohn added that Corgarff Castle, specifically 'to support the civil authorities in the suppression of smuggling', was garrisoned by a captain, a subaltern, and fifty-six other ranks:

> Previous to the alteration in the distillery laws, this parish was one of the strongholds of smuggling. The inhabitants of Corgarff, the glens, and not a few in the lower part of the parish, were professed smugglers. The revenue-officers were set at defiance. To be engaged in illicit distillation, and to defraud the excise, was neither looked on as a crime, nor considered as a disgrace.[564]

In Mortlach in the 1790s, there were about ninety persons self-employed outwith agriculture, including three distillers of whisky. It was observed there that – within the eighteenth century – '[t]he drinking of whisky instead of good ale is a miserable change'.[565] Before 1836, 'illegal distillation . . . was carried on to a great extent'.[566] In nearby Boharm, smuggling was 'a tempting employment – for which the parish had great facilities'. Of Boharm's inns in 1834, it was reported that 'the whole four are spirit-shops also', and the absence of effective policing allowed them to operate at all hours of the day and night.[567] In Aberlour, a 'change for the better' in the people's moral and religious character was said to have taken place 'since the suppression of smuggling', which was 'scarcely' heard of by 1836.[568] It was commonplace in this region for the *New Statistical Account* of 1834–45 to describe smuggling as recently or mostly ended where the *Old Statistical Account* of 1791–99 failed to mention it at all – suggesting that the Kirk winked at smuggling up to the *very moment* that the Treasury and the military cracked down on the smugglers with all the force that the post-Waterloo state could suddenly command.

Some parish ministers writing in the *Old Statistical Account* did admit to it, of course. In the Cabrach, according to Rev. James Gordon, writing in the 1790s, distilling consumed the entire surplus of 200 bolls of barley – 1,200 bushels or about thirteen tons. In contrast to the censorious Rev. Robert Scott in Glenbuchat, who credited the 'annihilation of smuggling' with every positive development from population growth to good manners to 'a strong desire for

*Hidden stills were far from being exclusively rural. The clock tower of Dufftown – built after 1817 – once contained an illicit still, whose chimney was disguised as a lightning-rod.*

reading and general information',[569] Gordon in Cabrach showed no apparent awareness that the practice might be considered immoral. As late as 1914, a retired Revenue officer lamented that 'well-to-do people . . . engage in the traffic through sheer wantonness, just for the romance of the thing' and that 'the Highland clergy, with one exception, are guilty of the grossest neglect and indifference in this matter.'[570]

Throughout northern Aberdeenshire and Banffshire, smuggling created curious symbiotic relationships. Coastal farms sent grain 'up to forty miles inland' to be distilled,[571] and distillers sent the finished product back the same distance to retailers and exporters, including the Aberdeen firm of Christie & Mitchell, described by historian Jean Pike as a 'successful smuggling syndicate'.[572] As late as the 1850s, many so-called 'farms' in Cabrach were distilleries in all but name. The returning officer for the Cabrach census in 1841 and 1851 was William Ronald, who served as schoolmaster of Cabrach from 1823 to 1876. Both his returns are unusual in that they seek to explain the parish's recent population decline. Even more striking than the offer of an explanation is the explanation itself. In the 1841 return, Ronald wrote that

> A very Considerable decrease of the population has taken place since 1831. For some time previous to that, the profits arising from illicit distillation . . . induced many to settle in [Cabrach] with a view of engaging in this contraband trade[.]

He kept up the same line of argument in 1851, by which time the population had fallen by almost a third in twenty years. This, he said, 'was in great measure due to a change in the Excise laws, which affected considerably the circumstances of the people, and led many of them to seek a livelihood in other parts of the country'. The widespread notion of distilling as a marginal, almost solitary activity that made no one rich is belied by the schoolmaster's assessment that the 'profit' from it attracted a very sizeable labour force into the Cabrach from other parts of the kingdom. Moreover, Ronald's further comments that the smuggling days were now ended, must not be taken at face value. Indeed, they may represent 'attack as the best form of defence', in that the *specific information* contained in the returns, and especially that of 1851, would inherently tend to arouse suspicions that smuggling was still going on.

First, we must look at the question of farm size. In the agriculturally and socially equivalent area of Micras on Upper Deeside in the 1830s, people lived extremely precariously on the produce of one acre per person. Seven acres per person had been a more comfortable margin for survival in the previous century, but still no absolute guarantee against scarcity and want.[573] So it is surprising indeed to learn that Alexander Gordon in Auchmair described himself in 1851 as a farmer of four acres employing two labourers, supporting a family of four, and entertaining a visitor, Robert Milne from Forfarshire, 'Hawker of Cloth'. Given that male wage rates in Cabrach were 2s a week or more, Auchmair was apparently generating not merely 150–200 per cent of the maximum theoretical food supply for a farm of its size – at the height of the Highland Potato Famine! – but an additional £11 sterling per year in cash. Only a profitable, undeclared business could explain this cash flow, or indeed, why the workmen who received some share of it were needed at Auchmair in the first place. The presence of the travelling salesman in the house is also highly suggestive of a contraband distribution strategy. Such 'farms' were not the majority: even in Cabrach, genuine farming was occurring, with sixteen acres per hired man being the norm. Yet, many examples similar to Auchmair could be identified. Implausible as it sounds, Gauch in Cabrach – now a single farm – was as late as 1861 a village of forty-four persons in six households. There were also six houses at Auchmair, which supported a population of two dozen, including two itinerant traders, William Dobbie from Annan and Mary Dobbie from Stonehaven. However, in this particular census return, the finger of suspicion points most strongly at John Mitchell in Tomnavowin, 'farmer of three acres', supporting three adult siblings and a niece and nephew, and employing two servants.[574] There had been a *licensed* distillery on Tomnavowin as recently as 1842.[575] On the whole, census data makes it seem quite obvious that something other than agriculture was going on in the Cabrach, a full generation or more after the supposed end of the smuggling era in the 1830s.

There was, in fact, a now-forgotten 'Indian summer' of illicit distilling in this region in the 1880s. It was an immediate consequence of the repeal of the malt tax. This new laxity was underscored by the Crofters' Holdings Act 1886, which took eviction off the table as a potential legal weapon against smugglers. One of the most prolific and successful illicit distillers of this later period was James 'Goshen' Smith, one-time gamekeeper on the (Spanish wine merchant-owned) Beldornie estate, and 'the most cunning chemist in Strathbogie'. Sir William Grant, who had sampled Goshen's whisky 'whilst on holiday at Beldorney', inadvertently led to the distiller's downfall, by praising the quality of the brew to a man in London who turned out to be 'a high ranking official in the Excise Department'! This occurred in early 1888, and led to a careful search of 'every farm and croft between Stoniley (Goshen's croft) and the Grouse Inn'. Goshen was tried at Keith on 17 April 1888 and fined £10.[576] It was also around this time – and perhaps on the same occasion – that 'a local worthy by the name of Pizgah, hid his plant and stock of whisky in such haste that he never succeeded in recovering them'.[577] Excise officers from Ian Macdonald (*fl.* 1900) to Steve Sillett (who retired in the 1960s and is still with us) believe that Cabrach smuggling could have lasted much longer even than this later period. The proprietor of the Gordon Arms Hotel in Keith was, after all, arrested for distilling in the hotel as late as 1934. By this time, prison terms were more frequently handed out – instead of or in addition to fines, which were themselves stiffer in real terms. But as Sillett puts it,

> in any of the once notorious smuggling districts . . . whilst most people are genuinely of the opinion that the practice of illicit distilling was discontinued long before they were born, and never resumed, others . . . know a good deal more than they care (or dare) to admit.[578]

Another point seemingly lost on the many writers of books about whisky and smuggling is that every distillery produced, as by-products of its distilling operations, a large quantity of fertiliser, as well as 'valuable additional food for cattle', especially in winter.[579] In 1788 it was computed that, 'on a farm of 213 English or 168 Scotch acres, a distillery with a still of 50 gallons would produce a difference of £613 per annum' due to fertiliser alone, as against unfertilised land of the same size; whereas an equivalent improvement using animal manure would require the dung of hundreds more beasts than such a small farm could otherwise support.[580] It was further estimated that, for this reason, the presence of a distillery on a farm of 1,500 Scots acres would double the value of the land, from 15s to 30s per acre. If these statements are broadly true, there may well have been a hitherto nearly secret contribution of illicit distilling to the 'Age of Improvement' in Scotland generally.

Ian Macdonald and others have complained that the word 'smuggling' should properly be applied to illicit transport, not production, but in this they are at odds with the Norse root word *smuga*, which applies only to concealment, not movement from place to place. The Scots are simply using the borrowed word more accurately than the English.

## THE ENFORCERS

The shopworn 'mists-of-time' arguments about whisky tend conveniently to ignore the question of when suppression of the illicit trade began. Illicit distilling as such was virtually unknown until the imposition of the Excise tax on alcohol,

first by the Covenanters in 1644 and then by the occupying army of Oliver
Cromwell from 1655. The number of Excisemen, and smugglers, increased as –
due to a near-permanent state of war with France – French products including
brandy were banned. Initially, whisky filled this gap in the market; it was even
hailed as patriotic by the JPs of Aberdeenshire in a proclamation of 1744, ordered
to be printed and published in all parish kirks of the county.[581] In this proclamation, the Quarter Session swore

> by our own Example to lessen the Consumpt of all foreign
> Commodities Particularly . . . Brandy or foreign spirits Except from
> our own plantations nor drink in any publick house where we know
> the same to be sold . . . we will give all proper Encouragement to the
> distilling and brewing [of] Good malt Liquor and malt Spirits for the
> service of our Country in a reasonable way for the Consumpt of our
> own Grain.

They would assist Customs and Excise, but only mentioned that this would be
in the suppression of 'Brandy, Tea, or any uncustomed Goods', i.e., imported
wares and not the patriotic 'Good . . . malt Spirits' they were busy encouraging,
and perhaps planning to produce themselves. The wording of the Resolution
also implies that, up until now, the worthy justices *had* been drinking smuggled
foreign alcohol in dodgy taverns. The oldest Excise document I have seen that
describes Scottish illicit distilling as a growing problem dates only to 1775, and
home distillation for (supposedly) personal use, in a still of up to twelve gallons,
remained legal until after 1786.

It has been argued that legislation of 1736, which prescribed the death
penalty for smugglers who wounded officers, may actually have led to an
increase in violence, as perpetrators became increasingly keen to evade capture.
And by 1746, harbouring smugglers and even 'assembling' to smuggle goods also
became death-penalty offences – at which point the individual's choice between
killing, wounding and not shooting at the officers became theoretically irrel-
evant. But in practice, most smugglers who were *not* killers could escape
punishment by informing on their confederates.

J.W. Fortescue argued in 1905 that, in addition to there having been 'no
distinct police force of the slightest efficiency in these islands' except under the
Cromwellian Protectorate, '[o]ur existing police are, in fact, a standing army,
and such a standing army as would have been permitted to no English Sovereign
in the seventeenth and eighteenth centuries'.[582] The 'principal duty' of the British
Army's cavalry in the period 1688–1714, 'and for, I suppose, nearly a century

later', was 'to act as a preventive service in aid of the Custom House, to suppress the smuggling which throve so amazingly'.[583] This comment would take in, in the Scottish case, not only the Scots Greys but also (from 1690) the rather more mysterious Cunningham's Dragoons, a.k.a. the Queen's Own Dragoons and subsequently the 7th Hussars. This unit was used as a police force in Scotland almost immediately upon its formation.

The problem of smuggling was not intermittent or seasonal: Excise officers obtained evidence of, but were unable succesfully to prevent or prosecute, a serious offence 'almost every other day'. The officers picked their battles carefully, challenging only the 'smaller parties', but still often lost these encounters and were severely beaten up. Only 'a sufficient Military Force, dispersed throughout the Country', and 'particularly . . . a large number of Dragoons', the Excise Commissioners argued, could tip the balance of power in their favour. The Commander in Chief for Scotland was unable (though willing) to assist them, 'owing to the scanty number of Troops that now are, and for some time past have been, sent to, and quartered in Scotland'. Aside from permanent garrisons in forts, there were in July 1789 only six troops of horse and eighteen companies of foot; that is, probably nearer 1,000 than 2,000 men, dispersed between 'only eleven places'.[584] That the Commissioners dared to make this extraordinary request at all – at the risk of appearing weak or inefficient to their superiors – suggests how serious the situation was. The large force of dragoons, of course, never appeared, though some were deployed in Glen Shee, and the authorities remained outgunned by the smugglers well into the nineteenth century – indeed, until after the smuggling trade began to die out for

*Preventive-men, early nineteenth century.*

other reasons. Even in the late 1820s, army and naval assistance was 'more often needed than might be expected'.[585]

Being an Excise officer could be ruinously expensive. From the earliest days of the Excise's existence, the Treasury took only fifty per cent of the value of seized goods, the other half going to 'the Seizor, Discoverer, or other, who seizes, makes, or brings Information of the breach':[586] i.e., it was divided between the officers and their informers according to some formula of their own negotiation. Aberdeenshire-based Malcolm Gillespie – considered one of the most diligent officers – estimated that between court costs and payoffs to informers, the whisky he seized had left him out of pocket £1 per anker. Desperate for cash, he turned his hand to forgery and was hanged. Perhaps for related reasons, Excise regulations specified that new officers had to be debt-free, and if they were married, have two children or fewer.[587] Officers were mounted or unmounted, not as a mark of rank, but in response to the practical matter of the geographic spread of the premises they were inspecting. Those deemed to need horses had to pay for them themselves.[588] The average daily ride for those with horses was estimated at eighteen miles, and the length of the working day for all officers averaged twelve to thirteen hours.

Disappointingly, an Excise manuscript titled *An Account of the Number of Illegal Stills Seized and Condemned in Scotland for the Year ended 5th July 1805* gives no breakdown by county or parish, only by still capacity (see opposite).[589] This information is, however, rather interesting in itself and I have not seen it published elsewhere.

This account was drawn up some eight years after the repeal of rewards linked to still capacity (2s 6d per gallon), which had led to the same still being cyclically discovered, 'destroyed' and 'discovered' again and again.[590] Collusion between Excise officers and smugglers certainly occurred at other times, too, and it may have been given added urgency in Aberdeenshire by the presence of known Jacobites within the Excise service, perhaps even after 1746.[591]

If the pre-1815 detection regime seems relaxed, the punishments for non-violent smugglers could be positively risible. Some officials at the Treasury felt that persons sentenced to a fine and imprisonment for private distilling should be kept in prison until the fine was paid off, but in practice this was never done: imprisonment 'for a time not exceeding Six Months, unless the fine or penalty be sooner paid' was generally allowed to stand in for full payment of the fine.[592] JPs often found offenders guilty but then let them go without punishment.[593] This was a structural problem: in contrast to England, which had the Court of King's Bench to keep them in check, in Scotland 'there was no superintending jurisdiction over JPs in revenue matters'.[594] At an Excise Court held in Old Deer

*Total seized and condemned: 1,222*

| Size in gallons | How many stills of this size |
| --- | --- |
| 60 | 1 |
| 57 | 1 |
| 50 | 1 |
| 45 | 1 |
| 44 | 1 |
| 40 | 95 |
| 38 | 51 |
| 36 | 2 |
| 35 | 3 |
| 34 | 252 |
| 32 | 4 |
| 30 | 264 |
| 28 | 4 |
| 25 | 333 |
| 24 | 5 |
| 20 | 2 |
| 18 | 1 |
| 16 | 2 |
| 15 | 2 |
| 14 | 1 |
| 13 | 1 |
| 'Broke on the Spot, Contents not ascertained' | 195 |

in 1821, the culprits were found to be so poor that they were merely given repri-mands. Fining them, it was thought, would have simply redoubled their criminal efforts.[595] The Excise board fumed at this but all their officers could do was make empty threats. National anti-smuggling supremo Donald McNicol inves-tigated the abetting of smuggling by lower-ranking Excise officers, as well as by JPs: specifically, 'whether the fines imposed had operated as a Licence to, or as a discouragement of, this practice'.[596] By October 1808, the JPs were in open revolt, showing 'their unwillingness to enforce the act passed last Session, respecting Private Distillation' by which they were required to fine offenders £20 minimum or imprison them 'if the money is not immediately paid'.[597] Even when they were locked up, moreover, smugglers 'were treated with greater consideration than other prisoners', being sometimes allowed to go home on

Sundays, for example;[598] and all Excise prisoners in Scotland were released for the coronation of King George IV, unless their crimes were 'flagrant'.[599]

It is even possible to read the duke of Gordon's famous 1820 House of Lords speech, in which he pledged to co-operate with the Excisemen on his lands, as evidence that he had *not* been co-operating with them hitherto. As Steve Sillett points out,

> successful smuggling on a large scale had the immediate effect of raising the price of barley, which in turn, afforded the proprietors . . . increased rents for inferior lands; frequently as much as three times their true value . . . The illicit distiller, tenant and landlord were thus entirely inter-dependent[.][600]

On the Gordon estates, Joseph Mitchell recalled, '[t]he smugglers had to be rooted out', but the duke 'handled the business with great delicacy. He pensioned some, gave others better crofts and houses, and, in short, managed matters so adroitly that no complaint or grievance was heard in regard to the changes he adopted.'[601] Very intriguingly, the duke personally expended £68 10s in legal fees to defend Charles Stewart in Haddoch – unsuccessfully – against a smuggling charge brought in the Court of Exchequer in early 1825.[602]

Barley in the early 1820s cost 32s a boll in Mortlach, as compared to just 18s in the non-distillery coastal town of Macduff. 'Since a great many of the magistrates were, themselves, landowners, and as such, materially interested in the proceeds of smuggling,' it was 'only politic that they should settle for face-saving fines of £2 or £3, even in cases where the offender had benefited to the extent of several hundred'.[603] William Grant, a JP in Auchorachan and known as the 'Cripple Captain' because of his wooden leg, often let suspected smugglers go free, and was widely suspected of smuggling himself.[604] In the late nineteenth century, Mitchell recollected 'a Highland laird toasting, "Cheap barley, and success to smuggling"'.[605]

An interesting sidelight on the illicit trade is provided by the Banff JPs' licensing book for 1769–1828.[606] This documents their remarkably patchy efforts to maintain control over retail sellers of 'exciseable liquors'. It has two suspicious features. The first is an extreme concentration of activity in Keith and the coastal towns – Gardenstown, Crovie, Doun/Macduff and Cullen are frequently mentioned[607] – at a time when we know from the *Old Statistical Account* that spirit-selling was rife in Cabrach, Tomintoul and other parts of the county's Highland zone. Amid the complete returns of licences for the period, the first Cabrach seller is John McInnis in Braehead of Auchindoun, in 1787. James Gow alias Smith in Nether Ardwell first declared his business in 1808. William Gordon in Priestwell of Mortlach did not commence licensed operation until 1810; and Aberlour was issued with licences only in 1787, 1789, 1790, 1805 and 1813. The first licence in Tomintoul was issued several years *after* Rev. John Grant commented of the village that '[a]ll of them sell whisky, and all of them drink it'.[608]

The second suspicious feature is a tendency for the total number of licensed premises to float down toward nil over a period of years, during which any particular seller might drift in and out of licensed status many times. The afore-mentioned Mr McInnis took out licenses only in 1787, 1788, 1799 and 1800. Tomintoul, which admitted to having three or more sellers throughout 1801–03 and in 1808, admitted to none from 1813–18, then, suddenly, had four again (including one of the original men). And there is no very good reason to suppose that Robert Gordon, vintner in Keith for thirty-six years from 1790 to 1825, actually ceased trading for the twenty-one years within that period during which his licence lapsed. The Banffshire JPs were considered so slack in this aspect of their responsibilities that one of the earliest official 'form letters' was produced. The Banffshire session received one of these on 18 December 1794, notifying them that they had failed in their statutory obligation

> to make up a true and exact List, in a Book or Register to be kept for that Purpose, of the Names, Additions, and Places of Abode, of all persons within their respective Divisions to whom Licences for retailing Ale, Beer, or other exciseable Liquors, shall be delivered[.][609]

It appears that on this occasion they were fined £10.

For Excise purposes, the Highland zone in our area was anywhere to the west of a line drawn from Fettercairn to Fochabers via Kincardine O'Neil, Clatt, Huntly and Keith. Though this was hardly its intent, the government's peculiar combination of action and inaction in the two decades after 1786 – including lower licence fees in the Highland zone, but also total non-enforcement in some places – amounted to a gigantic experiment in stimulating the Highland whisky industry, chiefly at the expense of the Lowland one. It is an experiment the effects of which are still being felt worldwide.

## LOST HISTORY OF A LOST LAND: THE CABRACH

Overwhelmingly, the history of the North-east has been written as the history of certain powerful families – understandably so, since the power they wielded, particularly in the judicial sphere, was 'extreme' by European standards.[610] While there is nothing wrong with this publishing trend in itself, it has left many questions unanswered, particularly about remote areas where barons and their retinues tended not to linger. The Cabrach, straddling an especially cold stretch of the Aberdeenshire-Banffshire border, is a case in point. Its key role in illicit distilling and smuggling has already been mentioned, but the rest of its lost history is no less intriguing.

Sometimes called 'Scotland's Siberia', the Cabrach is even today an awesomely desolate-looking and remote place. On my second visit to the area, I encountered only one other being: a collarless yellow Labrador with a dead black lamb in its mouth. Historians are frequently guilty of exaggerating the difficulties of transport and communication in the early-modern world, but Cabrach is one of the exceptions proving the rule: a zone that was genuinely cut off from the rest of Scotland by bad roads and worse weather for several months each year.

J.T. Duncan, sheep farmer in Buck of Cabrach, recorded in his diary on 10 January 1912 that 'Jas Law here this morning tells us that James Kellas Hillhead is dead, starved in hill of Gaugh coming from Glenbucket on Monday night died 5 a.m. on Tuesday'. Many others met similar fates over the centuries. Duncan described 10 April 1912 as 'A fearful stormy day ewes & lambs unable to stand against it & I have no shelter on this Devil of a place with the wind out of the North gathered ewes round cots at night'.

This isolation, among other factors, may have contributed to the Cabrach becoming a refuge for law-breakers from an early date. Gordon of Lesmoir was found in possession of a stolen mare belonging to Robert Coutts of Auctercoull in Cabrach in July 1573.[611] In 1588, six Jesuit priests were denounced for prose-lytising in the North-east from their bases in Moray and Strathbogie. Part of the problem, as the Kirk saw it, was that five churches including Cabrach and Kildrummy were firmly in the grip of the earl of Huntly, who threw out the ministers and prevented other Kirk officials from entering the area.[612] The seeds of the extreme lawlessness of the seventeenth century were perhaps being sown. In or before 1614, a 1,000-merk reward was offered for McGillieworicke, 'ane starke theiff and captane of theifis . . . [who] trubled all the Cabroch and Braa of Marr'.[613] Though they were strikingly well-born, many of the Cabrach tenant farmers of the early 1600s ran into serious trouble with the law. There was, for example, a mass outlawry in March 1635 of Alexander Leith 'brother to Harthill', James Gordon 'sone to Baldornie', William Ros 'sister sone to Letterfoure', Adam Gordon 'callit of Parke' and thirty-nine other men, 'all in Cabrache', who were the authors and committers of the manie slaughters, fireraisings, heirships, depradations, and others barbarous oppressions, wherewith his Majesteis peaceable subjects in the north parts have beene greevously infested these diverse yeeres bygane, to the dishonour of God, disgrace of his Majesteis government, and disturbance of the publict peace and quyetnes[.][614]

In the absence of either a police force or a standing army, it was, indeed, a family affair. The men ordered to *enforce* the commission against these outlaws included John Gordon of Park, James Gordon of Letterfourie, and George Gordon of Beldornie!

Even so, it had some effect. By 11 June, seven of the accused men had been hunted down and killed, including Adam Gordon the younger of Auchnacrie, whose severed head was set up on the 'Nather Bow' in Edinburgh. However, James Gordon of Letterfourie and others (including, newly, Robert Gordon of Pitlurg) were then summoned to appear before the privy council.[615] William Ros, Letterfourie's nephew and 'ane of the principall rebellis and dissobedient persons in the north', was captured by one Patrick Grant,[616] but rescued with considerable violence by William Gordon and Alexander Farquharson (both tenants in Migvie), and James Farquharson, WS. This gang returned Ros to Strathbogie, where apparently he was in no further danger from royal justice. Alexander Leith the younger of Harthill – repeatedly identified as one of the worst of the outlaws, and probably their leader – was still on the loose on 3 July 1636.[617]

Not long after this, the Civil Wars began. Though Scotland's government quickly changed beyond recognition, Highland Banffshire remained a place of refuge for those out of step with authority. The townspeople of Strathbogie began using 'Glenfiddiche and Auchindoun' as hiding places for their moveable goods.[618] Anna Gordon, accused of nonconformity by the Presbytery of Turriff, fled to the comparative safety of Lesmoir in 1643. 'Patrik Leyth of Arthill' was excommunicated for royalism in 1647.[619] In the greater Cabrach – as perhaps nowhere else – there is some grain of truth in the commonplace Puritan smear, that royalist officers were drawn from the pre-war criminal element.

In 1654, due to the English military occupation of Scotland, and the Gordon clan's opposition to this, ownership of the Cabrach was transferred from the Gordons to the collaborator Campbell of Lorne, whose nominees kept hold of it until at least 1662. But by 1669, Kirkton of Cabrach had been returned to Charles Gordon (1638–1681), first earl of Aboyne, and fourth son of the second marquess of Huntly. The Kirkton was granted an official fair, as it was one of the kingdom's 'publict places of resort . . . upon the hie way betuixt the heelands and lowlands'. For 'bying and selling of horse, nolt, sheip, fish, flesh, meill, malt and all sorts of grane, cloath, lining and wollen and all sort of merchant commodities', the fair was to begin on the third Tuesday in August annually, and last three days.[620] Perhaps the most interesting aspect of the act granting this, is the presumed equivalency between Aboyne on Deeside – nowadays, a very prosperous large village of 2,200 persons – and Kirkton of Cabrach, as 'lost' a community as one is likely to find, or rather not find, anywhere. In any case, the first Cabrach fair must have been a great success, since in 1686, the Huntly family requested and obtained permission to hold three others in Cabrach: 'the second Tuesday of Apryle . . . the third Tuesday of September, [and] ane otheir there the second Tuesday of November'.[621]

The Cabrach's surprisingly large cash flow, already noted in the context of the 1840s and '50s, was already apparent in the seventeenth century:

> In 1600, the Rental of the Upper Cabrach was '366 merkis silver maillis' and 17 stones butter. In 1696, the Rental had risen to £454 Scots, or nearly double. It is suggestive that while most of the low country rents were partly paid in grain and meal, neither entered into the Rental of the Cabrach.[622]

From 1654 to 1713, most rents in Cabrach were paid in money only, an unusual feature indeed, in an economy which was dominated (p. 60, above) by payment in kind.[623] Gauch alone, when tenanted by Peter, Alexander and John Gordon, rented for six hens and £100 cash – another strikingly large sum to have been generated by a small farm in an infertile district.[624]

Prior to the early sixteenth century, the Aberdeenshire part of Cabrach was apparently not farmed at all, and it seems to have had no permanent residents other than Alexander de Narne, keeper of the king's untamed horses there in 1438, and John Rede, keeper of the queen's horses in 1451–52. Lesmurdie, under the spelling 'Losmorthie', came into existence (at least as a place-name) by 1473, and Belcherrie by 1488.[625] The Gordon clan acquired Cabrach from the crown in April 1508, and the first resident proprietor, James Gordon of Achmyling, moved to the lands of Gauch in Cabrach in December 1508 or early 1509. The Grant Gordon family, some of whom still live at Reekimlane of Gauch, trace their ancestry to him.

'Achmyling' has been tentatively identified as Auchmullen, near Wester Clova in the adjoining parish of Kildrummy. As such, it is further believed that this James Gordon of Cabrach and Achmyling was the brother of John Gordon of Longar. Longar was the founder (in 1539) of the extraordinarily talented dynasty of Gordon of Pitlurg, which included the cartographers Gordon of Straloch (1580–1661) and Gordon of Rothiemay (1617–86), as well as Gordon of Auchleuchries, one of Imperial Russia's most famous generals (see above, p. 166). In 1903, Gordon historian Capt. Douglas Wimberley wrote that '[t]he Gordons of Dauch or Gauch, of Elrig, of Bank of Corinacy, and of Pyke are, I understand, all related to one another, and claim to be descended from the Pitlurg Gordons'.[626]

Though more populous in the seventeenth century than now, the Cabrach was already considered distant and desolate when the famed poet Arthur Johnston (c.1579–1641) chided his well-educated friend Sir John Gordon of Craig and Auchindoir for spending all his time in the Cabrach:

Why, O Gordon, are you thus glued to the Cabrach's heather,
Hiding away far from the city, among rocks and caves?
What good is it to have conquered Minerva in wit,
If thus you allow your gifts of the mind to rust unused?
You have lurked there nearly five years, seeing nothing
But wild animals, deaf rocks, the birds of the air.
You have nobody who can utter or answer an educated voice,
Or who is able to learn anything from you.
The people are entirely barbarian, the land is stark,
It is always raining, and even in the Dog-Days, it is mired in snow.

According to Douglas Wimberley, the famine years of the 1690s lasted somewhat longer in the Cabrach than elsewhere – i.e., from 1693 to 1700 – and the area experienced 'almost absolute depopulation'. However, 'some . . . who had removed elsewhere returned' as soon as the famine ended.[627]

As of 1747, Glengairn was the principal route by which cattle stolen on Deeside were transported to Speyside. When stealing cattle from Lowland Banffshire, on the other hand, the thieves would drive them through the Cabrach and Glenbuchat to Strathdon, 'by Inchrory and into Glen Aven and so westward to the hills of Speyside and beyond . . . [T]he men who plied this trade were well accustomed to long marches and dangerous living'.[628] Witnesses against these marauders were hard to come by. Victims also hesitated to bring legal actions, which cost an average £25 sterling, or five-eighths of the net worth of the average potential claimant.[629] The government's serious, and largely successful efforts to stamp out Speyside cattle-rustling, aided by the new military roads, seem to have begun in earnest in 1744.[630] By 1766, a large section of the rustling community had gone legitimate, and transformed cattle-droving into a large and prosperous trade. However – as with distilling after 1823 – a hard core of desperadoes assiduously maintained their underground network, which was readily adapted to the smuggling of articles other than stolen cattle. The Cabrach remained as important a route for the legal cattle traders as it had been for the thieves.[631]

All was not crime, of course. Peter Scott in Milton of Cabrach established a 'Mutual Instruction Class' in 1852. The members sought to educate each other in such topics as meteorology and the 'Elevation of the Working Classes', with new essays and other writings by the membership appearing at a rate of more than one per week.[632] Poetry was a popular Cabrach activity, and not just for the Mutual Instructors. On one occasion, the post office was given a letter with the following 'address':

> The Cabrach is the parish, and Milton is the toun
> And Robie Robson is the man, a handsome clever loon
> Now, Charlie, man, tak' care o' me, and ye shall never want,
> Hae me up to the Haugh o' Glass, gie me to Peter Grant,
> And Peter, man, ye ken yersel' that I gae by Dummeth,
> Sae never lose a gripe o' me, till ye gang past Forteith,
> And leave nae me at Drywells, Boghead, nor yet the Mains,
> But gie me unto Rob himsel', or ane o' Milton's weans.[633]

In the early nineteenth century, the only postman to serve Cabrach did so in a purely private capacity: James Sheed, servant at the manse, went nine miles each way to Rhynie for letters, once per week, for many years. The other Cabrach residents rewarded him with a large purse of money in the spring of 1847.[634] Lest this activity alone were not proof of Sheed's physical strength, he took seventh prize in a ploughing competition two years after his retirement.[635] There was also a carrier between Cabrach and Aberdeen, who served in that capacity for fifteen and a half years before emigrating to America in 1855.[636]

Lt James Taylor, farmer in Dalriach, Cabrach, was drowned in floods on the way to his farm in December 1848.[637] On the same occasion, the Deveron's 'mighty noise',

> dashing upon the rocks, seemed to be mocked and hushed in silence
> by the rival element, which drifted the spray like the billows of the
> mighty ocean in a raging storm. The fields were strewed with the
> wreck of stack-yards . . . a scene of destruction never witnessed in this

*Carrier in the Den of Kildrummy, c.1900. An inadequate railway system ensured that many places in this region would go directly from horse-drawn carts to petrol engines without passing through the steam age at all.*

*James Davidson making a delivery to the farm famously named Lost, 1920s.*

quarter . . . houses unroofed . . . windows were blown in . . . The wooden bridge over the Deveron, at Lesmurdie, was raised from its resting place and tossed into the river. Scarcely a bee hive escaped.[638]

In the winter of 1859–60, snow drifts were up to fourteen feet deep, burying flocks, and the conditions of travel were widely and bitterly complained of. Cabrach was by this time officially the poorest parish in Aberdeenshire, with a valuation of £1,105. The only other parish in the county valued at less than £2,000 was neighbouring Glenbuchat (£1,187). At the same date, sixteen parishes in the shire were worth over £10,000.[639] Nonetheless, the honesty of Cabrach's inhabitants was the stuff of legend: James McCombie, merchant in Crofthead, reported in 1860 that he had recently been repaid (with interest) a sixpence owed to his father – who died in 1846.[640] Nor did the poverty of the land mean that the inhabitants were cash poor; one Cabrach cattle dealer, who 'had been drinking, and could tell very little about the matter', was pickpocketed of £275 at Rhynie Fair – in modern terms between £20,000 and £170,000.[641]

Briefly, Cabrach's staple product was sold openly. Richard Smith, grocer at 86 Broad Street, Aberdeen, advertised 'Cabrach and Glenlivat WHISKY' alongside coffee, London porter, candles, sugar, pickles and fish sauces in the *Aberdeen Journal* on 18 October 1826.[642] In the same issue, Charles Fyfe & Co. proclaimed their stock of whisky 'equal to the best Smuggled'; subsequently they claimed to be selling 'very fine' Cabrach whisky to other dealers, 'at the Distillers' prices'.[643] An 1829 meeting of the Elsick Farmers' Society debated,

*Urn in Burnside of Delgaty, Turriff, following blizzards in January 2010. (Photo by Eleanor MacCannell)*

but failed to settle, the question of 'whether the Cabrach and Glenlivat whisky, which they some years since were in the practice of receiving, or the Glenury, which they were then drinking, was preferable in toddy'.[644] Later the same year, William Clark's shop at 8 King Street, Aberdeen was selling 'Fine Malt Whisky' for 8s 6d a gallon, but Cabrach whisky for 10s 6d a gallon – a twenty-four per cent premium.[645] A month later, Clark added merely 'Good' whisky to his repertoire, at 6s 6d to 7s 6d a gallon, while the prices for 'Fine' and Cabrach remained unchanged.[646]

Access to so much whisky had its dark side, of course. In 1822, William Gordon, forty-five, a 'respectable' and highly literate native of Cabrach, was convicted of murdering his wife with scissors while both of them were so intoxicated as to be incapable of reason. Despite petitions to the throne, both by Gordon himself and by 'many people of considerable influence, both in town and country', he was hanged in Aberdeen on 31 May.[647]

A very funny poem was produced in 1917 in aid of the Gordon Highlanders' Prisoners of War Fund. Written by John Mitchell and reprinted several times, it was called *Tibby Tamson o' the Buck: or, a Cabrach Wife's Views on Things in General*, price 2d. Entirely in dialect, it is a curious but still-familiar mixture of bloodthirsty patriotism and suspicion of the British establishment.

> An' Jock's a wicked, wittrous wratch, that aye cud stan' his grun',
> An' just the contermashous kin' that likes a fecht for fun;
> But noo wi' medals on his breest an' strips upo' his airm,
> He'll fecht his battles ower again gaun pottrin' roon the fairm.
> An' if ye e'er sit fit aroon the Shoother o' the Buck,
> Jist speer your wye to Bodiebae – you're welcome to pot-luck;
> An' tho I dinna haud wi' drink or biblin aye ower drams,
> I keep a knaggie in the press for incomes, stounes, and dwaums;
> An' ower a blaw o' Bogie an' a skirp o' barley-bree
> Ye'll hear the story o' the war fae Sergeant John MacPhee . . .
> They've commandeert the tatties, an' they've commandeert the hay,
> They've commandeert the corn an' meal, forbyes the neeps and strae,
> They've commandeert the fusky that keeps oot the caul an' wet
> If they commandeert some common-sense, we'd get tae Berlin yet.[648]

# FURTHER READING

In my opinion, the best starting points for a more in-depth investigation of this region include John Pratt's *Buchan* (1858); Marshall B. Lang's *The Story of a Parish* (1897), regarding Meldrum; John Wilken's *Ellon in Bygone Days* (1921); James McBey's *The Early Life of James McBey* (1977), regarding Newburgh; Charles McKean's *Banff and Buchan: An Illustrated Architectural Guide* (1990); Richard Oram *et al.*'s *Historic Fraserburgh* (2010); and Banff Preservation Society's *The Book of Banff* (2009). The impending publication of David Walker's *The Buildings of Scotland: North Aberdeenshire* (Yale University Press) is highly anticipated, and I am grateful to David for his learned advice, especially regarding Huntly Castle and the towns of Huntly and Peterhead.

Though they cover a significantly wider area, I can also highly recommend David Ferguson's *Shipwrecks of North East Scotland* (1992); Colin Martin's *Scotland's Historic Shipwrecks* (1998); and Angus Martin's *Fishing and Whaling* (1995). For those interested in a particular rural area, the *Old Statistical Account* and *New Statistical Account* are almost uniformly helpful. Some *OSA* entries, for example Kirkmichael and Peterhead, are very engagingly written and nearly of book length. One you might want to avoid, however, is the *OSA* for Forbes and Kearn, whose author was clearly mad.[649]

In a lesser tier of excellence, but still useful, are William Temple's *The Thanage of Fermartyn* (1894) and A.I. McConnochie's *Donside* (1900).

For additional reading suggestions, please refer to the endnotes.

# ACKNOWLEDGEMENTS

I would like to thank all of the personnel of the Royal Commission on the Ancient and Historical Monuments of Scotland who helped me in the research for this project. I would also particularly like to thank Eleanor MacCannell, Barry Robertson, Alison Hay, Peter Davidson, Jane Stevenson, Sir Moir Lockhead, Anna Brown, Rae and Ellie Younger, David Butler, David Walker, Alistair Mason, Julian Watson, Finlay Lockie, Kirsten McKenzie, Marc and Karen Ellington, Dean and Juliet MacCannell, Vicky Dawson, Andrew Simmons, Paul Dukes, Stuart Petrie, Steve Sillett, Neil Sheed, Phyllis Goodall, Paul Hambelton, Lindsay Milligan Dombrowski, Chloe Ross, Dan Wall, Davy Shanks, Chris Fenton and the Underwater Archaeological Society of British Columbia, Peter Donaldson and all the volunteers and staff of the Grampian Transport Museum, the Alford History Group, and all the empoyees of the National Library of Scotland, Aberdeen City Library, Aboyne Library, the National Archives at Kew, the Library of Congress, the British Museum and Aberdeen University. Any errors in the book are, however, my responsibility alone.

# NOTES

CHAPTER 1

1 Charles McKean, *Banff and Buchan: An Illustrated Architectural Guide* (Edinburgh, 1990), p. 4.
2 *New Statistical Account* of 1834–45 (hereafter '*NSA*') for Aberdour.
3 John B. Pratt, *Buchan* (Aberdeen, Edinburgh and London, 1858), p. 24.
4 Skene manuscript 'E', quoted in William Forbes Skene, ed., *Memorials of the Family of Skene of Skene* (Aberdeen, 1887), p. 137.
5 McKean, *Banff and Buchan*, p. 3.
6 The one exception appears to have been the 26th Foot (Cameronians), who elected a Presbyterian elder from each company. However, the 26th gained few if any recruits from up here.
7 James McBey, *The Early Life of James McBey: An Autobiography 1883–1911*, ed. Nicholas Barker (Oxford, 1977), pp. 8, 9, 22.
8 McBey, *Early Life*, p. 6.
9 McKean, *Banff and Buchan*, p. 3.
10 *NSA* for Crimond.
11 *Old Statistical Account* of 1791–99 (hereafter '*OSA*') for Cullen.
12 McKean, *Banff and Buchan*, p. 87.
13 *OSA* for Mortlach.
14 Pratt, *Buchan*, p. 37.
15 Richard Pococke, bishop of Meath, *Tours in Scotland 1747, 1750, 1760*, ed. Daniel William Kemp (Edinburgh, 1887), p. 197.
16 *OSA* for Aberdour.
17 *OSA* for Peterhead.
18 *Barbour's Bruce*, ed. M.P. McDiarmid and J.A.C. Stevenson (Edinburgh, 1980–85), pp. 221–22.
19 G. Donaldson, 'Scotland's Conservative North in the Sixteenth and Seventeenth Centuries', *Transactions of the Royal Historical Society*, fifth ser., vol. 16 (1966), pp. 65–79, p. 67.
20 R.D. Oram *et al.*, *Historic Fraserburgh: Archaeology and Development* (Oxford, York and Edinburgh, 2010), p. 45.

CHAPTER 2

21 Alan Young, 'The Earls and Earldom of Buchan in the Thirteenth Century', in G.W.S. Barrow and Alexander Grant, eds., *Medieval Scotland: Crown, Lordship and Community* (Edinburgh, 1998), p. 183.
22 Thomas Mair, *Records of the Parish of Ellon* (Aberdeen and Edinburgh, 1876), p. 1.
23 Ellon Burgh Council, *Ellon, Aberdeenshire: The Official Guide* (Cheltenham and London, 1952), p. 9.
24 *NSA* for Logie-Buchan.
25 *NSA* for Logie-Buchan.
26 Pratt, *Buchan*, pp. 7–8.
27 Alexander Grant, 'Thanes and Thanages, from the Eleventh to the Fourteenth Centuries', in Barrow and Grant, eds., *Medieval Scotland*, p. 46.
28 Banff Preservation and Heritage Society, *The Book of Banff: Royal and Ancient Burgh* (Wellington, Somerset, 2009), p. 14.
29 William Donaldson's introduction to Gavin Greig, *Logie o' Buchan: An Aberdeenshire Pastoral* (Aberdeen, 1985 {1899}), p. v.
30 *OSA* for Alvah.
31 *NSA* for Pitsligo, but see also *OSA* for Tyrie.
32 Christopher Harvie, in *Scotland and Nationalism* (Abingdon and New York, 2004), claims there were 150, which may include failures; the more conservative figure is from J.R. Coull's more detailed *The Evolution*

*of Settlement in the Buchan District of Aberdeenshire Since the Late Sixteenth Century* (Aberdeen, 1984).

33 *OSA* for Rathven.
34 McKean, *Banff and Buchan*, p. 5.
35 Quoted in McKean, *Banff and Buchan*, pp. 96–97.
36 Pratt, *Buchan*, p. 39.
37 So spelled in 1685: Records of the Parliament of Scotland (hereafter RPS) 1685/4/92 .
38 Coull, *Evolution of Settlement*, 33.
39 Coull, *Evolution of Settlement*, 28, 33, quotation at 28.
40 *OSA* for Lonmay.
41 Coull, *Evolution of Settlement*, 30.
42 Coull, *Evolution of Settlement*, 33.
43 *OSA* for Slains and Forvie.
44 Coull, *Evolution of Settlement*, 35.
45 *NSA* for Slains.
46 It is very frequently claimed that New Slains was the inspiration for Dracula's castle. Be that as it may, Stoker wrote a novel actually set in Cruden Bay, called *The Mystery of the Sea* (New York, 1902) which describes the castle's surroundings as 'as wild and rocky a bit of coast as any one could wish to see. Behind Slains runs in a long narrow inlet with beetling cliffs, sheer on either side, and at its entrance a wild turmoil of rocks are hurled together in titanic confusion': p. 408.
47 James Grant, ed., *The Old Scots Navy from 1689 to 1710* (London, 1914), p. xiv.
48 Keith M. Brown, *Noble Power in Scotland from the Reformation to the Revolution* (Edinburgh, 2011), p. 144.
49 *Some Considerations on the Present State of Scotland* (Edinburgh: W. Sands, 28 March 1744), p. 19.
50 'The yawl's crews are old men, who fish near the shore, if possible.' *OSA* for Rathven.
51 *OSA* for Rathven.
52 Alex M. McAldowie, 'Personal Experiences in Witchcraft', *Folklore* Vol. 7, No. 3 (Sep. 1896), pp. 309–14, at p. 313.
53 *NSA* for Peterhead.
54 *OSA* for Longside.
55 http://en.wikipedia.org/wiki/Rosehearty – which wisely marks this passage 'citation needed'!
56 http://www.portknockiewebsite.co.uk/knocker/Autumn_2003.pdf
57 *OSA* for Cullen.
58 *OSA* for Slains.
59 *OSA* for Rathven.
60 David M. Ferguson, *Shipwrecks of North East Scotland* (Edinburgh, 1992), p. 1.
61 Richard Hakluyt, quoted in Ferguson, *Shipwrecks*, p. 6.
62 Ferguson, *Shipwrecks*, p. 9.
63 Ferguson, *Shipwrecks*, p. 11.
64 *OSA* for Crimond.
65 *NSA* for Crimond.
66 *OSA* for Foveran.
67 Robert Smith, *Buchan Land of Plenty* (Edinburgh, 1996), pp. 22, 25–26.
68 Pratt, *Buchan*, p. 26.
69 Ferguson, *Shipwrecks*, p. 7.
70 Pratt, *Buchan*, p. 55.
71 See *Scotland's Historic Shipwrecks* by Colin Martin (London, 1998).
72 Ferguson, *Shipwrecks*, p. 27.
73 McBey, *Early Life*, p. 13.
74 McBey, *Early Life*, p. 3.
75 Angus Martin, *Fishing and Whaling* (Edinburgh, 1995), p. 56
76 http://www.scran.ac.uk/packs/exhibitions/learning_materials/webs/40/boiling.htm
77 *NSA* for Longside.
78 http://www.scran.ac.uk/packs/exhibitions/learning_materials/webs/40/timeline.htm. Some other sources claim there were thirty-two Peterhead whaling ships in 1857.
79 Martin, *Fishing and Whaling*, p. 14.
80 Daniel Defoe asserted in the 1720s that there was already an important international trade in Buchan herring at that time, but if it indeed existed, all observers of a century later seem to have been unaware of it.
81 Martin, *Fishing and Whaling*, p. 20.
82 McBey, *Early Life*, p. 49.
83 Martin, *Fishing and Whaling*, p. 74.
84 Smith, *Buchan Land of Plenty*, p. 8.
85 Samuel Smiles, *Life of a Scotch Naturalist* (London, 1901), p. v.
86 *Banffshire Journal* article, quoted in *Book of Banff*, p. 81.
87 *OSA* for Peterhead.
88 *OSA* for Peterhead.
89 Pococke, *Tours in Scotland*, p. 197.
90 *OSA* for Peterhead.
91 *NSA* for Peterhead.
92 *OSA* for Turriff.
93 *OSA* for Strathdon.

94  *OSA* for Strathdon.
95  *OSA* for Foveran.
96  *NSA* for St Fergus.
97  *NSA* for Methlick.
98  *NSA* for Turriff.
99  *NSA* for Ellon.
100  *NSA* for Old Deer.
101  *OSA* for Peterhead.
102  *OSA* for Cullen.
103  *OSA* for Monquhitter. The *NSA* for the same parish denied that the original linen manufactory was 'dropt', claiming, 'it has been kept up ever since'.
104  Pococke, *Tours*, p. 194.
105  *OSA* for Grange.
106  *OSA* for Monquhitter.
107  *OSA* for Kirkmichael.
108  http://canmore.rcahms.gov.uk/en/site/18499/details/lintmill+of+boyne/
109  *NSA* for Deskford.
110  *OSA* for Keith. In the 1730s there was also an extensive trade in a cloth called 'white web', but declining standards of quality caused demand to collapse: *OSA* for King Edward. As well as flax, the women of Crimond spun tow, which was made 'into a coarse kind of narrow cloth, called *harn,* which labouring people use for shirts . . . [and] a still coarser kind, which is made into bags for carrying grain': *OSA* for Crimond.
111  *NSA* for Turriff.
112  *NSA* for Boharm.
113  Perhaps confusing cause with effect, Edmund Spenser famously claimed that 'nothing doth sooner cause civility in any country than many market towns': *A View of the Present State of Ireland*, ed. W.L. Renwick (Oxford, 1970), pp. 164–65.
114  Quoted in Smith, *Buchan Land of Plenty*, pp. 79–80.
115  Harvie, *Scotland and Nationalism*, p. 50.
116  *OSA* for Rothiemay.
117  *OSA* for Turriff.
118  *NSA* for Longside.
119  *OSA* for Marnoch.
120  *OSA* for Alvah.
121  *NSA* for Alvah.
122  *NSA* for Ordiquhill.
123  *NSA* for Meldrum.
124  *OSA* for Monquhitter.
125  *OSA* for Longside. Across the region, ideas of how big a 'croft' might be varied considerably, from six to as much as thirty acres.
126  John Wilken, *Ellon in Bygone Days* (Peterhead, 1921), p. 23.
127  Scottish Enterprise and Aberdeenshire Council, 'Agriculture in Aberdeenshire: looking to the future', http://www.aberdeenshire.gov.uk/support/agriculture/agriculture__in__aberdeenshire__ summary.pdf, accessed 28 February 2012.
128  *OSA* for Tyrie.
129  *NSA* for Peterhead.
130  *NSA* for Pitsligo.
131  *OSA* for Forglen.
132  *NSA* for Alvah.
133  *OSA* for Auchterless.
134  *OSA* for Inveraven.
135  *OSA* for Marnoch.
136  *Book of Banff,* p. 27.
137  *NSA* for Cruden.
138  *NSA* for Gartly.
139  *OSA* for Rothiemay.
140  *OSA* for Turriff.
141  *NSA* for Old Deer.
142  *OSA* for Aberdour.
143  *OSA* for Aberdour.
144  *OSA* for Tyrie.
145  *NSA* for Alvah.
146  *NSA* for Strathdon.
147  *OSA* for Pistligo; *NSA* for Tyrie; Pratt, *Buchan*, p. 22.
148  *Report by Thomas Tucker Upon the Settlement of the Revenues of Excise and Customs in Scotland* (1656; first printed Edinburgh, 1825), p. 15.
149  *OSA* for Forglen.
150  John Swinton, *A Proposal for Uniformity of Weights and Measures in Scotland, By execution of the Laws now in force* (Edinburgh, 1789), p. 39. Legislators had attempted to reform the system in 1661, 1685 and 1707, and would do so again in 1824, but informal use of some of these measures lasted into recent times.

151 A hundredweight of 112 pounds could be divided into an exact number of fourteen-pound stones, whereas a 100-pound hundredweight could not.
152 Oram *et al.*, *Historic Fraserburgh*, p. 158.
153 Scottish Law Commission, *Report on Feudal Tenure* (Edinburgh, 1999), p. 5, quoted in Scottish Parliament Research Paper 00/09, 3 May 2000, p. 12.
154 *OSA* for Deskford.
155 Scottish Archive Network catalogue, single person code NA7972 (Statute Labour Trustees). The system was later extended to British colonies including Prince Edward Island.
156 *OSA* for each of the parishes mentioned in brackets.
157 *OSA* for Keith.
158 Scottish Archive Network catalogue, single person code NA7972 (Statute Labour Trustees).
159 *Report by Thomas Tucker*, p. 11.
160 *OSA* for Turriff.
161 *OSA* for Udny.
162 *OSA* for Turriff. In neighbouring King Edward at the same date, the combination of multures and payment-in-kind meant that thirty-one per cent of all rent was payable in meal.
163 *OSA* for Rayne.
164 Aberdeen Sheriff Court Records, vol. 2, p. 372.
165 Aberdeen Sheriff Court Records, vol. 2, p. 375.
166 AUL MS 3,175/M (II)/A33, dated March 1742.
167 *OSA* for Grange.
168 *OSA* for Rothiemay.
169 *Book of Banff*, p. 67.
170 Untitled review of *The Pattern under the Plough* by George Ewart Evans, *Folklore* , Vol. 78, No. 1 (Spring, 1967), pp. 67–69, quotations at p. 69.
171 James Porter, 'The Folklore of Northern Scotland: Five Discourses on Cultural Representation', *Folklore*, Vol. 109 (1998), pp. 1–14, p. 6.
172 *OSA* for Keith.
173 *OSA* for Cabrach.
174 The medieval *twal'-owsen pleugh* was never painted, which allowed rainwater penetration to increase its already great weight.
175 *OSA* for Mortlach.
176 *OSA* for Grange.
177 Pratt, *Buchan*, p. 18.
178 *OSA* for Forglen.
179 *NSA* for Lonmay.
180 *NSA* for Turriff.
181 http://www.bbc.co.uk/news/uk-17311542
182 *Book of Banff*, p. 51.
183 *Book of Banff*, p. 51.
184 Marshall B. Lang, *The Story of a Parish, Being a Short Account of Meldrum and Its Ministers* (Aberdeen, 1897), p. 21.
185 *OSA* for Rathen.
186 *OSA* for Clatt.
187 S.W. Sillett, *Illicit Scotch* (Aberdeen, 1965), pp. 59–60.
188 *Book of Banff*, p. 61.
189 *NSA* for Grange.
190 *NSA* for Turriff.
191 Pratt, *Buchan*, p. 31.
192 1851 Census of the UK.
193 http://www.bbc.co.uk/news/uk-scotland-north-east-orkney-shetland-12633678
194 http://www.aberdeencity.gov.uk/council__government/equality__and__diversity/pos __gypsy.asp
195 *Book of Banff*, p. 23.
196 Oxford *Dictionary of National Biography* online edition (hereafter *DNB*).
197 This title became extinct in 1803.
198 *Aberdeen Journal* no. 4,868, 28 April 1841.
199 *Book of Banff*, p. 48.
200 *Book of Banff*, p. 25.
201 'The witchcraft act of 1563', in Lawrence Normand and Gareth Roberts, eds., *Witchcraft in Early Modern Scotland* (Exeter, 2000), p. 89.
202 *OSA* for Banff.
203 *OSA* for Kirkmichael.
204 Pococke, *Tours in Scotland*, p. 194.
205 *NSA* for Ellon.
206 *NSA* for Turriff.
207 Lang, *Story of a Parish*, pp. 6, 12, 14.
208 Lang, *Story of a Parish*, p. 9.
209 Lang, *Story of a Parish*, p. 13.
210 Lang, *Story of a Parish*, p. 13.
211 http://www.abdn.ac.uk/slavery/banner7.htm

212  *NSA* for Strathdon.
213  McKean, *Banff and Buchan*, p. 88.
214  *Book of Banff*, p. 38.
215  William Temple, *The Thanage of Fermartyn* (Aberdeen, 1894), pp. 498–99; Mair, *Records of the Parish of Ellon*, pp. 166–67.
216  Temple, *Fermartyn*, p. 499.
217  Temple, *Fermartyn*, p. 500.
218  Temple, *Fermartyn*, p. 503.
219  http://canmore.rcahms.gov.uk/en/site/266031/details/kinmuck+friend+s+cottage+north+wing/
220  *DNB.*
221  *DNB.*
222  *DNB.*
223  *DNB.*
224  *OSA* for Strathdon.
225  *OSA* for Grange.
226  *OSA* for Forbes and Kearn.
227  *NSA* for Alvah.
228  *NSA* for Glenbuchat.
229  *Book of Banff*, p. 55.
230  *NSA* for Peterhead.
231  *NSA* for Lonmay.
232  *OSA* for Botriphnie.
233  *OSA* for Fyvie.
234  John Mason, 'Scottish Charity Schools of the Eighteenth Century', *Scottish Historical Review* 33(115) (Apr. 1954), pp. 1–13, p. 1.
235  *OSA* for Turriff.
236  *NSA* for Turriff.
237  *OSA* for Aberdour.
238  *OSA* and *NSA* for Logie-Buchan, quotation from *OSA*.
239  *OSA* for Cullen.
240  *NSA* for Meldrum.
241  Wilken, *Ellon in Bygone Days*, p. 16.
242  Temple, *Fermartyn*, p. 481.
243  Sillett, *Illicit Scotch*, pp. 50–51.
244  Temple, *Fermartyn*, p. 481.
245  Quoted in Oram *et al.*, *Historic Fraserburgh*, p. 33.
246  'Ferm, Ferme, Farholme, or Fairholm, Charles (1566–1617)', *DNB* print edition of 1885–1900, Vol. 18.
247  Oram *et al.*, *Historic Fraserburgh*, p. 33.
248  Oram *et al.*, *Historic Fraserburgh*, p. 34.
249  *OSA* for Fraserburgh; Oram *et al.*, *Historic Fraserburgh*, p. 35; quotation from *OSA*.
250  Oram *et al.*, *Historic Fraserburgh*, p. 36.
251  Oram *et al.*, *Historic Fraserburgh*, p. 34.
252  Oram *et al.*, *Historic Fraserburgh*, p. 139.
253  Oram *et al.*, *Historic Fraserburgh*, p. 11.

CHAPTER 3

254  *OSA* for Auchterless.
255  McAldowie, 'Personal Experiences in Witchcraft', p. 312.
256  *OSA* for Tullynessle and Forbes.
257  *OSA* for Rhynie and Essie.
258  *NSA* for Marnoch.
259  *OSA* for New Deer.
260  *NSA* for Peterhead.
261  Pratt, *Buchan*, p. 33n.
262  Pratt, *Buchan*, p. 39.
263  *OSA* for Inveraven.
264  *OSA* for Keith.
265  *NSA* for Belhelvie.
266  *NSA* for Tarves.
267  *NSA* for Gartly.
268  *NSA* for Fyvie.
269  *OSA* for Rathven.
270  *NSA* for Meldrum.
271  *NSA* for Deskford.
272  *NSA* for Alvah.
273  *OSA* for Rathven.
274  *OSA* for Clatt.
275  *OSA* for Cullen.

276 Pococke, *Tours*, p. 195.
277 *OSA* for Banff.
278 *Book of Banff*, p. 20.
279 *NSA* for Inveraven.
280 *NSA* for Auchterless.
281 Pratt, *Buchan*, p. 17.
282 *OSA* for Kirkmichael.
283 *OSA* for Alvah.
284 *NSA* for Alvah.
285 http://canmore.rcahms.gov.uk/en/site/20861/details/foveran+chapel+of+the+holy+rood/
286 *NSA* for Turriff.
287 *OSA* for Gartly.
288 *NSA* for Aberdour.
289 McKean, *Banff and Buchan*, p. 72.
290 *NSA* for Fyvie.
291 *OSA* for Slains.
292 Lang, *Story of a Parish*, p. 7.
293 *OSA* and *NSA* for these four parishes; quotation is from *NSA* for Strichen.
294 *NSA* for Crimond.
295 *NSA* for Marnoch.
296 *NSA* for Gartly.
297 McKean, *Banff and Buchan*, p. 38.
298 A.I. McConnochie, ed., *The Book of Ellon* (Ellon, 1901), p. 194.
299 *NSA* for Tarves.
300 *OSA* for Deskford.
301 *NSA* for Strichen.
302 Alexander Fenton and Bruce Walker, *The Rural Architecture of Scotland* (Edinburgh, 1981), p. 65.
303 Fenton and Walker, *Rural Architecture*, pp. 65, 67, 68.
304 *OSA* for Turriff.
305 Mair, *Records of the Parish of Ellon*, p. 152.
306 *Ellon, Aberdeenshire: The Official Guide*, p. 9.
307 http://canmore.rcahms.gov.uk/en/site/20878/details/moot+hill+mains+of+ardiffery/
308 *OSA* for Strathdon.
309 *NSA* for Strathdon.
310 *OSA* for Forglen.
311 William George Black, *The Scots Mercat 'Cross': an Inquiry into its History and Meaning* (Glasgow and Edinburgh, 1928), p. 16; Craig Mair, *Mercat Cross and Tolbooth: Understanding Scotland's Old Burghs* (Edinburgh, 1988), pp. 52–55.
312 http://canmore.rcahms.gov.uk/en/site/17655/details/clatt+market+cross/
313 http://canmore.rcahms.gov.uk/en/site/20342/details/newburgh+market+cross/
314 http://canmore.rcahms.gov.uk/en/site/18884/details/inverurie+market+cross/
315 Oram *et al.*, *Historic Fraserburgh*, p. 81.
316 McKean, *Banff and Buchan*, p. 37.
317 Oram et al., *Historic Fraserburgh*, p. 36.
318 Pococke, *Tours in Scotland*, p. 197.
319 http://canmore.rcahms.gov.uk/en/site/21192/details/peterhead+harbour+street+wine+well/
320 *Book of Banff*, p. 24.
321 Wilken, *Ellon in Bygone Days*, p. 18.
322 Wilken, *Ellon in Bygone Days*, p. 18.
323 Wilken, *Ellon in Bygone Days*, p. 20.
324 McConnochie, ed., *Book of Ellon*, pp. 196–97.
325 *OSA* for Banff.
326 *NSA* for Turriff.
327 'History for sale as Maud Mart is auctioned off', the *Scotsman* online, 27 September 2003.
328 *OSA* for Kirkmichael.
329 *NSA* for Monquhitter.
330 Smith, *Buchan Land of Plenty*, p. 20.
331 McKean, *Banff and Buchan*, p. 118.
332 http://canmore.rcahms.gov.uk/en/site/20361/details/castle+of+esslemont/
333 McKean, *Banff and Buchan*, p. 80.
334 http://canmore.rcahms.gov.uk/en/site/18128/details/dunnideer/
335 Smith, *Buchan Land of Plenty*, p. 32.
336 Letter of Major James Dundas of Halkett's Regiment to Thomas Forbes III of Waterton, 20 October 1748; printed in full in Anon., *Memoranda of the Family of Forbes of Waterton* (Aberdeen, 1857), p. 49.
337 Article reprinted in full in *William and Mary Quarterly*, 3rd Ser., 22(4) (1965), p. 653.
338 http://canmore.rcahms.gov.uk/en/site/19299/details/castle+of+cullen+of+buchan/
339 *OSA* for Grange.
340 *NSA* for Tarves.
341 James Imlach, *History of Banff* (Banff, 1868), p. 13.
342 William Cramond, ed., *The Annals of Banff* (Aberdeen, 1891), vol. 1, p. 94.

343 http://canmore.rcahms.gov.uk/en/site/19149/details/turriff+castle+rainy/
344 The medieval period did have its equivalent of the lairds' houses of the seventeenth century, but only three of these 'Ha' Hooses' have survived from before 1350. These are Rait Castle in Nairnshire; Morton Castle, Dumfriesshire; and Tulliallan in Fife. But these three probably only survive because they are 'the most elegant and well-built examples of what was once a much larger group of broadly similar buildings constructed of less durable materials', such as wattle-and-daub (known in Aberdeenshire as stake-and-rice), timber, and/or clay: John G. Dunbar, *The Historic Architecture of Scotland* (London, 1966), pp. 33–35, quotations at p. 35.
345 Dunbar, *Historic Architecture*, p. 65.
346 Dunbar, *Historic Architecture*, pp. 66, 67; the lateness of the use of both in Leslie Castle, Aberdeenshire in 1661 is absolutely extraordinary. By 1701, Scotland's first 'retro' or mock-castle, Lochryan House, had been constructed in Wigtownshire.
347 Dunbar, *Historic Architecture*, pp. 68 and 77–78.
348 Dunbar, *Historic Architecture*, pp. 71, 75.
349 The following link is provided as a condition of publication: http://www.geograph.org.uk/photo/672370
350 Dunbar, *Historic Architecture*, p. 81.
351 McKean, *Banff and Buchan*, p. 78.
352 David MacGibbon and Thomas Ross, *The Castellated and Domestic Architecture of Scotland* (Edinburgh, 1887), vol. 2, p. 463.
353 Dunbar, *Historic Architecture*, p. 84. Further evidence of Dunbar's bias is shown by his conceding, in the case of Dunbarney House, Perthshire, only that it was probably built before 1752. RCAHMS, in contrast, states unequivocally that Dunbarney is from the seventeenth century.
354 Sheila Forman, *Scottish Country Houses and Castles* (Glasgow and London, 1967), p. 34.
355 George Scott-Moncrieff, 'Introduction', in Forman, *Scottish Country Houses*, pp. 3–5, p. 5.
356 Forman, *Scottish Country Houses*, pp. 23–24.
357 For instance, Ranald MacInnes, Miles Glendinning and Aonghas MacKechnie, *Building a Nation: The Story of Scotland's Architecture* (Edinburgh, 1999) and James Macaulay, *The Classical Country House in Scotland 1660–1800* (London, 1987). It perhaps goes without saying that Scotland has been given short shrift within the history of British architecture as a whole, as Macaulay points out: *ibid.*, p. xxi. See also Frank Arneil Walker, 'Tradition and discontinuity in architectural heritage', *Architectural Heritage* 11 (2000), pp. 80–90, p. 85; Ranald MacInnes, Miles Glendinning and Aonghas MacKechnie, *Building a Nation: The Story of Scotland's Architecture* (Edinburgh, 1999), p. 41. The beginning of the period is difficult to determine precisely, except to say that Glamis Castle (as remodelled 1670) and Sir William Bruce's first house design, Balcaskie (also 1670), were in an older idiom; while Bruce's designs for Dunkeld House (1676) and Moncreiffe House (1679) were in the style we are discussing. His Leslie House (1672) and Thirlestane (1673; spoiled by baronialisation 1841) occupy an uncomfortable middle position. Quotation is from Macaulay, *ibid.*, p. xxii.
358 Oram *et al.*, *Historic Fraserburgh*, p. 135.
359 Smith, *Buchan Land of Plenty*, p. 55.
360 Smith, *Buchan Land of Plenty*, p. 51.
361 http://canmore.rcahms.gov.uk/en/site/20825/details/boyndlie+house/
362 McKean, *Banff and Buchan*, p. 100.
363 Buildings at Risk Register for Scotland, item 1,367.
364 McKean, *Banff and Buchan*, p. 47.
365 McKean, *Banff and Buchan*, p. 63.
366 W. Douglas Simpson, 'Lesmoir Castle and the Church of Essie: with some additional notes on Auchindoir', *PSAS*, 14 December 1931, pp. 86–101, p. 90. The assertion that the castle was first built in 1508 is unconfirmed: *ibid.*, p. 91.
367 Simpson, 'Lesmoir Castle', p. 91.
368 Simpson, 'Lesmoir Castle', p. 94.
369 He had been a student at Marischal College, Aberdeen from 1722 to 1726 and remained in the Cabrach for seven years, thereafter spending the rest of his life in Auldearn.
370 *Miscellany of the Spalding Club, Vol. 4* (Aberdeen, 1849), pp. 279–80. He might also have been the 'Younge Harthill' who leased Quhythillock, Cabrach, from 1601–1605.
371 Cassilis, *Rulers of Strathspey* (Inverness, 1911), pp. 100–101.
372 References are included in Patrick Gordon, *Britane's Distemper*; Sir William Fraser, *The Melvilles, Earls of Melville, and the Leslies, Earls of Leven*, vol. 2; *Act. Parl. Scot.*, vol. 6 pt. 1; *Act. Parl. Scot.*, vol. 6 pt. 2; and W. Gordon, *History of the Family of Gordon*.
373 In J.M. Bulloch, *The House of Gordon* (Aberdeen, 1903), vol. 2.
374 *Aberdeen Journal* No. 616 (Tue. 30 October 1759), p. 2.
375 Pratt, *Buchan*, p. 48.
376 There is no mention of an Armada ship called the *Michael* or *St Michael* in either Ferguson's *Ship-wrecks* or R.N. Baird's more comprehensive *Shipwrecks of the North of Scotland* (Edinburgh, 2003).
377 http://canmore.rcahms.gov.uk/en/site/21190/details/peterhead+meikle+battery/
378 *OSA* for Banff.
379 Pratt, *Buchan*, p. 47.
380 http://canmore.rcahms.gov.uk/en/site/19037/details/montrose+s+camp/
381 http://canmore.rcahms.gov.uk/en/site/19039/details/campfold+of+ardlogie/
382 Jim Hughes, *A Steep Turn to the Stars: A History of Aviation in the Moray Firth* (Peterborough, 1999), p. 158.
383 Hughes, *A Steep Turn to the Stars*, p. 153.

384 Army memorandum of 9 June 1940.
385 George Allan Dey, *Fraserburgh at War and the Coronation* (Aberdeen, n.d. c.1998), p. 37.
386 Hughes, *A Steep Turn to the Stars*, p. 146.
387 Hughes, *A Steep Turn to the Stars*, p. 152.
388 Hughes, *A Steep Turn to the Stars*, p. 140.
389 http://canmore.rcahms.gov.uk/en/site/20525/details/hilton+farm+windmill/
390 McAldowie, 'Personal Experiences in Witchcraft', p. 312.
391 Ordnance Survey of 1876, quoted in
http://www.visionofbritain.org.uk/descriptions/entry_page.jsp?text_id=121580
392 http://canmore.rcahms.gov.uk/en/site/21270/details/inverugie+castle/
393 *NSA* for St Fergus.
394 http://canmore.rcahms.gov.uk/en/site/21092/details/rattray+castle+hill/
395 John Thomas and David Turnock, *A Regional History of the Railways of Great Britain, Volume 15: North of Scotland* (Newton Abbot, 1989), pp. 7, 17, all quotations at p. 7.
396 Thomas and Turnock, *Railways of Great Britain*, p. 22.
397 McBey, *Early Life*, pp. 3, 20, quotation at 20.
398 D.J. Withrington, 'Introduction', in A.I. McConnochie, *Donside* (Aberdeen, 1985), p. v.
399 Thomas and Turnock, *Railways of Great Britain*, p. 200.
400 Thomas and Turnock, *Railways of Great Britain*, p. 177.
401 Down to 1863, this was operated by a separate company, the Banff Portsoy and Strathisla Railway.
402 Macduff itself was not added until 1872.
403 Thomas and Turnock, *Railways of Great Britain*, p. 206.
404 Thomas and Turnock, *Railways of Great Britain*, p. 199.
405 Thomas and Turnock, *Railways of Great Britain*, pp. 163–64.
406 http://www.scotsman.com/news/scottish-news/top-stories/are-they-taking-the-euryth-mick-annie-lennox-image-used-to-push-project-she-opposes-1-791018

CHAPTER 4

407 Anna Ritchie, *Picts* (Edinburgh, 1989), p. 5.
408 F.T. Wainwright *et al.*, eds., *The Problem of the Picts* (Perth, 1980), p. 10.
409 Wainwright *et al.*, eds., *Problem of the Picts*, pp. 1, 2, 130.
410 Ritchie, *Picts*, p. 10.
411 Ritchie, *Picts*, p. 62.
412 *OSA* for Fraserburgh.
413 Alex Woolf, *From Pictland to Alba* (Edinburgh, 2007), p. 276.
414 Woolf, *Pictland to Alba*, p. 340.
415 Ritchie, *Picts*, p. 17.
416 *NSA* for Auchindoir.
417 *OSA* for Belhelvie.
418 Douglas Tate, 'Blue Bloods of Gunmaking', *The Field*, April 2012, pp. 60–65, p. 61.
419 Richard Holmes, 'Foreword [II]', in M.M. Gilchrist, *Patrick Ferguson: 'A Man of Some Genius'* (Leeds, 2003), p. ix.
420 Louis L'Amour, *The Ferguson Rifle* (Leicester, 1983), pp. 2, 3, 7, 9, 13–14.
421 Graeme Rimer, 'Foreword [I]', in Gilchrist, *Patrick Ferguson*, p. iv.
422 Gilchrist, *Patrick Ferguson*, p. 9.
423 Gilchrist, *Patrick Ferguson*, p. 14.
424 Gilchrist, *Patrick Ferguson*, p. 41.
425 Gilchrist, *Patrick Ferguson*, p. 43.
426 *DNB*.
427 Gilchrist, *Patrick Ferguson*, p. 64.
428 Gilchrist, *Patrick Ferguson*, p. 69.
429 Robert L. Dallison, *Hope Restored: The American Revolution and the Founding of New Brunswick* (Fredericton, 2003), pp. 91, 96, 97, quotation at 97.
430 Gilchrist, *Patrick Ferguson*, p. 77.
431 *DNB*.
432 Smith, *Buchan Land of Plenty*, p. 43.
433 Not 1800, given as the approximate date by biographer I.C. Pray, and thereafter copied as definite fact. See for instance James Burnley, *Millionaires and Kings of Enterprise* (1901), p. 390. One other source opts for 1794.
434 'The Newspaper Press of America', in *Temple Bar* Vol. 7 (March, 1863), p. 190.
435 *DNB*; I.C. Pray, *Memoirs of James Gordon Bennett and His Times* (New York, 1855), pp. 25–30, p. 267.
436 Pray, *Memoirs*, p. 31.
437 Chapter 44 of *Sunshine and Shadow in New York* (1868), at p. 511.
438 *DNB*.
439 Pray, *Memoirs*, p. 248; G.E. Currie, *The United States Insurance Gazette* (1872), p. 125.
440 Brown, *Noble Power*, pp. 76–77.
441 Brown, *Noble Power*, p. 125.

442  Brown, *Noble Power*, p. 132. I have often wondered if 'Mad-ganil', a Scoto-Russian officer of the 1620s, was a relative of mine.
443  Brown, *Noble Power*, p. 136.
444  Brown, *Noble Power*, p. 144.
445  Ned C. Landsman, 'Nation, Migration and the Province', p. 466.
446  *OSA* for Aberlour.
447  *OSA* for Monquhitter.
448  *OSA* for Strathdon.
449  *OSA* for St Fergus.
450  Marjorie Harper, *Emigrants from North-East Scotland, Volume 2: Across the Broad Atlantic* (Aberdeen, 1988), p. ix.
451  McBey, *Early Life*, pp. 50, 57–58, 131.
452  Wilken, *Ellon in Bygone Days*, p. 3.
453  J.M. Bulloch, *The Gordons of Coldwells, Ellon, Now Represented by the Family of Von Gordon of Laskowitz, West Prussia* (Peterhead, 1914), p. 4.
454  *DNB.*
455  *DNB.*
456  *DNB.*
457  This is almost certainly a compositor's mistake for the improbable-sounding Dunlugas. *OSA* for Turriff.
458  Respectively, George Forbes of Skellater and John Gordon of Glenbuchat (then spelled Glenbucket).
459  *NSA* for Strathdon.
460  *DNB.*
461  Mair, *Records of the Parish of Ellon*, p. 90.
462  James Imlach, *History of Banff* (Banff, 1868), p. 45.
463  *DNB.*
464  *DNB.*
465  *DNB.*
466  Duncan Fraser, *The Smugglers* (Montrose, 1978), p. 9.
467  NAS E366/109, Informations of Seizures 1742.
468  Quoted in James Grant, ed., *Records of the County of Banff 1660–1760* (Aberdeen, 1922), p. 406.
469  *OSA* for Abernethy and Kincardine.
470  French brandy-smuggling into Britain was based chiefly at Dunkirk until 1755, when an effectively managed English blockade forced it to relocate to Ostend; in any case, many brandy-*producing* operations in France were, by this time, Irish- or Scottish-owned. Scottish- and Scottish-connected brandy houses in the Garonne included Johnstons, Delaps and Forster Brothers. A family of Scottish smugglers, the Murdochs, moved to Ostend from Dunkirk in 1779 – part of a new concerted effort by the town's magistracy, using tax breaks and other perks, to lure in English and Scottish smugglers who had previously been based in Dunkirk and Flushing. See especially Jan Parmentier, 'The Sweets of Commerce: the Hennessys of Ostend and their Network in the Eighteenth Century', in David Dickson *et al.*, eds., *Irish and Scottish Mercantile Networks in Europe and Overseas in the Seventeenth and Eighteenth Centuries* (Ghent, 2006), pp. 67–92, at pp. 76–80.
471  Letter from the Annual Committee of the General Convention of Royal Burghs, originally produced on 3 September 1736, subjoined at p. 22 to *Some Considerations on the Present State of Scotland* (Edinburgh: W. Sands, 28 March 1744), second pagination, p. 14.
472  *Some Considerations*, p. 5, italics in original.
473  NAS CE87/1/1, Copies of Letters to the Commissioners, 1728–30.
474  NAS CE87/1/1, Copies of Letters to the Commissioners, 1728–30, letter dated 6 December 1728.
475  NAS CE87/1/1, Copies of Letters to the Commissioners, 1728–30, letter dated 17 June 1730.
476  NAS CE87/1/1, Copies of Letters to the Commissioners, 1728–30.
477  *Some Considerations*, pp. 8, 16–17.
478  NAS CE87/1/1, Copies of Letters to the Commissioners, 1728–30, letter dated 23 June 1729.
479  Pratt, *Buchan*, p. 26.
480  NAS CE87/1/1, Copies of Letters to the Commissioners, 1728–30, letter dated 28 March 1729, describing incident of 5 March 1729.
481  NAS CE4/3, Scottish Excise, Board to Collectors, 1804–18, letter dated 20 June 1815, p. 294.
482  Pratt, *Buchan*, p. 27n.
483  Pratt, *Buchan*, p. 27.
484  Pratt, *Buchan*, pp. 27–28.
485  Vivien E. Dietz, 'The Politics of Whisky: Scottish Distillers, the Excise, and the Pittite State', *Journal of British Studies* 36(1) (1997), pp. 35–69, p. 46.
486  Paul Monod, 'Dangerous Merchandise: Smuggling, Jacobitism, and Commercial Culture in Southeast England, 1690–1760', *Journal of British Studies* Vol. 30, No. 2 (April 1991), pp. 150–82, p. 170. See also W.A. Cole, 'Trends in Eighteenth-Century Smuggling', *Economic History Review*, New Series Vol. 10, No. 3 (1958), pp. 395–410, at pp. 408–09. However, others argue (directly against Cole) that 'the quantitative importance of smuggling during the eighteenth century is irretrievably lost': Hoh-Cheung and Lorna H. Mui, '"Trends in Eighteenth-Century Smuggling" Reconsidered', *Economic History Review*, New Series Vol. 28, No. 1 (1975), pp. 28–43, p. 43.
487  Brian M. Halloran, *The Scots College, Paris 1603–1792* (Edinburgh, 1997), p. 92.
488  Douglas Wimberley, *A Short Family History of the Later Gordons of Beldorney* (Banff, 1904), p. 24.
489  Fraser, *Smugglers*, p. 9.

490 As compared to the 1680s or any earlier period: see Monod, 'Dangerous Merchandise'. For a counter-vailing view that the increase in smuggling between the 1680s and 1690s could have occurred for purely economic reasons, see B.R. Leftwich, 'The Later History and Administration of the Customs Revenue in England (1671–1814)', *Transactions of the Royal Historical Society*, Fourth Ser., Vol. 13 (1930), pp. 187–203. However, Leftwich's ideas about the difficulty of travel in this period have since been outmoded.

491 Daniel MacCannell, *News Before the 'News Revolution': Britain and Ireland, 1460–1642* (forthcoming).

492 Jan Parmentier, 'The Sweets of Commerce: the Hennessys of Ostend and their Network in the Eighteenth Century', in David Dickson *et al.*, eds., *Irish and Scottish Mercantile Networks in Europe and Overseas in the Seventeenth and Eighteenth Centuries* (Ghent, 2006), pp. 67–92; Guy Chaussinand-Nogaret, 'Une élite insulaire au service de l'Europe: Les Jacobites au XVIIIe siecle', *Annales* Vol. 20 (1973), pp. 1,098–99; Cole, 'Eighteenth-Century Smuggling', p. 407.

493 Monod, 'Dangerous Merchandise', p. 171.

494 Francis Collinson, *The Life and Times of William Grant* (Dufftown, 1984), p. 4.

495 L.M. Cullen, 'The Smuggling Trade in Ireland in the Eighteenth Century', *Proceedings of the Royal Irish Academy* Vol. 67 (1968–69), pp. 149–75, p. 160.

496 Dietz, 'Politics of Whisky', p. 50.

497 Dietz, 'Politics of Whisky', p. 59.

498 'Amor Patriae', *Remarks on the Present State of the Distillery of England and Scotland* (London, 1788), pp. 4, 26–27, italics in original.

499 Dietz, 'Politics of Whisky', pp. 60, 65, 67.

500 Jean Pike, *Scottish Smugglers* (St Ives, 1975), p. 5.

501 NAS E510/4/1–39, Collector's Incident Accounts, Collector Theophilus Ogilvie, Aberdeen, Quarter ended 5 January 1770–Quarter ended 10 October 1775.

502 The Scottish Excise Commissioners to the to the Lords Commissioners of the Treasury, 22 February 1790, within PRO T 1/678, pp. 1–3.

503 Quoted at length in Ross Wilson, *Scotch Made Easy* (London, 1959), p. 115. We should not ignore the fact that illicit importation of rum was also occurring, particularly via Glasgow, by the 1750s: Wilson, *ibid.*, pp. 103–04. 'It has been variously suggested that the term *aqua vitae* or *water of life* is a corruption of *aqua vite* or *water of the vine*, namely brandy; [or,] that the term was first used to signify a spirit distinct from brandy, but as yet undefined': Sillett, *Illicit Scotch*, p. 3.

504 Hugo Arnot (1749–86), who married an Exciseman's daughter, quoted in Sillett, *Illicit Scotch*, p. 21.

505 John Burnett, *Liquid Pleasures: a Social History of Drinks in Modern Britain* (Abingdon and New York, 1999), p. 163.

506 Burnett, *Liquid Pleasures*, p. 179.

507 *Exchequer Rolls of Scotland*, Vol. 10, p. 487.

508 *Oxford English Dictionary*, 'usquebaugh, n.'

509 John French, *The Art of Distillation, or A Treatise of the Choicest Spagyricall Preparations . . . Together With The Description of the chiefest Furnaces and Vessels used by Ancient, and Moderne Chymists* (London, 1651), pp. 45–46, 64–89, 91, 93–94, 98, 100.

510 Though Smith lived in Westmorland, the book was published in London. Here we cite the 1725 edition, pp. 38–40 and 132, quotation at p. 132.

511 *Oxford English Dictionary*, 'whisky, n.' Ian Macdonald suggested that native distilling was stimulated by the 1622 Scottish government proclamation against the importation of wine to the Isles; in other words, that it was a substitute for wine as in later generations it was a substitute for brandy: Ian Macdonald, *Smuggling in the Highlands: An Account of Highland Whisky with Smuggling Stories and Detections* (Stirling, 1914), pp. 31–32.

512 *OSA* for Kirkmichael.

513 Michael Brander, *The Original Scotch* (London, 1974), p. 27.

514 Quoted in Brander, *Original Scotch*, p. 35.

515 Michael S. Moss and John R. Hume, *The Making of Scotch Whisky: A History of the Scotch Whisky Distilling Industry* (Edinburgh, 1981), p. 58.

516 CE4/2, Scottish Excise, Board to Collectors, 1791–1804, p. 9.

517 Moss and Hume, *Making of Scotch Whisky*, p. 98.

518 For the former view, see for example Sillett, *Illicit Scotch*, pp. 18, 24, and for the latter, for example, Brander, *Original Scotch*, p. 5 and Moss and Hume, *Making of Scotch Whisky*, pp. 26–32.

519 Moss and Hume, *Making of Scotch Whisky*, p. 36. The statute itself is RPS 1579/10/74.

520 Wilson, *Scotch*, pp. 36, 48; Brander, *Original Scotch*, p. 14.

521 Sillett, *Illicit Scotch*, p. 9.

522 Brander, *Original Scotch*, p. 25. Allowing for possible linguistic or other confusion between usky and brandy, another example might be the Lady Bridekirk met by Alexander Carlyle in the mid-1720s: *ibid.*, p. 68.

523 Brander, *Original Scotch*, pp. 38–41.

524 Quoted in Brander, *Original Scotch*, p. 44.

525 Brander, *Original Scotch*, p. 46.

526 *Rules, Orders, and Instructions, Made and Published by the Commissioners of Customs and Excize in Scotland, To be observed by the several Officers conjunctly of both* (Edinburgh, 1656), p. 40.

527 For whisky history as virtually pure obfuscation, see especially Wilson, *Scotch*, chapter 1.

528 BL 08227 b22, William Thomson's collection of news clippings from the *Weekly Scotsman*, *Kilmarnock Standard* and *Inverness Courier* regarding the smuggling era (1910).

529 Macdonald, *Smuggling in the Highlands*.

530  BL 08227 b22, fos. [10–10v] and [24]
531  Pike, *Scottish Smugglers*, p. 3.
532  BL 08227 b22, fo. [26].
533  BL 08227 b22, fo. [28]v.
534  T.M. Devine, *Clanship to Crofters' War: The Social Transformation of the Scottish Highlands* (Manchester, 1994), p. 127.
535  *Inverness Courier*, 18 March 1910.
536  Devine, *Clanship*, pp. 124, 129.
537  *Aberdeen Journal*, issue 3,780, 21 June 1820. Not this, but a similar incident probably led to a 'Large Quantity' of Highland whisky being offered for sale by auction at the Permit Office in Netherkirkgate: *Aberdeen Journal*, issue 3,762, 16 February 1820.
538  Issue 15,871, 24 May 1823.
539  NAS, *Crim'l Letters . . . Ag't Alexander Gordon 1823*, pp. 2–3.
540  NAS, *Crim'l Letters . . . Ag't Alexander Gordon 1823*, p. 3.
541  NAS, *Crim'l Letters . . . Ag't Alexander Gordon 1823*, p. 4.
542  NAS, *Crim'l Letters . . . Ag't Alexander Gordon 1823*, p. 5.
543  NAS, *Crim'l Letters . . . Ag't Alexander Gordon 1823*, p. 6.
544  NAS, *Crim'l Letters . . . Ag't Alexander Gordon 1823*, pp. 7, 9.
545  NAS, Alexander Gordon's statement to William Kennedy, 1822, pp. 1–2.
546  Kenneth McCulloch and Thomas Dunnigham.
547  NAS, Alexander Gordon's statement to William Kennedy, 1822, p. 2.
548  *Edinburgh Advertiser* (1823), p. 264.
549  NAS JC11/70/84r; NAS JC11/74/102r; NAS JC11/82/42v.
550  F. Paul Pacult, *A Double Scotch*, (Hoboken, New Jersey, 2005), p. 78, an assessment based on primary source documents in the possession of the University of Glasgow.
551  *Trial of Malcolm Gillespie* (Aberdeen, 1827), pp. 37–38.
552  *Proceedings*, pp. 245–46.
553  By the 1860s, this sort of massed musketry seems to have been sublimated into an annual shooting match contested between Upper Cabrach, Lower Cabrach and Glenbuchat, with a total of forty prizes: *Aberdeen Journal* no. 5,903, 27 February 1861.
554  *Aberdeen Journal* no. 4,757 (13 March 1839) and no. 5,119 (18 February 1846).
555  16 December 1822, NAS CE4/4, p. 125.
556  Issue 5,248.
557  A 1990 bottle, as quoted in Dietz, 'Politics of Whisky', p. 35.
558  F.G. James, 'Irish Smuggling in the Eighteenth Century', *Irish Historical Studies* 12(48) (1961), pp. 299–317, p. 314.
559  *OSA* for Kirkmichael.
560  *NSA* for Kirkmichael.
561  According to Collinson, this was the parish where Alexander Grant, Jacobite great-grandfather of Maj. William Grant, hid out in the immediate aftermath of Culloden: *Life and Times of William Grant*, p. 5.
562  *OSA* for Inveraven.
563  *OSA* for Strathdon.
564  *NSA* for Strathdon.
565  *OSA* for Mortlach.
566  *NSA* for Mortlach.
567  *NSA* for Boharm.
568  *NSA* for Aberlour.
569  *NSA* for Glenbuchat.
570  Macdonald, *Smuggling*, pp. 117, 129.
571  Devine, *Clanship*, p. 129.
572  Pike, *Scottish Smugglers*, p. 30.
573  Daniel MacCannell, *Lost Deeside* (Edinburgh, 2011), p. 101.
574  1861 Census of the UK.
575  *NSA* for Cabrach.
576  Sillett, *Illicit Scotch*, pp. 72, 74, 75, 98, quotations all at p. 75.
577  Sillett, *Illicit Scotch*, p. 30, my italics.
578  Sillett, *Illicit Scotch*, pp. 109–17, quotation at p. 116–17.
579  Devine, *Clanship*, p. 124.
580  'Amor Patriae', *Remarks*, p. 8.
581  NAS JP26/2/1. Signatories included James, Lord Forbes and the lairds of Auchmacoy, Kininmonth, and Foveran, among others.
582  J.W. Fortescue, *The British Army 1783–1802* (London, 1905), p. 2.
583  Fortescue, *British Army*, p. 21. Fortescue's separate, magisterial work on the relationship between the County Lieutenancy and the army suggests (by omission) that the involvement of the Lieutenancy/Militia with smuggling prevention was non-existent, and that only regular troops were used in support of the gaugers.
584  The Scottish Excise Commissioners to the Lords Commissioners of the Treasury, 22 February 1790, within PRO T 1/678, pp. 3–6.
585  Devine, *Clanship*, pp. 126, 131.
586  *Rules, Orders, and Instructions*, p. 92.

587 J. Bateman, *Excise Officer's Manual* (London, 1840), p. 249.

588 Bateman, *Excise Officer's Manual*, pp. 250–51.

589 Found within PRO T 1/935.

590 See within PRO T 1/1353.

591 Supervisors of Excise in Scotland, *A List of Persons Concerned in the Rebellion . . . 7th May 1746* (Edinburgh, 1890 {1746}). For a more detailed, but perhaps 'paranoid' exploration of this theme, see *The Spirit of Loyalty, and of Rebellion, During some late Troubles, Detected, In the Conduct of the Commissioners of Excise in Scotland* (Westminster: H. Griffiths, 1755).

592 Letter from James Sedgwick, Edinburgh Excise office, to the Lords of the Treasury, 26 October 1813, found within PRO T 1/1353.

593 See for instance Scottish Excise report to the Treasury dated 20 October 1813 (found in PRO T 1/1353), and its attached letter from Angus Mackentosh JP, who point-blank refused on moral grounds to levy enormous fines on every 'Half Fed, half Naked Wretch' who came before him charged with this crime, reducing them and their 'large Families to complete Beggary and Ruin'. See also letter from James Sedgwick in PRO T 1/1353.

594 Devine, *Clanship*, p. 125.

595 *Inverness Courier*, 25 March 1910.

596 NAS CE4/3, Scottish Excise, Board to Collectors, 1804–18, p. 7.

597 NAS CE4/3, Scottish Excise, Board to Collectors, 1804–18, p. 114

598 Macdonald, *Smuggling*, p. 71.

599 NAS CE4/4, Scottish Excise, Board to Collectors, 1818–26, p. 91.

600 Sillett, *Illicit Scotch*, p.45. But even having said this, Sillett cites 'seasonal unemployment . . . poverty and boredom' as the chief reasons distilling was taken up! (*ibid.*)

601 Joseph Mitchell, *Reminiscences of My Life in the Highlands* (Newton Abbot, 1971), Vol. 2, p. 35.

602 Letter from George Gordon, solicitor, to an unknown clergyman, 1 June 1825, NAS GD44/51/433/90.

603 Sillett, *Illicit Scotch*, pp. 42–43, 56.

604 Pacult, *Double Scotch*, p. 52.

605 Mitchell, *Reminiscences*, Vol. 2, p. 61.

606 NAS JP5/3/1, *Banff Licensing Court Book 1769–1868* [*sic* for 1828].

607 Though Banff itself is not, being mentioned fewer than half a dozen times in the whole half century covered.

608 John Grant, *OSA* for Kirkmichael.

609 Bearing the date 15 December 1794, and found within NAS JP5/3/1 [item 2].

610 Brown, *Noble Power*, p. 89.

611 *Sheriff Court Records*, Vol. 1, pp. 257–59, here spelled 'Cultis'.

612 For more details see David Calderwood, *The History of the Kirk of Scotland*, ed. Thomas Thomson (Edinburgh, 1843), Vol. 4, pp. 658–59. Quoted in Calderwood, *History*, Vol. 4, p. 659.

613 The earl of Dunfermline to John Murray, 9 December 1614, quoted in full in Abbotsford Club, *Letters and State Papers . . . James the Sixth* (Edinburgh, 1838), pp. 240–42, quotation at p. 242.

614 Commission to the Marquis of Huntly, Edinburgh, 19 March 1635, quoted in full in John Spalding's *Memorialls* (1850 edition), Vol. 1, pp. 425–27, quotation at p. 426.

615 Spalding, *Memorialls*, Vol. 1, p. 428–29, quotation at p. 428.

616 Before 31 August 1635: *ibid.*, Vol. 1, p. 429.

617 *Ibid.*, Vol. 1, pp. 422, 423, 431, the co-leader being Adam Gordon, brother of the first laird of Park, and therefore also a brother of Patrick Gordon, third laird of Glenbuchat.

618 *Ibid.*, Vol. 1, p. 298.

619 *Extracts from the Presbytery Book of Strathbogie 1631–1654* (Aberdeen, 1843), pp. 39, 75.

620 RPS 1669/10/40.

621 RPS 1686/4/115.

622 Macdonald, *Place Names in Strathbogie*, p. 169; see also Wimberly 'Notes on the Cabrach', fo. [11].

623 NAS GD44/51/747/4; NAS GD44/51/739/63–70; NAS GD44/51/75/2; NAS GD44/51/73.

624 John A. Henderson, *Aberdeenshire Epitaphs and Inscriptions* (Aberdeen, 1907), p. 242.

625 Wimberley, 'Notes on the Cabrach', fo. [3].

626 Wimberley, 'Notes on the Cabrach', fo. [14].

627 Wimberley, 'Notes on the Cabrach', fo. [13].

628 A.R.B. Haldane, *The Drove Roads of Scotland* (Colonsay, 1995 {1952}), p. 119.

629 Haldane, *Drove Roads*, p. 120n.

630 Haldane, *Drove Roads*, pp. 119, 121, 127.

631 Haldane, *Drove Roads*, pp. 121, 125.

632 *Aberdeen Journal* no. 5,503, 29 June 1853.

633 *Liverpool Mercury* no. 4,416, 7 April 1862.

634 *Aberdeen Journal* no. 5,179, 14 April 1847.

635 *Aberdeen Journal* no. 5,278, 7 March 1849.

636 He was named James Law. *Aberdeen Journal* no. 5,597, 18 April 1855.

637 *Caledonian Mercury* no. 19,844, 25 December 1848.

638 *Aberdeen Journal* no. 5,268, 27 December 1848. It is perhaps unsurprising that severe agricultural depression followed, leading to a public meeting at Lindsay's Inn, Ardwell, chaired by James Robertson in Tomnaveen: *Aberdeen Journal* no. 5,342, 29 May 1850.

639 *Aberdeen Journal* no. 5,830, 5 October 1859.

640 *Caledonian Mercury* no. 22,064, 14 June 1860.

641  *Aberdeen Journal* no. 5,886, 31 October 1860.
642  Issue 4,110.
643  *Aberdeen Journal*, issue 4,581, 28 October 1835.
644  *Aberdeen Journal*, issue 4,250, 24 June 1829.
645  *Aberdeen Journal*, issue 4,269, 4 November 1829.
646  *Aberdeen Journal*, issue 4,274, 9 December 1829.
647  *Caledonian Mercury* no. 15,719, 3 June 1822.
648  Unnumbered first page and pp. 5–6.
649  Rev. Benjamin Mercer believed his parish was in the grip of widespread and chronic scurvy, which was both hereditary and highly contagious – but controllable using goat's whey.  In fact there was no incidence of scurvy in the area, and Mercer was noted by his successor as having a 'diseased imagination': *NSA* for Tullynessle and Forbes.

# INDEX